# Eglė Juodvalkė

# SUGAR MOUNTAIN

### My Life and Misadventures
### as a Lithuanian Diabetic in America
### and Other Exotic Places

Mildred,

Hope you are well —
Here is a copy of my book —
it just came out this year —
a glance at an eventful life —
please enjoy it.

Eglė

DIPTERA

2016, Aug. 25

LA GRANGE

Diptera
8945 West 103rd Street, Palos Hills, IL 60465
Diptera is a division of Peeps, Inc. The Diptera name and
logo, and EASY READ™, are
trademarks and/or registered trademarks of Peeps, Inc.

First Edition

ISBN 978-0-9970771-9-3

This is a Diptera EASY READ™ book. The typeface
is Adobe Caslon Pro 12 point on 15 point leading. This
combination facilitates reader enjoyment by increasing word
recognition and reducing eyestrain, especially
in low light conditions.

Printed in the United States of America

Judith M. Vale Publishing Enterprise

*Wine comes in at the mouth*
*And love comes in at the eye;*
*That's all we know for truth*
*Before we grow old and die…*

from "A Drinking Song" by W. B. Yeats

To Henryk, a heartless editor, shrewd critic, cruel taskmaster, and my one and only…

# About the author

Born of Lithuanian parents, Ona Norkutė and Antanas Juodvalkis, in 1950 in East Chicago, Indiana, Eglė Juodvalkė received her B.A. from the University of Chicago. While working on her master's degree at Southern Illinois University at Carbondale, she was offered a job by Radio Free Europe/Radio Liberty, Inc., initially in New York City then in Munich, Germany, where she worked for 20 years and left RFE/RL as a Senior Correspondent of the Lithuanian Service. She covered the disintegration of the Soviet Union and the rebirth of the Baltic States. One of her volumes of poetry, *Veidrodis ir tuštuma/ The Mirror and the Void*, was presented at the Frankfurt International Book Fair in 2002. Writing mostly in Lithuanian, she is the author of an autobiography *Sugar Mountain* that became a literary event. Since the year 2000 her bio appears in *Marquis Who's Who in the World and Marquis Who's Who in America*. She and her husband, writer and traveler Henryk Skwarczyński, live in La Grange, a suburb of Chicago, and she spends much time in Vilnius.

# Contents

# 1. A portentous announcement is made, and the heroine is introduced.

"I have news for you—both good and bad," Dr. Rubenstein said, opening my file. "Your eyes are fine—the retinopathy looks stable."

What could be wrong?

"In about three years your kidneys will stop working."

"But, but..." I spluttered.

The meaning of the words escaped me. What was renal failure, and what could it possibly have to do with me? Was the end coming inexorably closer?

Lithuanian by parentage, American by place of birth, a poet by inclination, and a diabetic by an accident of fate, I have dealt with my diabetes in a variety of ways—an obedient child became a rebellious teenager, changed to a health anarchist at the university, and finally stabilized as an adult.

Henryk calls me a warrior. He refers to the mixture of Lithuanian genes, peasant sturdiness, and American determination that comprise my nature. I have lost diabetic battles, but like the Knight of the Woeful Countenance, after a beating I rise again to struggle with adversity.

When Henryk told his mother that I was traveling by myself somewhere in the Philippines, Australia, or Macau, she thought me rash. When I told a colleague that I had fallen in love in Paris, she warned me against disclosing my diabetes because the man might back off. "Wait," Aušra said, "too soon would be... imprudent."

Her advice came too late. I had told Henryk about the diabetes and the kidney within an hour of meeting him. In South Africa when I roused the camp doctor near the border with Mozambique to ask for antibiotics because the catheter needle of my insulin pump had caused an infection at the insertion site on my belly, she wondered at my temerity—I was the first organ transplant she had encountered on safari. When I could find no rubbing alcohol to clean a pus-filled wound in Melbourne, my friend Raimonda advised me to make do with a bottle of Eau de Cologne, and I was on a plane to Hong Kong the next morning.

*  *  *

The United States took in a number of refugees after World War II. Among them was a non-English-speaking couple in their thirties, the woman pregnant. They had a sponsor to Chicago and then were redirected to East Chicago, Indiana, where steel factories were looking for strong men. My Father sought work to feed his family—my pregnant-with-me mother with a ferocious toddler, my brother. People were reluctant to rent to a foreign couple with a two-year-old and an about-to-be born baby. A Hungarian American family offered them the only space it had—a basement room next to the coal bin. Four months later I, a seven-and-a-half pound raven-haired baby girl, hanging upside down in midair, greeted the world.

Soon the swatch of black hair fell out and the light brown fuzz of babyhood sprouted and grew into thin, fine strands. I had blue eyes, and no identifying marks.

Mother took me, age five, to our family doctor because of a nosebleed, excessive thirst, and uncontrolled urination. Dr. Gustaitis ran some blood tests, among them for glucose. Diabetes mellitus! Where had it come from? No one in the family had been known to have it.

The diagnosis came crashing down like the blade of a guillotine. My parents had to tell me I would be hospitalized. Blessed with a healthy fear of doctors and a will of my own, I crawled into the comfort and safety under our heavy oak dining room table, one that was to grace our home for half a century. Mother and Father could neither cajole, nor drag me from my haven. Only the dire threat that police would extricate and deliver this squalling brat to St. Catherine's Hospital in Hammond, Indiana, finally brought me wailing and hiccuping into my mother's arms.

\* \* \*

My parents-to-be who had not even met then, left Lithuania separately in 1944, fleeing the war front as the Soviets pushed out the Germans. My father, Antanas, an accountant in a sugar factory and distributor of an underground paper against the Nazis, knew that the plant was scheduled for detonation, but hoping to return before the evacuation of workers, had accompanied the factory's director to a neighboring town on business for a few days.

Dad left a new bicycle and a clothes-packed suitcase with his boss, Edvardas Gedgaudas, locked two satchels in his desk, one with a change of underwear and a shirt, the other with ham, bread, and cheese.

"Don't forget my new bike. Just throw it on the truck if

it comes to relocate the workers before I get back."

"Rest easy. I'll take care of your things."

When Antanas returned two days later, the factory was deserted—no co-workers, no suitcase, no bike. Only the satchels were still locked in his desk. The sole remaining guard assured him that no extra suitcase, certainly no new bike, had been on the truck that relocated the workers of the sugar factory.

Father found his co-workers and his superior in a neighboring town. The stay was bound to be brief, as the Germans were losing the war, he comforted himself. After the first Soviet deportation of Lithuanians to Siberia he'd discovered his name on a list for the next expulsion. This elimination of "anti-Soviet elements" was interrupted by the German occupation. The Reds left everything—secret lists, orders, and files—as they retreated from the German drive east in 1941.

The Russians had begun deportations from Lithuania, Latvia, and Estonia to labor camps in Vorkuta, Magadan, Kolyma, the Urals, and elsewhere in 1940 and continued them until Stalin's death in 1953. My father's eldest sister Ona, pregnant and with six small children, was taken to Siberia because her farmer husband was not home when the Soviets came to arrest him. It took her twenty-five years to return to Lithuania.

After the Germans dynamited the plant, the director of the sugar factory, Balys, traded the company car for two wagons for his extended family, but made room for Antanas. Claiming to be a German from Klaipėda returning to the "Vaterland," Balys finagled a permit for them all to cross the border. He had worked in Klaipėda and spoke some German. Everyone else kept silent. He ferried the wagons to a border crossing by side roads, avoiding the main thoroughfares used by large German convoys gathering up stray civilians, escorting them to the nearest camp and away from the borders

Once the wagons crossed the border into Germany without being stopped, the sweat on Antanas's brow dried and he began to look for a way to survive until the projected Allied victory and his return to Lithuania. Thirty-two he hired himself out as a farmhand for food and shelter. After Germany surrendered on May 8, 1945, the Allies collected refugees in Displaced Persons camps in four zones, where, despite food shortages, all forms of daily life began to burgeon. Word came that Edvardas, his supervisor from the sugar factory, was in the American zone at a camp in Landshut, Bavaria.

Why not go there?

At the railroad station he accidentally jostled a man, who turned angrily asking what he wanted in Lithuanian and then in foreigner German.

"*Nesistumdyk, Tamsta. Was wollen?*"

They looked at each another.

"Antanas? Remember me? Justinas from Kaunas."

"When did you leave? How did you get out?"

The outline of their stories was the same. Both were marking time, waiting for the Allies to move the Soviets out of Lithuania.

"My parents decided to stay," Justinas confided. "'No one will touch us, we're too old,' they said. Hope they were right. I was on the deportation list, so I packed a bag and headed for the border. My sister and her family are in Landshut, so that's where I'm going."

"Landshut? Me too. My supervisor is there with his

family. Why don't we join up for the trip?" my father offered.

"How will we ever get past that mob at the train?" the other exclaimed in dismay.

"Get close to the window. I'll try to push my way in."

"Coming through, excuse me." Antanas elbowed and bulldozed his way into a railroad car and to the window. Throwing open the sash, he leaned out and yelled, "Justinas, over here! Throw me the bags." Up went one suitcase, the other followed, and then Justinas grabbed the top of the open window and raised himself, feet scrabbling for a foothold. My father gripped his arms and heaved.

Doors slammed. Conductors whistled. Train wheels rolled.

My father's boss Edvardas at the sugar factory was my mother's uncle. My parents had not yet formally met, though Mama described a first, unofficial encounter that she had reason to remember. When Antanas was delivering sugar to Kaunas from Panevėžys, he brought my mother a loaf of rye bread from her Uncle Edvardas. Mother said that wasn't all.

"A stranger in a calf-length fur coat burst into my office at the State Insurance building, snatched me in his arms, and kissed me," she told me. "Greetings from Uncle Edvardas!" Then he put a loaf of rye bread and a sack of sugar on my desk, turned on his heel, coat tails flying, and left."

I looked at Dad for confirmation.

"It's possible," nodded my father sagely. "Could well have happened that way."

Looking for a way to get his family out of Kaunas before the Russians arrived, Uncle Edvardas bribed acquaintances in the railroad administration because only the families of railroad workers could board trains to Germany and even the Germans were a safer bet than the Soviets who had given a preview of their occupation. Suddenly Edvardas was employed by the railroad. His wife, Mara, and their four children were family, but Ona was not considered close enough kin. To take her out of Lithuania with his family Edvardas came up with the plan of marrying her by civil ceremony to a Lithuanian railroad worker. For a sum. It would let her cross the border.

More than twenty years later, I, a teenager, snooping in my mother's chest of drawers, came across a note affixed to a certificate of marriage issued in Munich between my father and a woman, Ona, whose last name was not my mother's maiden name. The note was brief: married, a name and date in 1944, died, the same name and a date two weeks later. I was intrigued, but I didn't dare ask about the matter I'd discovered poking where I had no business. My curiosity remained unsatisfied for another decade.

One day, in response to a little gentle prodding, Mother told me of her escape from Lithuania. "Didn't I ever tell you the story? I thought I had. I had to marry a railroad worker in order to get out. A paper marriage. I didn't even know him. How did he die? Child, people were dying right and left. I haven't the least idea how. I'm just glad I was notified of his death because all my German documents of the time were with his last name."

In Silesia some railroad cars, including the one containing my uncle and my mother, were uncoupled from the train. The Lithuanians were herded up and put to work in a factory manufacturing metal parts needed for the German war machine. They continued living in the train car in Silesia for months and working—where could they go? Edvardas made forays into cities and found out about the refugee camp in Landshut. He, Mara, their four children and Ona obtained permission to join relatives there and left Silesia.

Though the details of my parents' meeting and courtship in the Landshut Displaced Persons Camp in the American Zone were never told me, I do know that they progressed from joint bike rides to marriage in two years. They exchanged vows in a Munich church, my mother's cousins and sisters looking on, a Lithuanian priest officiating. The newlyweds celebrated in a small eatery next door with what they had managed to save on their food ration cards.

A year later the Landshut DP camp saw the birth of my brother, Uosis, whose name means ash tree. An eleven-pound blond baby who became a chestnut-haired, blue-eyed youngster, he resembled my father, but grew taller, replanted in American soil. For that's what lay ahead though they did not yet know that. The parents had turned a page of history and the earlier pages had been ripped out or rewritten. They found themselves with nothing, the future a question mark.

The second Soviet occupation, which was to last fifty years, engulfed Lithuania in 1944. The USSR demanded return of the displaced Lithuanians. Since the Allies, except Russia, did not recognize the occupation of the Baltic States, the DP's were offered the possibility of emigration to Australia, the USA, England, France.

Antanas and Ona arrived at Ellis Island in the autumn of 1949. After the war healthy men like thirty-seven-year-old Antanas were wanted for work in steel mills and factories. My mother was pregnant. Neither of the grown-ups spoke English, their one suitcase held meager belongings and they had no money. I arrived four months later on January 28, 1950. Antanas had just gotten a job at Inland Steel

Company in East Chicago, Indiana. A week later the union called a strike, which lasted a month and a half.

Dad hadn't received his first paycheck yet. The baby and the two-year-old had to be fed. Beans were the order of the day for the grownups for six weeks. The Lithuanian grocer gave Ona milk for the children on credit. "You'll pay me when Antanas works again."

Once the strike ended life settled into the routine of work, children, church, cultural activities and for the next five years Antanas and Ona happily limited their social contacts to other Lithuanian émigrés. Only at work my father enjoyed the variety of America's ethnic mix— Czechs, African Americans, Serbs, Puerto Ricans, Poles, Greeks, Hungarians.

Mom had a clear memory of the time wives were invited to see their husbands' workplaces. She was issued a hard hat and taken to the huge machines that melted iron into sheets of steel, each one manned by laborers wiping sweat from their brows on the wringing-wet sleeves of blue denim work shirts. At home that evening she gathered Uosis and me close and told us, swallowing tears, "Be good, for your father's sake. He works in hell."

My parents come of stubborn Lithuanian stock, though my father hails from Aukštaitija, the Highlands, and my mother from Žemaitija, the Lowlands. The inhabitants of these sectors differ from one another like a stolid native of Massachusetts from a voluble Southerner. Obstinacy was a characteristic common to both parents.

My mother, Ona Norkutė, one of seven siblings, was born in Russian-occupied Lithuania, but grew up in an independent country. She experienced the Bolshevik Revolution and the famine of 1917 in St. Petersburg, renamed Petrograd, then Leningrad and today once again called by its old name. My grandfather was forcibly recruited into the Czar's army just before World War I began in 1914. My grandmother followed him to St. Petersburg with their seven children, the youngest, Dozė, in swaddling clothes. Konstancija had no means of support, but she had a sister working as maid for a well-to-do Russian family there. They agreed to help and invited Konstancija and her brood to come. At the time famine raged there. The adults and the older children could tighten their belts, grouse and make do with rotting vegetables or moldy bread, but Konstancija feared malnourishment for the younger children. She took three of them, Ona, her younger siblings, Lialė and Alis, to the Czar's Summer Palace, which had been set up as temporary housing for youngsters.

At the palace, the rooms were arranged with rows and rows of children's beds made up in pristine white linen. My grandmother did not know that the palace had no food. All of the kids foraged in the surrounding forests for roots and berries. Both Ona, nine, and Lialė, seven, were old enough to cram whatever they found into their mouths. Alis, only five, collected his berries and roots in his pockets and when their mother came in a couple of days, he pulled them out, confiding, "Mama, these are for you. You must be hungry, too." She collected her brood and took them back to the city with her, muttering, "We'll starve together, if starve we must."

When the Bolshevik Revolution broke out in 1917, my mother, age ten, watched communists carry red coffins through the streets, mourn their fallen comrades, brandish weapons and shout victory. On her way to the Russian school Ona was attending, a soldier grabbed her by the braids and snarled, "Where are the red ribbons in your hair? I'll chop off your braids, if I ever see you without signs of joy at our Bolshevik victory!"

Once World War I ended the founding fathers of Lithuania restored it to sovereignty and statehood, which it had lost to Russia one hundred and twenty three years earlier. In 1918 Konstancija with her husband and family returned. She continued her children's education in Šiauliai, then Kaunas, first in Polish schools, then in Lithuanian ones, as the new Ministry of Education began to build and equip schools, including the university in Kaunas. My mother went on to become one of three females in her graduating class to complete studies in mathematics in 1930, when the university was renamed for Vytautas the Great.

\* \* \*

Seven years after coming to America my father bought their first car, a white Buick. My mother asked him for driving lessons. When she stepped on the brake instead of the gas, Father lost his temper and told her that she'd never drive. Mother bridled at my father's tone and attitude. Some weeks later she stalked into the kitchen and laid a spanking-new driver's license on the table.

A builder by affinity, my father reconstructed the interior of the run-down house he and my mother bought: he made stools, benches, tables, plastered the walls, learned the rudiments of plumbing, and hung doors my mother sanded and varnished. Thereafter, for several consecutive years every summer he built a house to sell. The whole family worked on each one. I earned pin money pounding nails into slabs of rock lath, filling in nail holes, sweeping floors. The smell of wood shavings brings back memories of those hot July and August days and feelings of achievement.

"Build it as though we're going to live in it," Dad advised.

Determination and persistence were qualities shared by both my parents, who were similar in many ways, though my mother held in what bothered her while my father let his temper flare. He held strong opinions that he was willing to vent and defend. At times I would have argued passionately that the man was a dictator, but this was in my adolescence. In temperament and character I was very much like him. My obstinacy I took from both. Two strong wills— like father, like daughter—would pit themselves against each other and two strong voices would rise to heights that would make my mother leave the room. I lost arguments because I was young and dependent, as Father pulled rank, "While you live in my house, you do as I say."

After I graduated from Washington High School and left for the University of Chicago, coming home only on weekends, I decided that, being independent, except financially, I had the right to defend my position. The battle of wills continued every Saturday and Sunday, until I moved to Carbondale to work on my master's. Distance and absence worked wonders. We didn't have the same heart for arguments as before.

## 2. The diabetes surfaces. Mother's diary relates the diagnosis of epilepsy, and Eglė achieves her heart's desire.

"Could the doctors be wrong?" my parents asked.

Shaken by the calamity that had befallen their child, my parents were ready to try anything. When friends told them about a chiropractor who had a "remedy" for diabetes, they fell for it. They knew it couldn't be true, but what if this was the one possibility for a cure and they passed it up? They reached into savings, scrimped on things for themselves, and paid and paid.

Excerpt of Mother's Diary

July 11
7:15 A.M. I was about to sterilize the syringe when Eglytė suddenly began to shake her head in her sleep. At first I thought she woke up and was shaking it on purpose. But I saw that she was unconscious. A little bit of bloody saliva dribbled from her mouth. She was grinding her teeth. This lasted about 3 minutes. Then she began crying terribly, quieted down, then cried again. She was hot, her little face was red, quite warm, and her hair was wet. She had wet the bed. And kept crying.

I couldn't give her anything to drink because her teeth were clenched. She turned all white. And cold. (…)

July12

6:30 P.M. The doctor came. Eglė's sugar is okay and he said that it is epilepsy. The same as they said two years ago. In between times she feels fine. She sucks the ice cubes, but the vomiting has not stopped. (…)

July 16

About noon we left the hospital. They prescribed her pills for epilepsy to be taken three times a day. In two weeks I'll take her to have her blood sugar checked. They found a high level of sugar in her blood.

August 1

This morning it took her a long time to wake up. I kept touching her, talking to her as I tried to rouse her but she didn't react. I gave her the insulin injection.

7:30 A.M. She's not getting up. I talk to her but she says a word and turns on her side again and doesn't talk. I gave her some grape juice to drink. She revived around 9:00.

End of Diary Excerpt

Only the doctors in Michigan City diagnosed "epilepsy." Small wonder that my mother grew grey hair dealing with diabetes, a disease that was misdiagnosed and incorrectly treated in smaller towns even in 1957. It was *terra incognita* to many physicians.

*　*　*

Coming home from school one day at age eight, I found my favorite two-foot doll peering forlornly over the rim of the garbage can. Blubbering and hiccupping, I rescued her.

"You have so many other dolls, pretty dolls with hair. This one is bald," Mother said, hiding a smile at my wild sobs and gesticulations.

"But that's why I love her," I begged through my tears. "She's deformed. She needs me."

*　*　*

During my school years doctors told me over and over that I could live a "normal" life, healthier than people who don't pay attention to their eating or exercise habits, on one condition—that I follow doctors' orders. I found that impossible. At ten I was injecting insulin into my body. The fact that I needed daily injections of insulin, that I had to do what other children did not—follow a strict diet, weigh my food or have someone weigh it for me, that too much or too little play would mean too much or too little energy expenditure, everything needed to be balanced with insulin or fast-acting carbohydrate, like orange juice. Every time I turned around someone was calculating something for me, or I was doing it myself. This all spelled a-b-n-o-r-m-a-l.

If I ran around the block twice, I had to compensate with a piece of fruit. If I delayed supper for an hour because I was rehearsing the second act of the school play, I was in danger of an insulin reaction. If I was furious with the girls on the volleyball team, if I cried when no one asked me to dance, everything, but everything had to be compensated with insulin or some form of glucose.

Sweets were forbidden except nickel size Dairy Queen ice cream cones, which were a rare and longed-for treat. I wanted delicious and taboo candy badly enough to go to great lengths to obtain it. I could not for the life of me understand why I couldn't have it, when every other child indulged in handfuls. I was outraged at six when my mother took Uosis and me to the doctor for inoculations. He got a lollipop, and I—a pat on the head.

When the time came, it was hard enough to be pubescent without the complications that diabetes brought. Some well-meaning friends of my mother's would offer me a cookie and withdraw the plate before I could react, "Oh, I'm so sorry, but you can't have that, dear, can you?" I would have preferred that the lady not offer the sweet rather than have her point out that I was ill, and imply that I would act irresponsibly and take it. I resented the fact that I was not allowed to politely refuse the cookie. I considered the right to decide, to take charge of my life, crucial.

In elementary school the teachers, Sisters of St. Casimir, had been informed about treating an insulin reaction. They cooperated, but I didn't. Sometimes I let a half hour of symptoms, starting with drowsiness, and then yawning, go by, not wanting to interrupt the class. A few of the nuns were loving, most were strict, and some were known for the punishment they meted out. Raising a hand for an insulin reaction was a daunting experience.

In twelfth grade, when Sister Mary Marion canvassed the graduating girls a second time to see who had a vocation to join a religious order, I abjured what I, like half of the other girls in our class, had professed to have a scant half year before. I had grounds for bravery. I knew that I would not be going to Bishop Noll, the Catholic high school a bus ride away. Though it was an academically better school, my parents had opted for a public school several blocks away, George Washington High, so that I could lunch at home. The deciding factor was the diabetes. Sister Mary's recommendation would not be necessary for a public school.

When I began kindergarten in the parochial grade school, I spoke only Lithuanian. From the first day I loved school. I had already learned the rudiments of reading, albeit reading in Lithuanian, at home. School opened up a new world. The nuns provided me with an excellent basic education in all subjects and instilled English grammar, spelling, and syntax in me.

I won our local spelling bee and went to the state competition. All but two of us had been eliminated. One would be champ. The disembodied voice pronounced, "apostrophe." I stood on the floodlit stage of the auditorium, unable to see my mother and brother who were mouthing the proper letter, said "a-p-o-s-t-r—" and stopped dead. Could be "a," I thought, but maybe "o." I hesitated, started again. Time was passing. I closed my eyes and said "a." As soon as the letter was out of my mouth, I knew I had failed. My stomach churned and my eyes filled with tears. I was down the steps when I heard applause for the winner. I had flubbed it because, as my mother said, I didn't *think* in Lithuanian. I would have known from the Lithuanian *apostrofa* that the two middle vowels were o's.

When I first got sick, my mother wrote about my illness to my great-aunt in Lithuania, bemoaning the fact that I would not be able to enjoy sugar again. Magdutė consoled her, "Don't worry. Eglė can substitute honey as a sweetener." There were many misconceptions about diabetes then, fewer today, but they still exist.

Mother learned to sterilize the syringes and needles, to inject insulin into my arm or thigh, to watch for any sign of fatigue, incoherence, slowness in speech, slurring of words, or sluggishness that might indicate a hypoglycemic reaction. I was ten before I started injecting my own insulin after learning to shoot water into an orange.

As parents of diabetic children still must, my mother had to take up the cudgels in defense of her diabetic child's rights against ignorance of what the disease means, what it requires, and what it permits. When I was twelve, I wanted to be a cheerleader more than anything in the world. I could do all the jumps, bends, kicks, and even a full split. St. Francis in East Chicago, Indiana, had a basketball team, the Maroons. After a successful tryout, I listened to Sister Mary tell me that I would not be able to be a cheerleader. Why? Because of my diabetes. I bawled inconsolably.

My mother put on her coat and went to talk to the nun. The next thing I knew, Mama was measuring me for a maroon corduroy skirt. As I did my splits at the games, twirling my pompoms, the 180-degree diameter knee-length skirt billowing, I was ecstatic. "And for maroon and white we'll fight, fight, fight..."

For a time, while Uosis and I were in grade school, summers my father would pack my mother and the kids into the white Buick and take us down to the Indiana dunes for vacation. To allow the children summers at the lake in Beverly Shores Father worked overtime whenever he could, Mother made her own and my clothes and saved wherever possible. *Tėtis* would return to work in two weeks, but Mother would stay with the children till August and bring us back to the city just before Labor Day for the start of the school year. The Villa "*Jūratė*," where we rented a large room, was named for the Lithuanian goddess of the sea who lived in an amber palace on the sea floor.

Oh, the fragrance of summer mornings when my eight-year-old eyes opened to see my mother walking the length of the huge room, shaking the remaining drops of distilled water from the saucepan in which she boiled my syringe. The sunlight caught and sparkled in the drops as they fell. The taste of blueberry ripple ice cream, a rare treat, still conjures up hot, sunny days, white dunes, the smell of unpolluted Lake Michigan, tall grasses bending in a cool breeze—

The dunes were a fifteen-minute walk from the villa. We'd pack lunch, a thermos, and scoot down to the beach for a day of building sand castles, swimming, and collecting rocks. *Mamytė* hardly took her eyes off me.

Once, when I was about nine, I had a hypoglycemic reaction and a sun stroke in the water. Mother saw me go down, once, twice, and then she was running and screaming for help.

A Lithuanian man dove in and pulled me from the water unconscious. Mother, holding me in her lap as the car raced toward Michigan City Hospital miles away, kept one hand on the horn, while telling the driver to run red lights.

I was in a coma for eight hours in my wet bathing suit, doctors all around, while she waited at my side until I opened my eyes and whispered, "*Mamytė*."

## 3. Cravings for sweets lead to moral failings. The first World Lithuanian Youth Congress takes place in Chicago, and Eglė spends the last day crying.

There were frequent hospitalizations in elementary school to adjust the treatment of my diabetes. These were exercises in futility—everything would function in the hospital and fall apart as soon as my parents brought me home.

The hospital day was regulated—insulin at 6:45 AM, breakfast at 7:30, snack at 10:00, lunch two hours later, snack at 4:00 PM, dinner at 6:00, snack at 8:00, lights out at 9:00 PM. I spent all day in bed reading, putting puzzles together, playing Monopoly, but the minute I was out, the schedule would disintegrate. I'd race to the car, sprint around the block when I got home, and bam! I'd be out with an insulin reaction.

Breakfast would be a solid forty-five minutes later than in the hospital, as I whirled out the door to school, clutching my hat to my head and waving goodbye. Dinner was at four because that was when the insulin peaked and my father got home from the day shift. My day could not have been less like the hospital's! It wouldn't take long to create diabetic havoc. Even the nights were not peaceful. About nine in the evening I'd grab an apple or a couple of saltines with a glass of milk and dive into bed with a flashlight so I could sneak-read under the covers.

My mother, who had a sixth sense about the things I was up to, would check to see if I was asleep. Long, deep, even breaths. Could she hear the pounding of my heart? Had I stifled the glow of the flashlight with my body? Heaven help me if she caught me! The book would be confiscated, and a stern voice would pronounce, "This goes back on the shelf. No more books until next week."

"But, Mother!"

All kinds of books went the bed route—historical romances, like *Les Misérables*, classical literature, adventure stories—all in Lithuanian, until I finished elementary school.

My report cards were good enough to satisfy my parents. They drummed the value of education into my head, not only as a prerequisite for the security of a better job, but also as indispensable for a cultured individual.

In grade school I was tractable in diabetic matters more often than not—the rebel was still dormant in me until age twelve. Then I discovered that I could disobey my parents and keep my transgressions secret by prevaricating.

Difficulties of coping with the disease began to multiply with the onset of puberty, and I started to feel out possibilities. I craved candy, all of it—the Butterfingers, Baby Ruths, Mr. Goodbars, Reese's Peanut Butter Cups, Hershey's Chocolate Almond Bars, boxes of Good & Plenty, M&M's, Sugar Babies, SweeTARTS, and Milk Duds. What was missing much of the time was the wherewithal for their acquisition.

So, in my last year of elementary school, I reached a new level of depravity. I began to rifle my parents' pockets for change. Nothing major—a nickel, a dime, pennies. I would speed to the corner grocery and lay it all out for candy and bubblegum. Once I got my chocolate bar home, I would sneak a square of it into my mouth and let it melt, trying hard not to move my lips. Suddenly Mother would look up and ask, "What are you eating?"

The answer, "Nothing" got short shrift and, having determined that "nothing" was candy, she would ask,

"Where did you get it?"

"Bought it."

"Where did you get the money?"

"Had it."

"From where?"

"Someone gave it to me." My first out-and-out lie.

"Who?" This was clearly a dead-end road.

"I took a nickel from Father's jacket."

"You stole it!"

It's hard to imagine what this meant in a household where no one stole anything and in all probability never had. Once could have been written off as naughtiness—after adequate punishment, of course. Twice might still have been excusable. When my parents figured out that I was pilfering regularly, they were at a loss.

Their daughter was turning into a pickpocket; that is, a thief.

As if this were not enough, the thievery was accompanied by dissimulation, dishonesty, and deception. To crown it all, the candy was sure to be a straight path to diabetic complications and an early death. What was to be done?

Events culminated one Good Friday, when I told my mother I was going to church to pray the Stations of the Cross but at the corner of Grand Boulevard took a right instead of a left and, at a trot, headed for the store. The storekeeper had a round glass gumball machine full of small gumballs in various colors. There were also a few striped yellow and orange gumballs mixed in. These were special. If your penny got you a striped one, you could turn it in for a nickel bar of Hershey's chocolate. That Good Friday I spent a dollar's worth of pennies for bubblegum and turned in seven striped gumballs for chocolate bars.

When I reached home my mother was waiting for me. "Did she see me?" flashed through my mind. I thought I spied a form in the living room window as I crossed the street. With a sick feeling in the pit of my stomach, I quickly stashed the loot behind a bush by the Presbyterian Church on the corner. In response to the question, "Where were you?" I muttered, "In church," and tried to slither by, but the Day of Judgment had arrived.

My mother retrieved the purse with the candy and called my father. Mother spoke. Father listened. I sobbed. Finally, rubbing his forehead with a tired hand, he turned to me, "What are we to do with you? Send you to Reform School? What choice do we have?" I too could see the inevitability of my future. " For your own good you must be punished." He declared this well-known truism in a heavy voice, but I was sobbing and shaking. I howled, though I knew he was right. The belt was used rarely in our house. My father was a loving, if strict, man. The lines were carefully drawn, and we children knew what to expect if we crossed them. Punishment was meted out for real transgressions only. Then, of course, as any self-respecting child, I thought I was being punished for no good reason. Commanded to lean over the bed and bare my behind I accepted my three thwacks of the belt in despair and cried more from the insult than pain.

I never stole from my parents' pockets again. Reform school receded.

At that time the way to check the state of the disease was urine-sugar testing, which involved a tablet of Clinitest, a test tube, an eyedropper, and urine. The liquid in the tube would turn one of seven colors from deep blue to muddy brown. Blue was great, yellowish brown, or brown, terrible. The problem was that sometimes I would test high, which was very bad, and fifteen minutes later be out cold with an insulin reaction, that is, very low. It took many years before I learned that the urine tests were inaccurate partly because the urine was collected in the bladder over a period of hours, always behind the actual situation.

I was "advanced" compared to many classmates. They were still playing with dolls when I was performing chemistry experiments with my test tube and pipette in the bathroom at home and logging the results. A test for ketones, a dangerous sign of chemical imbalances, was another part of the routine. A drop of urine on a white Acetest tablet could result in shades of purple from pale lavender to deep violet.

In ninth grade I began to perfect the art of guile. I was all too successful at it. When I was little, my mother had a foolproof method of determining whether I was lying. She told me she saw tiny crosses in my eyes. Tiny crosses! I would examine my eyes in a mirror, trying to discern them. They must be there if Mother saw them. The only way to avoid being discovered was not to lie. As I got older, I realized that there were no crosses and that I could deceive her, though I was never sure to what extent. When my urine sugar tested either bad or very bad because I had eaten something I shouldn't have, I started telling her a false result.

For a long time I thought Mother didn't suspect a thing. But then possibly my voice quavered, or I hesitated too long, maybe there was a note of uncertainty, or perhaps the good results just came too often, but when I called from the bathroom as sweetly as I could, "Ne-ga-tive!" she began asking me to repeat the urine test in her presence. If I desperately needed to have a decent result and couldn't get it honestly, I'd use water and show Mother the sky blue result.

Diabetes had its advantages in high school. I used it, albeit rarely, for nefarious purposes. Reading Balzac at night instead of chapter thirteen of the civics textbook was risky. The teacher could announce a surprise quiz from last night's homework. Immediately my hand would shoot up and I would murmur in a faint voice, "May I go to the nurse, please. I'm having an insulin reaction." Teachers were helpless in the face of it. Even if they suspected something, they would send me, weak and wan, to the medical office. Looking pale was no problem, since diabetics are prone to sickly complexions. The nurse would treat my supposed reaction with orange juice and keep me in the medical office until I "felt better." The quiz would be rescheduled for after school and by that time I would have reviewed the necessary chapter.

The craving for sweets did not lessen. I could ferret out a hidden dessert like a truffle-hunting pig. The oven drawer in which we kept rarely used pots and pans was often the repository of apple cakes, streusel, hard candy, even an occasional donut or sweet roll, clearly cached there for the men of the family. The hidden sweets were never mentioned because I would demand my share, weeping, wailing, angry, defiant, and making life miserable for everyone. Mother steeled herself against flattery, blackmail, begging, wheedling, seemingly impervious to it all.

Iron-willed and disciplined, my father applied his principles universally and expected no less of his children. He, a smoker of at least thirty years, was diagnosed with pancreatitis. Told he would have to avoid fat and quit smoking and drinking if he wanted to live, Father didn't touch a glass or a cigarette again. The only liquor I ever saw him consume thereafter came in chocolate candies filled with Armagnac that I brought from Europe on visits home many years later.

In ninth grade I began to borrow books from the public library to read at home. Until then my reading for fun had been confined to Lithuanian books and school homework assignments in English. I went through most of the literature in my parents' extensive library, anything I could get my hands on, very little of it children's fare. I read *Decameron* and *Kon-Tiki* in Lithuanian. Novels depicted country and city life, people's relationships, and historical feuds. Did I ever wonder why I was reading so little in English? I doubt it. My parents' library was adequately large—for a while.

Once I began high school, I started racing through English books, gobbling them voraciously, practically swallowing them whole. In summer I would cart eight books home from the library, incarcerate myself in my room and turn them in the next day for eight more.

Many years later my mother and I were discussing the teaching of a second language to children in the diaspora. We were clucking our tongues at the difficulties of making kids bilingual when she asked me,

"Do you know why you speak Lithuanian so well?"

"Probably because it's all we ever spoke at home," I hazarded.

"Partially," she nodded. "But you expanded your vocabulary by reading books."

That made sense to me, as by this time I was writing and publishing poetry in Lithuanian.

"And the reason you read so much in Lithuanian," mother continued, "was that I forbade the Indiana Harbor public library to issue you books."

"You what?"

"You were speaking English in school all day, you were doing homework in English, so I told the librarians that you were not allowed to take books out. You could sit there and read, but that was all until ninth grade, that is, high school."

I paced up and down the kitchen, and threw enraged glances at the chair in which my Mama, the despot who had trampled my God-given rights, sat peeling apples.

I was twenty-eight and had published my first book of poetry in Lithuanian when I heard this explanation. I had obtained a once-in-a-lifetime well-paying job as a native speaker of Lithuanian. I was contributing articles and poems to Lithuanian periodicals and was well aware of how important the language was to me, so it was difficult to keep the fury of the cheated twelve-year-old alive. Was I cheated? In school I was good at English, fond of grammar, adept at languages, a voracious reader. All this stood me in good stead. Books were the be-all and end-all. Injunctions to go outside and play fell on deaf ears. Play? What? Delay finding out whether Jane Eyre would ever see Mr. Rochester again? Not learn until tomorrow that the lost necklace which had cost a lifetime of hard work to replace had been a fake? Not wallow in tears when the yearling died? Not follow Angelique carted off from France to the slave markets of the Orient?

In high school I wore unfashionable clothes, glasses, was terrible at sports and good at mathematics. What better formula for unpopularity? But I longed to be accepted. What to do? I opted out. Walked the corridors with my head buried in a book. After I turned sixteen I dared to ask the most unpopular boy in the class to the annual Turnabout (girl asks boy) dance. I figured he was like me and might say yes. He said no. Somehow the news got out. I was mortified and so was he.

Then I thought of a solution. Uosis, who considered me little more than a punching bag, had a friend in Chicago who would sometimes come down for a visit. I asked him to the dance. He said yes, probably as a favor to my brother. Draped in a dark blue satin dress with spaghetti straps that my Aunt Dozė had shone in at banquets, my hair augmented with a fake braid, I was supremely happy. When I entered the decorated gym on Šarūnas's arm, my classmates gasped. Then he smiled and exclamations of "Who is he? Where did she find him? He's got dimples!" rippled through the room. The public triumph gave me satisfaction, at least until he and Uosis sat down to a game of chess after the dance and I became invisible again.

I had hoped that I was Cinderella with Šarūnas cast as the Prince, but instead it was pumpkin and ashes even before midnight struck.

\* \* \*

Our parents signed Uosis and me up for a course in

ballroom dancing to learn the foxtrot, slow fox, rumba, cha-cha-cha. Once I mastered the steps, I had to keep in mind that leading was a man's business. My favorite partner for waltzes and tangos was my father. Embarrassed and stiff, I concentrated on keeping my feet off his toes. He and his friends, courtly elder statesmen in my eyes, bound by their upbringing and tradition, insisted that the young lady in their arms was a graceful nymph even if she set her feet down like blocks. They danced, whether at a sedate pace or a fast canter, with obvious enjoyment. I so wanted to dance.

We were ten at a table at the Lithuanian Youth Center's Benefit Dinner in Chicago one year when I was still in high school, guys and gals chattering about math and science, debating and oral interpretation teams, cars and basketball. I was at a disadvantage for at the time I was still at Washington High School in East Chicago. Indiana, while they were all local in and around Marquette Park in Chicago, taught by the same teachers, supporters of the same teams and privy to the same secrets. Then the band struck up. The young men shifted in their seats until, finally, one caught a girl's eye and nodded toward the dance floor, "Dance?" Two by two couples rose and began moving to the music. My lone hope pushed back his chair and, as my heart fluttered and I mangled the edges of the tablecloth with my sweaty hands, excused himself to tap a girl at the next table on the shoulder. When it became clear to everybody that no one wanted to dance with me, a friend of my father's appeared and courteously held out his hand. And so it went. Dance after dance.

I loved the singing. I didn't mind if I slid up and down the scale searching for a comfortable place to settle my voice: I enjoyed singing loudly, quietly, sadly, melodiously, raucously, joyously. "*Stoviu aš parimus prie rūtų darželio, Kai paspaudęs ranką, tyliai išėjai.*" ("I stand at the gate where you left me quietly after pressing my hand.")

Tomorrow I would be hoarse and my voice would sink an octave, but tonight I crooned and bellowed. My father signaled me when it was time to go home, but the signal needed repetition and parental patience. At the door of the banquet hall I turned back for a last stanza. The longer I sang, the happier I was.

Songs helped me learn languages. So it was with the little Spanish I remember. *Vaya con Dios, mi vida...* So it would be with Greek. *Sineuyasmeni kyriaki.* Even German would oom-pa-pa its way into my life.

The banquets and dances often involved more than just a good time. In East Chicago at a celebration for which the Lithuanians had hired an ethnic band, my father suddenly halted in the middle of a turn on the dance floor and began to bellow.

"Stop the music!"

The orchestra leader signaled and the medley of Russian tunes, *Katyusha* among them, broke off. It had been the marching song of the Red Army as it entered Lithuania in 1940.

The community in East Chicago celebrated on a grand scale, marking Lithuanian holidays and events. If there was to be food, then tables swayed under platters of sausages and sauerkraut, potato *kugelis* with great dollops of sour cream, dumplings strewn with bacon, bowls of chopped vegetable medley with mayo, homemade herring, heavy loaves of dark and light Lithuanian rye. Dinners ended with a rich slice of the twelve-layer *napoleonas* or a sliver of meter-tall *šakotis* of the sixty egg yolks.

The summer after I turned sixteen and had completed my junior year of high school, a major event took place in Chicago—the first World Lithuanian Youth Congress. Because of my age, I was only allowed to register for the pre-congressional camp with its evenings of song around the campfire.

The participants of the assembly organized a demonstration demanding freedom for Lithuania. I marched, sang and shouted. The year was 1966. The eyes of the world were on England, as its soccer team whirled through the games to win the World Cup competition after the final game with Germany's team 4:2.

The closing ceremonies of the Congress were in Chicago, and both my brother and I were permitted to attend. My father gave Uosis the car, admonishing him to look after his sister. He was three years older. After the official part of the festivities and before heading for parties at the Conrad Hilton where some participants were lodging, Uosis and I swung through the Lithuanian neighborhood in Chicago's Marquette Park to see some friends.

"Why don't we stop at the Gintaras Bar?" he suggested.

"Sure."

We parked and I entered. No problem. Uosis followed.

"ID?" A hand gripped his arm.

"Driver's license," Uosis tried to brazen it out.

"Underage. Don't try it again, or you'll lose your license."

So there I was, guzzling beer, which I don't even like, while Uosis eyed it longingly from outside. As I flitted from group to group, taking care to pass the window and give Uosis a wink, I could hear him grinding his teeth. Only when the bar began to empty, did I join him for the move to the Conrad Hilton.

"Listen, kid, we have our own friends, so I'll see you later," and he was gone. At half past four in the morning he appeared at the party where I was singing lustily and said, "I think we should move it. Getting late."

It was six by the time we reached home. Mother had been up all night.

"Streetwalker! Harlot! Where have you been all night?!"

This sounds bad in English, but in Lithuanian it sounds worse. With a muttered "Good night," Uosis slipped away to the basement where he was sharing a room with Father and left me to my mother's wrath. Because he and I hadn't concocted the story we would tell our parents, my lips were sealed.

"I'm dead tired," I mumbled under my breath, trying to ease past her into my bedroom.

"Good-for-nothing! Where have you been? Do you know what time it is?"

"Please, mama," I begged her. "We'll talk tomorrow." I slipped into the bedroom and was instantly asleep.

When I rolled out of bed in the afternoon to get ready for a second night of carousing, I was greeted by a committee of three, which clearly had been palavering about the night before. I wasn't surprised at the parents. What hurt was that Uosis sat there, nodding his agreement to every word they said about my being too much of a baby to understand how I should behave, and why I couldn't be allowed out. I was properly contrite and promised to do better that night,

"You're not going anywhere at all," my father pronounced. "You're staying home, thinking penitent thoughts, and considering what it means to be a responsible person."

I burst into tears. This possibility had not occurred to me. I had told my friends I was coming, we had made plans. Uosis didn't say a word, calmly took the keys from my father and left.

Almost a year later I was butting my head against another wall. My last high school dance was to be after the graduation ceremony. The whole senior class was going. My parents thought ten in the evening was too late.

"You're too young. There will be other dances."

"I'm going whether you let me or not," I hollered.

"Go, but don't come back if you do."

The front door was locked when I got home. I gritted my teeth and rang. Silence. I pressed the buzzer again. Tears welled up. I sat down on the stoop, my head in my hands.

After a good half hour the door opened and my mother said in a voice that sent shivers up my spine,

"Inside." Mother was so furious that true to her Samogitian nature, she did not speak to me directly until I left for the university in the fall.

## 4. Eglė discovers important truths about life, fellow students, and herself, comes to far-reaching decisions. Uosis makes a suggestion she accepts with alacrity.

The University of Chicago was eighteen miles away. My high-school advisor tried to dissuade me from applying to "that commie school" but my heart was set on it.

Besides book knowledge, the university taught me to apply my mind, to think, to deduce, to analyze, rather than learning blindly. During my high school years the rules at home had been clear. I spent some time there angling for more freedom of choice and decision, but the agreement between the powerful and the powerless was that I would achieve this in time. The time came my freshman year.

I was seventeen. Like all first-year women in 1967, I was required to live in a dormitory, Woodward Court in my case. My roommate, Linda Brodzinski, was an American of Polish descent. I returned from a lecture one Thursday afternoon some four months into the academic year, flung open the door, yelling a greeting, and stopped dead. One half of the room was empty— no clothes, no books, no Linda. Stunned, I walked to the window, to the closet, to the bed and sank down.

Linda had not complained about my character, or my staying up until all hours, or my messiness, or anything at all. There was a letter saying it was not my fault, that this was a personal problem she had to work out, but my mind comprehended only one thing—there was something wrong with me if another girl couldn't bear living in the same room and couldn't talk to me about it.

*  *  *

During my first quarter at the university I discovered dating. There were fraternity parties, orientation events, movies. In the first ten weeks I saw twenty men, seven times as many as I had dated in my entire life till then.

Now I was on my own—no hours, as much responsibility as I was willing to accept, and a pleiad of men who indicated interest if I so much as glanced their way. The first to ask me out was a third-year math major. He brought me to his place, talking art and theorems, plays and hypotheses. Then he turned down the lights, snaked a practiced arm around my shoulders, and nuzzling my neck, bent me backwards.

"By the way," breathing heavily between kisses that I allowed, very curious about the progression of such matters, he whispered, "how old are you?"

"Seventeen," I gasped. He sat bolt upright, took a deep breath, tightened his tie, turned up the lights and looked at his watch.

"What's the matter?" I asked.

"Jailbait," he muttered succinctly. "Try me when you turn eighteen."

Another guy saw me in the Reynolds' Club cafe,

buried in a book, pushing a mass of long chestnut locks back from my face though they kept falling in my eyes.

"Wow! Great hair!" I looked up. A student was grinning down at me. "Mind if I join you?"

I moved my book bag from the chair.

"It's your hair. I love it."

By the time we separated to go to our respective classes, we had arranged to meet in two days. He had mentioned my hair twice more. When I got home I pulled off the chestnut wig with relief and ran my fingers through the flattened, matted mass of short blond curls. Should I tell him before I see him? Wiser to be honest, I thought, and called his number.

"I have something to tell you. I was wearing a wig today."

"The girl I spoke to had long, sexy hair."

"I'm telling you—that was a wig. Do you still want to see me?"

He hesitated. That told me everything.

At the end of the quarter I became depressed. So what did they want, all these men, so interested in me? What fascinated them—my intellect, my perspicacity, my wit, my charm? My frankness? They wanted my body. And I was seventeen and totally unwilling to share it.

The second quarter brought no relief. Every day after my classes I would stare blindly at the walls and review the first ten weeks—not the coursework, but the men. Discussions took place on how ridiculous it was that Common Core science courses were required for students interested only in the humanities and adjourned to my conversation partner's room for some "plausible" reason—either he had to return a book to someone who was waiting, or show me his collection of ancient Greek plays or get a different jacket. After the first few times, I recognized the pattern.

"Are you trying to seduce me?"

"Well, and if yes?"

"You don't know me. We might not even like each other. Don't you care? Anyway, if that's your intention, then forget it. I'm not interested."

"Sure, I care. Come on up to my room, and I'll tell you about it."

"Tell me about it? Is that how you express caring?"

"Sure you won't come up? Damn! Sorry," looking at his watch. "Is today Thursday? I just remembered that I've got chem lab. I'll call you."

After a number of such encounters I realized: that I, the real me, the person, the sensitive soul, the romantic, trusting, sincere, loving individual mattered not one iota to anyone except my parents, and much as I loved them, they just didn't count in this crisis.

I would close the door to my room behind me and sort of slide down the wall to the edge of the bed. Books slipped through my fingers. I stopped going to classes. Life did not seem worth the effort I had to expend to maintain it. Not that it was horrible, or painful, or unbearable. No. I just could not find a reason to be alive. I was polite to my new roommate when she came in but distant. I had nothing to say.

I began to think about not being. What difference would it make, if I ceased to exist? Vivian would wonder why, but roommates come and go. Teachers, classmates? My death wouldn't even cause them to raise their heads from their books. So who would care, if I didn't exist?

The guys I had gone out with? They wouldn't recognize my name if they read it in an obituary. I had no access to a gun, hanging was unappealing, slitting my wrists messy. Besides, something might go wrong—I might cripple, but not kill myself.

Presto! Diabetes! Hundreds of times I'd been told, "If you don't take your insulin, you'll die." How quickly? I read up on it. Death would take days. Fine. I wouldn't have to do a thing, just skip insulin injections. Perfect. I would wind down like a clock until I sank into a coma and died. I didn't want to simply wait for death, so I went to my lectures that day and the next.

In the afternoon the phone rang.

"Could you come and see me, Eglė? I've got to talk. No, I'm not all right." A sob.

"I'll be right over."

She met me disheveled, tears flowing.

"I don't matter to anyone, no one cares whether I'm alive or dead. Al and I split—it's not me he wants. He said so. I thought he loved me."

"You're wrong. Not about him, but about friends, me among them. Don't cry. I care. I know it sounds trite, but friends matter."

"Why should you care?"

"He's only one guy. You think you're zero because some jerk said you're not his one and only? When you hear me say that, doesn't it sound stupid? Think of stuff you like doing—art research, ceramics, books. I realize you're in love with him and Life Has Ended, but it hasn't. Cut the melodrama. Apropos, did I tell you I glued the pieces of the blue bowl I broke? Looks almost like new. If I search long enough, I'll find a better one. What's gone is gone. But you're still here and still great. Listen. You've got to believe in yourself, to know how fine you are. I considered myself a worthy human being as long as people told me that. Then I began to doubt myself. Then came a stretch of time when I had no faith in myself. But it's nonsense. I'm somebody, whether any male has the brains to see it or not. You're somebody whether that jerk loves you or not."

The longer I spoke, the more arguments I mustered. I talked half the night and convinced myself in the process. By morning we were holding hands and singing.

I felt sure of my own worth. I would doubt it at times in my life, but I knew I would not consider suicide again. That realization was my gift to myself. We hugged each other, faces glowing.

At home I injected a judicious amount of insulin with shaking hands and, as the sun rose, raced to the fraternity to apprise Uosis of the great news. He grinned.

"You're early. Most University of Chicago students contemplate suicide in their sophomore year."

Involved in various aspects of living I forgot my courses for a while. At the beginning of the Common Core chemistry course the professor had warned the class that anyone who cut lab would fail. There would be no late registration for the lab. I procrastinated. When I realized we had begun the third week of a ten-week quarter, I decided to act—literally. I went to the lab and walked up to the graduate assistant, speaking English with as good a French accent as I could fake.

"*Monsieur*, I 'ave just arrivé from France. *Je suis Lituanienne.* I 'ave probleme *avec l'anglais, n'est pas? Mais,* I must take zis course. Please to 'elp."

I was allowed to register late and was assigned a partner for lab work. No one else was so blessed. For the remaining eight weeks in chemistry lab I spoke with an accent.

I constantly feared discovery. Once the Swiss professor who spoke English with a heavy French accent of his own stopped at the lab to check our work. As he came up to my partner and me, I broke into perfect unaccented American English. The assistant's jaw dropped. The next time I spoke to him my accent was back in place.

*   *   *

And then there was the disease. I had begun my studies with the realization that I was on my own and had carte blanche as far as sweets went. Not only did I indulge in daily desserts at the dormitory, but I also discovered candy machines in the rec room on which I could spend any allowance left over from books and supplies. I began to indulge in donuts and sweet rolls but gained no weight because my insulin—food balance was out of kilter and my body was just excreting the calories I consumed. I was five and a half foot tall and weighed a svelte one hundred and twenty-four pounds.

I would lug a half-gallon of orange sherbet home from the Co-Op, and begin shoveling it in. "Oh, I feel so-o-o bad," I would groan, clutching my stomach after the last mouthful. "I need water." It would take a gallon or two to wash the sherbet down. By that time I was writhing on the floor, but I knew what was needed—insulin.

Then there were the Oreo cookies. First, I'd eat the

cream fillings and then the cookies. By the time I got through three quarters of a bag, I'd feel sick and stick a finger down my throat. I had student health insurance, but who had time for clinic?

I knew it would catch up with me.

Each time I overindulged and saved myself with insulin I kept coming closer to a coma. The proverbial straw was a badly miscalculated insulin dose that caused a humongous insulin reaction, the latest in a series. I finished the ice cream, swallowed the cookies, and reached for the insulin. I woke up in familiar surroundings. Everybody around me was wearing white.

"Insulin reaction? " I muttered.

"When did you last eat? When did you take insulin? How much? What's your daily intake of calories? Do you know you could have died?"

"I don't remember. I don't know. I don't know. Can I go home now?"

"No, we don't think that would be wise. We want to keep you here until we get your diabetes regulated."

"I can't!" I yelped. "I've got exams next week."

Problem was that what with my emotional upheavals I hadn't studied enough during the last two quarters. I could neither face my parents if I failed nor continue at the University of Chicago.

"I need to prepare for exams."

"We're not joking," the doctors answered.

Afraid to take the chance, I acquiesced. Three weeks later I was released from the hospital, diabetes in order. My grades had come in: five incompletes. I had to do something. Before I told my parents I got myself a summer job as a switchboard operator, sublet a room, arranged to move.

Then I broke the news: I had lost my scholarship because of the hospital. "Pack your bags. We're taking you home. We should never have let you go there."

But I refused to go.

I was feeling my freedom. The first thing I did that summer was to make up the incompletes.

It was a grand summer. Independence was heady— earning money, supporting myself. I paid just enough attention to the diabetes to keep out of hospital. On the last workday with the final salary of twenty-five dollars for the last month's rent hidden in my purse, I walked to the Ida Noyes Coffee shop for a cup of tea. When I heard footsteps behind me, I let my imagination run wild. I imagined a robber who would first see if I continued straight on into a rotten neighborhood. He'd wait to bash me on the head there. If I turned left, he'd jump me right away. I got a better grip on my purse and turned left.

Next thing I knew, I was on the ground listening to voices.

I opened my eyes to a semicircle of policemen around me, whispering to one another, "What should we do? Take her to the hospital?" I sat up, said, "Curse it, I'll walk," put a hand to my head, looked at the blood, and lost consciousness again.

A teenager had hit me with brass knuckles. Somebody coming out of Ida Noyes Hall scared him away and called the cops. I needed ten stitches and was left with a scar, but I kept my money.

Just before the start of my sophomore year, a Lithuanian student organization, Korp! Neo-Lithuania, held its summer camp at Lake George in upstate New York. Six of us piled into a Chevy and drove from Chicago, stopping every five hours to drink coffee, go to the bathroom, run around the car and change drivers. When we arrived, I hit crisis point. I was eighteen and couldn't remember life without diabetes. Why inject insulin?

It was glorious to savor cakes as everyone else did, to go to sleep without injecting and wake up the same. But when I tottered to bed the second night, I felt queasy. On the way to my cabin I ran into some fellows who tried to stop me for a chat.

"Hey, Eglė, what did you think of Tom's skit and Romas's reaction?"

"What?"

They could have been asking what I thought of a moon landing. I took a step past them and slipped on the stairs. Rimas reached out a hand to steady me.

"Did you see her? Too much of the hard stuff. Hey, kid, better go sleep it off," they hollered in my wake and laughed.

All I wanted was to reach my bed and collapse. Once there I closed my eyes, but the walls kept moving. The movement of the room nauseated me.

Next morning a counselor got worried. I could not be roused. People were aware of my diabetes only tangentially, it hardly impacted their lives. They thought I was drunk.

"No, no, in the forest, not on the table, I can't help it, no, no, I won't..."

I sank into delirium, kept calling for water and promptly regurgitating it. An ambulance was called. I was gasping for air. The paramedics gave me oxygen on the way to the hospital. I revived much later with various intravenous infusions hanging over me, dehydrated, one arm plastered to a board.

My mother was at my bedside, having flown in from Chicago.

I was alive.

"Water," I croaked through parched lips and sucked through a straw at cracked ice.

I swore this would be my last diabetic coma.

I got an earful from everybody about the permanence of the disease, the close escape I'd had, the fact that I could not ignore diabetes. This time the admonitions penetrated. I accepted the diabetes. I might try to fudge the rules in the future, but I knew I was in the game until the final whistle.

Mother accompanied me on the flight home. My parents were willing to continue educating me, even after the mess I had made, but I would live with them and attend the extension of Purdue University. What could I say? Purdue seemed a poor substitute for the University of Chicago. I agreed because I did want to study but secretly began negotiations to return to the university where I had been. The U of C was willing to lend me tuition money for one quarter, but my parents would have to guarantee repayment.

"Mom, Dad, will you co-sign this loan for me?"

"Your mother and I have never borrowed—not for the car, furniture, or clothes. Haven't we taught you anything? Don't buy on time, don't borrow, don't use credit cards. If you have the money, buy whatever you want. If you can't pay cash, do without."

"My education won't wait."

"Then attend Purdue."

"If you won't countersign, I'll ask my cousin Rimvydas to do it."

"You wouldn't. That would be going outside the family."

"I would be forced to." Though I wasn't proud of what I said.

They signed.

After that quarter at the university I took a job as a clerk at Encyclopedia Britannica to repay the tuition loan. I returned to the university when I could do so clear of all debts, scholarship in hand for tuition, and a part-time job to cover living expenses.

Uosis and I shared an apartment, while I worked. I was grousing about the job one day, when he shot a glance in my direction and said, "Want to come to Europe with Vida and me?"

What a brother!

We pooled our money and drove our grey 1951 Plymouth, its roof contact-papered in a yellow and orange paisley print, to New York City.

## 5. The siblings travel and hitchhike through Europe, and Eglė meets undesirable men in Germany, Italy, and England.

Kerouac had published *On the Road* more than a decade before Uosis and I began our travels. The year was 1969, just after the Democratic convention and demonstrations in Chicago, at the height of "flower power." We were "fringe hippies," going to Europe, meeting the third of our party, Vida, in Paris.

In New York we camped in the apartment of a friend who was in the Army Reserve and had left Uosis the key and the cockroaches. I stayed outside as much as I could to evade them. I'd buy two pounds of dark, firm, sweet cherries, sit on the steps in the sweltering New York summer heat and wolf them down.

Gorging on cherries would not have received my doctor's approval, but diabetes was not going to stop me. I had decided that physicians who insisted on no sugar for diabetics, as many of mine had, were not telling the full story. Confident that everything edible has an insulin value commensurate with its carbohydrate content, I found that most products considered "bad" for diabetics were not on diabetic exchange lists. How much insulin do I inject if I want to eat this candy bar? No one would tell me. Certainly everyone tried to dissuade me from even thinking in those terms, but I was for living life free of, as I saw them, false constraints. They made me want to do the forbidden, including ingesting a couple of pounds of cherries. I was positive there was a way to live as I wanted within the limits of diabetes.

In that cockroach-infested New York City apartment the bug phobia I had since childhood ran wild. Once when I was twelve I was taking a shower in the basement. Having left my glasses on a shelf, I turned on the water and soaping myself, looked down to see a dark blob moving on the ground near my feet. A towel wrapped around my soaped body I shot out of there to the backyard, where my mother was talking to a visiting priest. Thank heavens, it was summer. Both my mother and Reverend Kapočius laughed.

"A centipede," Mother said calmly, coming back with my glasses.

"A centipede," I echoed and shuddered. "Did you kill it?"

An affirmative nod sent me down to finish showering. With my glasses on.

The New York cockroaches would have been no problem had they kept to themselves. When I opened a kitchen cabinet door and came face to face with an immense momma roach on a can of peas, we eyed one another unmoving for what seemed like hours. Had it not been for the hordes of offspring that suddenly swarmed in all directions from beneath her skirts, we might have stood eye to eye until my flight to Europe.

I was on the eve of an amazing adventure that was Uosis's present to me.

His girlfriend had lived in Paris with a French family her junior year at university and visited with them now for several weeks before we joined her. Our Icelandic propeller plane landed in Luxembourg fourteen hours after we took off from New York, and Uosis and I boarded a train to Paris.

Vida was given the use of a two-room apartment outside of Paris for three weeks. That was our base as we widened our knowledge of the area. One afternoon she bought a ripe Camembert in the town market for our delectation.

"For today or tomorrow?" the aged vendor inquired, fingering each one and telling her, "*Non, non, s'il vous plait. Ce camembert la, ce n'est pas pour aujourd'hui, non, non, non. Mais, voila!*"

Like a conjurer pulling a rabbit out of a hat, with a flourish, he placed a cheese in front of Vida and motioned us to smell. Uosis and Vida complied, oh-ed, ah-ed, and bought it, but I wouldn't come close, shaking my head and hands in disgust.

Then we split up, Vida to Lourdes, Uosis and I to Germany. Wherever the two of us went, we made use of the network of Lithuanians that the latest World War had scattered throughout many countries.

A week of Lithuanian Studies in Europe was taking place at Annaberg Castle in Bad Godesberg. Uosis and I lost no time in making our way to West Germany to meet people who shaped the rest of our journey.

In Mainz we stayed with Arūnas, who asked only that I absent myself from the apartment when his cleaning lady came because he was forbidden to have live-in guests. I took my bag and air mattress to a park, where I stretched out on the grass for a couple of hours of reading. I noticed someone pacing back and forth in front of me. Then he stopped and said something, I looked up from my book, smiled, shook my head. The next time he passed he proffered something in a small square box. I refused what I thought was candy. He insisted, shouting as if to a moron, "Anti-baby condom." I looked up the phrase, "Go away, or I'll call the police," motioned him over and, not knowing how to pronounce the German words, pointed with my finger.

He read it and disappeared.

I hitchhiked to Munich where one of my new friends, Aurelija, was living with her parents. Uosis had gone to Copenhagen without me "just to see what's there." I would meet him again in Munich.

The Bavarian city greened, trees and flowers everywhere. My eyes, used to cement and granite, factories and warehouses, and the modernity of Chicago, feasted on nature, history and age.

"Listen, Eglė, my folks are taking me to Stuttgart for the weekend. I'll be back Sunday night. You're on your own till then."

"See you."

Too ashamed to admit I didn't have the money to pay for a hotel room, I spent what I had on a return train ticket to Garmisch Partenkirchen, planning to spend the night in the station and come back to Munich on Sunday. As soon as I ensconced myself on a bench there, I knew I was in trouble. A pair of Italians kept inching closer and closer. "*Mangare, mangare,*" they breathed, leaning in on me.

An American soldier entered the station and sat down.

"Could you do me a favor?" I approached him. "Sit next to me and pretend you know me."

The soldier sat, the Italians turned a few circles and departed. Great. I thanked the guy. He invited me out for a meal.

"Thanks," I said, but I'm a pay-as-you-go person and

I'm flat broke."

"That's all right, I'll pay."

I dithered. Nowhere to go, nothing to do, and the station was about to be locked for the night.

"Would you like to sleep at the base? Sometimes it's permitted. We'd take the Army bus up." When we missed it by minutes, he shrugged, "No matter. We'll take a taxi."

Without the Army bus we couldn't go to the Base, so we'd have to sleep in a hotel. "Uh-oh," I thought.

"My fault we missed the bus, so I'll just take two rooms."

After the restaurant he had tried to get cozy, but I advised him to keep his hands to himself. "Hands off the bod." It seemed to compute. He was doing me a favor, no strings attached. When we arrived at the pension, he told me only one room was available. Alarm bells rang. The door was bolted on the inside and you needed a key to get out. We had an argument about the beds, a single and a double. He left to check in at the Base after locking me in. I still thought I could reason with the man.

When he came back, he told me I would not be sleeping on the single bed, but promised not to touch me. Right. I spent the next half hour struggling. It was the first time I came to the humiliating realization that it was in a man's power to force me. I threatened to scream.

"Oh, come on, you know you want to. All women say 'no' but mean 'yes'."

"This one says 'no' and means 'no'," I screeched, as I shot out of the bed. "Unlock the door."

He didn't want me to scream again. Out of patience, he snapped, "Go!" and opened the door. I skedaddled down the stairs, clutching a stolen towel that I hoped would keep me warm in the mountain air. When I couldn't open the front door, I had to bring him down to unlock it for me.

"Goodbye, soldier."

It was cold, not like sultry summer nights in Chicago, and I hadn't taken a jacket. An open, narrow, empty garage beckoned enticingly. Did I dare?

Awake at dawn, I headed down the mountain road to the town and my train station, glad to be alive. Several hours later I was in Munich.

The next day Uosis trained in from Denmark.

"Copenhagen was great, the smell of grass everywhere, people smiling, friendly. I slept in the park and tucked the straps of my knapsack under my head, so the tug would rouse me if anyone tried to steal the backpack. When I woke up the straps were still there. The thieves had sliced through the straps and left them. I reported the theft, got a new passport, but the rest—the address book, traveler's checks, the safely stowed check numbers—all were gone."

Uosis acquired a new rucksack, but we were destitute. We had planned to hitchhike to Lucerne, Switzerland, by way of Austria, Yugoslavia, and Italy, to meet Arūnas, our host from Mainz, on Lucerne's Death Bridge at noon. He was flying in with tickets for us to a violin concert of the Music Festival. We wired our parents to send money to the American Express office in Dubrovnik and started out. The plan had a certain panache, and changing it would have given us a bigger headache.

All we had with us were air mattresses, Uosis's new knapsack and my bag. The weather was glorious, the warmest summer that Europe had had in ten years. Car drivers stopped for us. In Dubrovnik, we stashed our goods at the train station and wandered through the stone-paved streets of the Old Town. We stopped at the American

Express office, but—no money.

We continued on to Split, stopped for rolls and fruit in a farmer's market, hitchhiked farther. Italian truck drivers drove us across the border into Italy and dropped us off at a youth hostel. There was no room in the women's. "No problem," I said, looking around the spacious hallway. "If you'll allow me, I'll inflate my air mattress and sleep on it in the lobby. All I need is a square meter or two of space."

"Sorry. *Impossibile*," was the answer.

"But I have nowhere to stay." Panic was beginning to set in.

"Not our problem."

I huddled on the steps until morning.

I had a lot of time to think about my disease. It was not being very bothersome in Europe. My plan was simple—no hypoglycemic reactions, as they tend to elicit comments like "Are you sure you're all right?" and "Don't you think you'd better stay home tonight?" How could I be certain of not having reactions? By keeping my blood sugar constantly elevated. This was before blood glucose monitors, so I could not check how well or badly I was doing. I approximated. I made it through the entire three months taking care of insulin reactions before they overpowered me—a little candy here, a bit of sugar there. I had cut my insulin dose considerably so that the increased exercise, as I trudged the highways, would not send me into unconsciousness.

Uosis passed a great night on a bed in the men's hostel. The next morning another truck driver picked us up. One night of no sleep was hardly a big deal for a nineteen-year-old, but sleep had been scarce several of the previous nights as well. I was fading. Dropped off in Milan, Uosis and I considered taking a room for the night, but five thousand lire—the equivalent of three dollars at the time—was the extent of our finances. The marble slabs in the train station waiting room looked inviting.

An Italian accosted us.

"Italians love America," he burbled, face wreathed in smiles. "I have for you a great room tonight. You are..." Franco hesitated, "married?"

"Brother and sister," Uosis corrected him. "How much for the room?"

"Five thousand lire."

We burst out laughing and hastened to explain that this was all the money we had. We thought it charming that we were brother and sister, traveling penniless through Europe. Franco was probably humming the local equivalent of "Oh, happy day" under his breath, as he wished us all the best and disappeared.

The immense waiting room with rows of marble slabs was full of men. I felt conspicuous. Within minutes my brother was dead to the world on one slab, but I was as alert as a scout on patrol because as soon as Uosis closed his eyes, a half-dozen Italian men made their move. I could not make them comprehend anything and they would not leave me alone. I woke Uosis.

"Okay," he said, "I'll get our air mattresses, and we'll lie down next to each other."

The minute he left his slab, I had my groupies around me again. One, a Sicilian, kept saying "*je t'aime*" in French and rubbing his appendix scar suggestively. I began shouting in English in sheer frustration and was stunned when a voice asked, "Something wrong?" Facing me was our Italian acquaintance of not two hours ago.

"Could you tell these guys to leave, please," I moaned.

He rattled off a sentence in Italian and they were gone.

"I speak to my friend Tony about you and your brother," Franco continued talking, as though nothing had happened. "Tony feel very sorry for you. He want give you place to sleep."

"I can't decide anything till Uosis gets back," I shook my head. When he did, I apprised him in Lithuanian of the offer, and we decided to accept it, but not allow ourselves to be separated. Then Franco got his friend Tony, who spoke only Italian, and sang out,

"Tony like buy you dinner."

"Why?"

"You eat? *Mangare*?"

We were treated to pizza and wine, very dry pizza, very much wine. After four bottles Uosis and I were feeling no pain.

"So, you will be sleeping in a room with other girls and your brother with other men," Franco said. We nodded and piled into Tony's Alfa Romeo. After a while he pulled to a stop.

"You will sleep here," Franco told Uosis. A warning bell tinkled at the back of my fuzzy brain, but Uosis thought it would be all right. I let Franco drone on and on.

"Tony is rich. He want to give you one hundred dollars."

"For what?" I asked drowsily.

"For nothing. For drink coffee with him. Because he love Americans. Because he sorry for you." Pause. "But there is one thing. You must not tell your brother." If that's all, I thought, I'll lie to them and tell Uosis right away.

"Sure," I assured him aloud.

"I am glad to see that you are not a *bambina*, you are a woman," exclaimed Franco and patted me on the shoulder.

*Bambina*? Woman? Lights flashed. In one second I was sober. The car was slowing to a stop in a small park and Franco was climbing out. I was terrified. "Tony want talk to you," he said, disappearing into the darkness.

"In what language?" I yelled after him.

Tony leaned across me and pushed a button. My seat folded flat. He then did the same on his side, turned to me and whispered, "*Amore,*" putting a hand on my thigh. I removed it. The man's *amore* was followed by a spate of Italian words. "I want my brother" was my only response. In English. After ten minutes Tony began to get annoyed. His avowals of *amore* took on a more insistent tone until finally he asked, "*Virgine?*" No time to vacillate. "Yes." Within seconds our seats were upright, and Tony had called Franco back to the car to ask me, "You have never known a man?"

"Never," I shook my head.

"Two hundred dollars. Do nothing. Just play."

"I want my brother."

Franco tried to cajole me into smiling, but my only response was "I want my brother."

"We will take you to your brother."

Then we were stopping again, and Franco was stepping out with the clear intention of not coming back.

"Where do you think you're going?" I screamed in his wake.

"This is my hotel. I'm going to sleep here."

"What about me?"

"Tony will take you to your brother."

We drove until we reached the train station again. Tony led me to a stranger. I understood his gestures to mean that he would take me to my brother. I was low on trust, but didn't know what else to do. I got in the car. By now it was close to five in the morning. The new man gave me the Grand Tour of Milan. He was conversant in Italian and German.

"*Katedrale*," he pointed, zipping past it. Before I knew it we were well out of Milan and he was identifying "*Sporto pavilione*," inside which he turned off the ignition, "*amore*" on his lips and a hand headed for my thigh.

"*Wir gehen nach mein Bruder*," I tried to redirect him in bad German. Not to be dissuaded from his *amore* speech, he insisted that I wait and listen for ten minutes, then he would transport me to Uosis. I sat out a harangue of *amore* and *Liebe*, staring at my watch and counting seconds aloud.

After ten minutes of impassioned pleading he stopped to take a breath, and I spoke up, "*Wir gehen nach mein Bruder*." Tony's friend leaped out of the car cursing, took my bag and the roll of air mattresses from the trunk, and plopped them down in the middle of the field.

It was "*Ciao, bambina*."

A delivery truck had stopped at the edge of the Pavilion. Tears streaming down my cheeks, I approached the men, able only to enunciate "*polizia,*" at which they clutched their heads, one another, and cried, "*Polizia? Incidente automobilistico?*"

"No, no," I reassured them, pointing to myself and trying to make them understand that the police would take me to the "*trene stazione*."

The men put me between them in the cab of the truck like a sack of potatoes, my luggage at my feet. Taking turns both tried *amore* and a hand on the thigh. I thought light hysteria might have a greater effect than firm refusal. Then abruptly they stopped the truck. Diagramming with their hands that the truck was *molto grande* for the narrow streets leading to the train station, which was just around that corner, they put me down.

Six in the morning. Many people out. Without warning I saw a familiar face. Tony! Shocked, he turned his palms up, asking what I was doing there. He didn't make a pass and took me to the train station by car. Then he got Uosis. The hour was almost eight.

My brother came in, yawning and stretching like a cat. "How did you sleep?" he asked.

"When we get about five hundred miles from here, I'll tell you."

He reddened, "Tell me now." When I was done he said, "We'll make Tony pay you the money he and Franco talked about."

"But, Uosis, I'm okay. They didn't do anything."

"So what? For your lost sleep."

"Give my sister the two hundred dollars you promised her," Uosis grabbed Tony by his lapels, but the man had six or seven muscular friends with him. It was better to be circumspect.

When Tony pulled out his wallet, it proved to be all but empty, though his five thousand lire doubled our resources. One thought irked Uosis: "I slept at Tony's house and saw his possessions: stereo, radio, television. Had I known what you were going through, a few luxuries would have suffered consequences. As it was..." The shrug never materialized. Instead, his eyes lit up.

"Sit here, don't move," he told me and, pouring himself a cup of sugar, went out. Uosis had remembered where Tony had parked his Alfa Romeo. "It probably had the only unlocked gas tank in Italy," my brother chortled, as he gloated over the sugar he had dumped into it. "Tony won't forget the Americans."

For the ten thousand lire we bought train tickets in the direction of Lucerne.

We spent the rest of our cash on a couple of chocolate bars and were thrown off the train once our tickets expired. It started to rain, not droplets but sheets. We were hoping to hitchhike the rest of the way, but people were chary of giving rides in the rain. At high noon we were standing at the side of a highway, dabbing at rivulets running down our foreheads and noses, hours away from our destination.

We didn't know Arūnas was bringing the money our parents had wired to him after the cash sent through American Express was returned unclaimed. Why? Someone had misfiled it under Uosis's first name.

A pickup stopped for us. There was room for one in the cab—Uosis could communicate with the driver in German, so I curled up cold and wet in the open back and reviewed the recent behavior of my diabetes.

We had no money, so we weren't eating. Two candy bars for the whole day were not enough to send my sugar soaring, rather, I had to keep an eye on it to prevent it from plummeting. That summer saw the beginning of a habit. Whenever I went into a European cafe and ordered coffee or tea, which came with one or two lumps of paper-wrapped sugar, I pocketed them. They were souvenirs, until the time my blood glucose dipped and I needed one in earnest. After that, I kept a handful in my bag at all times for emergencies. I'd regret losing the picture of a Parisian rose or an odd Turkish cafe name, but I consoled myself with the promise of another visit there if I survived that particular attack of hypoglycemia.

Seven hours late we reached the concert hall in Lucerne,

where Arūnas was already trying to sell our tickets. The doorman looked offended at our attire, but didn't bar us from entering. Having checked our bags in the cloakroom, disheveled and drenched, we took our seats, second row center. The women on both sides flaunted diamonds and elegant Italian footwear, as their gentlemen flicked dust from the sleeves of their tuxedos. I tucked my sandaled feet behind me.

But I caught the star of the evening, the Czech violinist, grinning at me. Whatever impression I had created, I ruined within the next ten minutes. The comfort of the seats and the soothing melody of the violin combined to lull me to sleep. Uosis elbowed me in time to clap. Another couple of hours of cold and privation I could have endured, gritting my teeth and vowing to die rather than succumb to sleep, but ten minutes of warmth and comfort were my undoing.

The end of our journey was approaching. Uosis and I had spent almost three months and all our money traveling. London was still ahead, and then back to routine, whatever that would be. The thought of what I would do back in America did not so much as cross my mind all summer.

\* \* \*

In London we rented a room at the Lithuanian House, where I left some things and hitchhiked alone to the Theater Festival in Edinburgh. As I set out on the M1 heading east, I was dressed respectably in a skirt and blouse. So excited I could barely keep my feet on the ground, I had tickets to three plays and a reservation for a bed and breakfast in my pocket.

A physician and minister in his late thirties, who would

shortly be making his home in Gibraltar, stopped and drove me four hundred miles to Scotland's capital, pausing on the way at Stonehenge.

In Edinburgh, my driver apologized for having business in London, and left me at the door of my bed and breakfast. What a breakfast! I made it my main meal for the next two days: tea, kippers, toast, scones, a whole pot of butter and marmalade, eggs. I could barely stagger to my feet after these morning feasts, but Edinburgh called, and I was off and running.

The Royal Shakespeare Company's productions of *Richard II* and *Henry V* touched every nerve of my imagination. "The-a-ter," I began to mutter in my sleep, "Theater." When would I dare to try it?

Blissfully sated with almost a week of twice daily theater productions, I rose early on Monday to get back on the road. While I was stuffing the last bite of buttered scone into my mouth, the doorbell rang. A gentleman was waiting for me in his car. The doctor had returned to give me a ride back to London. Since I had told him I wanted to see Stratford, we would stop there. He hadn't forgotten.

Tired from the long drive to London and back, he wanted to rest in Shakespeare's birthplace. We tried every hotel in and around the city, but all double rooms were booked because of a festival. In the end I was willing to share a single, if he would promise to keep to his side of the room, but the Reverend would not compromise my honor in the eyes of an innkeeper. I urged him to change his mind. I was satisfied that my honor would be safe. Nothing doing. He slept in the front seat of the car, while I slept in the back.

As the damp and foggy day began to seep into the car through the cracks of windows and doors, I opened my eyes, cramped and crabby. My driver was still snoring, but after a half hour I poked him awake. I felt sweaty and not very clean. He stank, but seemed oblivious. After breakfast we hit the road.

Before we reached London, he proposed to me.

He did not proposition me. That I would have expected, relying on summer experiences in Germany and Italy. No. The man asked me to be his wife and to go to Gibraltar with him.

I gave him the telephone number of the Lithuanian House where I was staying, but didn't tell him that in a week, when he was to call, I'd be an ocean away. Perhaps he didn't really expect me to say yes. Still, the courtesy of a reply would have been a minor enough way of showing my gratitude for his kindness, time, and effort. When many years later I told Henryk the story he insisted I had made at least one person happy, but he let me draw my own conclusions as to whom he meant.

The journey was over. It had lasted almost three months and had taken us through countries we had only heard of and read about. We had lived in the French countryside, floated down the Rhine, bought melons in Dubrovnik, stood in the rain on Italian mountain roads, breathed great gulps of theater in Edinburgh, bought postcards in Soho.

I didn't know then how the varied threads of my trip to Europe would be woven into my future. As I sat in the airplane, I had much to think about. The voyage had ended, but nothing had finished. There would be time for evaluation, for words of approval or censure, Uosis would have something to say about my dependence, my whining for food, for a bathroom, my habit of walking two steps behind him—like a slave, he said—but the lasting effects would become visible later.

Europe perceived through literature and my parents' stories for a number of years, took on new meaning. It became a part of my consciousness. I felt European.

## 6. Catalogs the traumatic return to Chicago and the beginning of a new life.

I returned to my parents' home in Indiana. What would I do with my life? Where would I go? No money, no apartment. My parents firmly suggested I stay with them. I bowed. Work in East Chicago? Rather, I began to hunt for employment in the Windy City.

A job in accounting at the Art Institute caught my eye. In the interview with the Personnel Director, I thought I had all the right answers.

"So you're looking for a job in accounting. Why?"

"I've always been interested in numbers. I was good at algebra, geometry, and trigonometry in high school. Of course, the fact that I've just come back from Europe and need money to live on did play a not inconsiderable part in my decision."

"A temporary job?"

A red flag went up.

"Not at all. I intend to make this my life."

"You don't want to finish your degree? We're looking for someone who is interested in staying with the job."

"I've decided not to continue with my degree. "

"Have you ever had an accounting job?"

"I was a cashier part-time."

"What do you do in your spare time?"

"Go to the theater, concerts. I get lost in a book faster than you can blink—other worlds, thoughts, ideas."

I remembered why I was there and began to wax rhapsodic about debits and credits, but a tiny smile twitched one corner of her mouth and I trailed to a stop.

"I don't think you'd be right for this job." I gulped, as she continued, "But go see Judy Christian. She's the Financial Aid Director at the School of the Art Institute. She's looking for an assistant."

Judy Christian was an angel in a position of power. We liked each other on sight. I had the job in five minutes and was rarely to feel such affinity for a supervisor. Getting to work was a little troublesome. I would commute to work by bus from Indiana. I aimed for the 7:30 A.M. bus. This may not seem tragically early to some, but I was going to bed at 3:00 AM. Four hours later I would walk like a horse with blinders, seeing only a square yard in front of me, unless people addressed me or otherwise obtruded themselves into my space. I slid into the day a millimeter at a time like my nephew Ben, who until age five had to be carried around in a parent's arms for a good half hour after he woke to ease him into the day.

It was time to move to Chicago to live, but I dithered. First I went out to Providence, where my brother had landed. He invited me to hike up a mountain in Vermont and stay overnight in a cabin by the lake. "Can't," I told him. "No way. I can walk a long way on flat ground, but I just can't climb. I would keep lagging behind. Nice of you, but I'd better not." Uosis insisted.

As I placed one foot in front of the other for first one hour, then the next, I could barely believe it—I was hiking.

Uosis had been sure of it. We dined on trail mix, and the constant exercise meant I had no trouble with the diabetes. We stopped to drink at a stream, to listen to the soughing of pines, the stillness broken by small animals in the brush, a deer pausing to sniff the air and bound away. At the top of the mountain the moon shone on the mirrored silver surface of the lake. We closed our eyes in the wooden cabin, took deep breaths of cool, clean air and fell asleep.

We woke to the sound of tapping on the cabin roof and it took some moments to realize that we were hearing drops of rain. Uosis was wearing hiking boots. My open-toed, open-heeled sandals—lousy hiking gear in the best of conditions—proved totally inadequate. At the top of the trail I was still okay, but at the bottom I was wading in mud and six inches of water.

That weekend was a kick. I could accomplish more than I had thought. I was making reasonable money, but I hungered for the thick of the action, for a new and "hopping" neighborhood in the north of Chicago, New Town. Apartment hunting took me to rooms on the fourteenth floor of a high-rise. The flat was reasonably big, unreasonably expensive, the windows providing a close-up view of concrete walls, looking down into garbage bins below, surrounded by buildings. No greenery, no space, but I convinced myself that precisely this was what I wanted.

When my parents came to visit, my father looked around and asked in disbelief, "You want to write poetry here?"

"Poetry can be written anywhere. It doesn't need to be beautiful or about beauty. It just needs to be meaningful, real," I pontificated.

Father shook his head and left. It took me a few

more weeks to admit that indeed I couldn't write there. I hated coming home, despised feeling closed in, abhorred the men urinating in the street. Besides, my unfinished degree gnawed at my mind. Didn't I want to go back to the university? Go South, young woman, go South!

Someone took over the lease. My debt to the university was paid. I began to search for ways to finance the rest of my education. The Lithuanian Alliance of America and the Lithuanian Foundation came through with partial scholarships. I negotiated with Judy Christian about switching to part-time work at the School of the Art Institute, while attending classes at the University of Chicago. I never did better at studies, but the job suffered. Art students had difficulties accommodating to my reception hours, which zigzagged from morning to afternoon according to my class schedule. I had worked the job in around my lectures, but that simply wasn't good enough. I sighed. It had been a dream job with mutually caring people. I staved off hunger for another quarter with part-time secretarial work for a history professor on campus.

Advised to apply for welfare when money became scarce, I did. Crowded waiting rooms, angry, bitter mothers, myriad children clutching at skirts, indigent men in silk and satin strutting their stuff, some careful to roll up to the door of the Welfare Office in Lincoln convertibles. Social workers were harassed and impatient, folders in piles around them—I listened, as I sat there for interminable afternoons. Each case was sadder than the last, each family's plight more pathetic. I was lucky. Welfare saw me through one quarter, but I resolved never to reach the point of needing it again.

The last year and a half at the university I studied as I never had before and graduated. The blow came later.

## 7. Depiction of a singular event in the protagonist's life and unexpected attacks both physical and spiritual.

On a sunny Sunday in June three hundred undergraduates in caps and gowns, I among them, rose from their seats one by one and walked up the aisle of Rockefeller Chapel to receive a bachelor's degree under the beaming eyes of family and friends.

What would be next for me? Graduate school or job? I had not applied to any graduate school. As I handed my father the appropriately understated gray diploma of the University of Chicago, he patted me on my black-gowned back, "Good. Means a lot. You'll see."

I had made some peace with my diabetes. After a time, the injections, the blood glucose tests, the food limitations became routine. The diabetes receded into the background of my conscious mind. Were it to disappear—trouble. An inner monitor flashed whenever I reached a limit. Consuming spinach and cheese tortellini in cream sauce at Lago di Garda, I took care to cover the carbs of the delectables with an injection. Tasting wine in the Stellenbosch vineyards of South Africa, I balanced the hypoglycemic effect of it with crackers. I learned to be spontaneous carefully.

Between 1970 and 1980 I changed my name or at least the writing of it in Lithuanian. The endings of women's surnames change to show their marital state. Either Norkutė, unmarried daughter of Norkus, or Norkienė—married, wife of Norkus. Men's names do not change. Several friends and I began to look for a way to make our names simply indicate gender which the Lithuanian language requires. We discovered that the ending -ė by itself would serve our purposes well. Marija Saulaitytė found encyclopedic evidence that this ending had been used in parts of Lithuania in the eighteenth century. She and her husband Algis Stankus took the married name Stankus-Saulaitis for him and Stankus-Saulaitė for her. I stopped signing my last name "Juodvalkytė" and began to write "Juodvalkė."

After graduation I stayed where I was, working part-time and acting. A summer production of Ibsen's *A Doll's House* was in rehearsal, and I had the leading role of Nora. I was happy, but something was wrong. First, my back began to ache. I could get relief only by bending, so I would double over during rehearsals whenever I had no lines. It was hardly in character for Nora, but my director bore with me. Then I stopped eating. Never hungry, if I tried to swallow something, intense pains would radiate within minutes in all directions like the sun's rays. I began losing weight.

At the Emergency Room of the University of Chicago hospital an intern talked to me at length about the back pain for which he could find no physical cause. I answered questions about my job, my daily routine, my hobbies. What did I intend to do with my life? I shrugged my shoulders. His eyes lit up. He discussed the trauma of leaving the security of the university, entering the real world, finding a job and functioning. I stood there, bent in half with pain and thought that this could make sense. I was willing to look for an explanation for my physical pain outside of my corporal body. I had read Freud, Jung. All I wanted was to know the cause of the pain so I could begin the process of dealing with it. The fact that I had been a diabetic for eighteen years somehow escaped both the intern and me.

Within a month and a half I deteriorated from the "healthy" hundred forty pounds I had expanded to in Europe to a gaunt hundred four. I was hospitalized. Nothing was found. The director of my play came to see me and gently inquired whether I would be able to carry on, "The show must…" I grinned a death's head grin, but wiping away tears had to admit that performing would be beyond me.

I was released from the hospital, but the only relief from my back pain was in a tub of cold water. It was summer in Chicago. "Hot town, summer in the city…" Like royalty, I received my friends in the tub. Matters got worse.

I had gotten the name of a diabetes specialist at Loyola University Hospital, a Dr. Brooks, who hospitalized me again. After two weeks he told me that the sharp, shooting pain in my back which had spread to my legs, was a nerve pain that would, in all probability, be permanent. He was the first to diagnose neuropathy. But in order to help me make the difficult adjustment to life with incessant pain, Dr. Brooks wanted to transfer me to the psychiatric ward. "Fine," I consented. "If you think that's what I need."

Overruling my mother's vociferous objections and refusing to discuss the problem with her, I signed myself in.

Matters began to clarify for me when the steel door clanged shut behind me. I discovered a patient skulking in a corridor, naked, scraping the wall with a large spoon and using her nails for handholds to help her climb up. Clucking an orderly told me she had to be periodically sedated. Should I introduce myself to the man sitting in the room next to mine? He was wearing a suit coat, though I could see the pale print of his hospital gown peeping out from under the jacket, Gradually the realization was dawning on me that maybe, just maybe, I had erred. The girl who was scraping her knuckles raw attempting to climb the wall did not even acknowledge my existence.

I wanted out. But how?

Because I had committed myself the doctor was the only one who could let me out. He thought I must learn to deal with a pain which would be mine for good. In 1973 the medical practitioner's attitude to chronic pain was that the patient just had to bear it.

There was a pay phone in the corridor. I called collect.

"Mama," I begged, "get me out of here."

Presently I was summoned to Dr. Brooks's office. My mother and her brother, Alfonsas Norkus, a judge in Lithuania before the war and a Midland Savings and Loan Association manager in the United States, were there.

"Do you want to leave?" the doctor inquired.

"Yes. Yes."

"As I explained to you before, you must come to terms with and accept your pain before you can take up your life outside the hospital. Leaving now will do irreparable damage to your mental health. I know that it's not easy. Still, you would be well advised to stay, despite the difficulties. For your own good," Dr. Brooks explained.

"No, thank you, no, I thank you and again, I thank you," I echoed *Cyrano de Bergerac*.

My mother and my uncle were adamant as well—they were not leaving without me. The doctor, annoyed but helpless, released me into their custody, free again, albeit just as sick as I had been when I was admitted.

"The only crazy thing you did was to put yourself in there," my mother later said many times with the satisfaction that comes of having repaired her child's self–inflicted damage, sort of like cleaning and bandaging a bleeding knee.

The problem was, I wasn't improving. I was in pain every waking minute. Aunt Lialė asked a Lithuanian doctor for advice. "Dr. Rubenstein," he said. "Endocrinologist at the University of Chicago Clinics, head of the Department of Medicine, a specialist of diabetes. He'll figure out what's wrong. Dr. Rubenstein."

When I dragged myself into his office, he took one look and hospitalized me. His diagnosis was complete. The nerve disease was a complication of diabetes, peripheral neuropathy. Every function of my body was tested. Autonomic neuropathy. The pains in the back, in the legs, in the stomach, all had a name.

Dr. Rubenstein was special. Not censorious, when I confessed a "sin" against my diabetic diet, he helped me to stop considering deviations from it transgressions for which I would be punished. I had to discuss lapses if I wanted to learn how to compensate for them. I had to admit to bad choices before I could correct them. I had to work on eliminating the words sin, transgression, mistake, bad, wrong when referring to my behavior treating the diabetes.

"You were a wreck when you first came to see me, how long ago was it? Twenty years? More? Look at you now," he grinned, when I kept an appointment many years later.

Panicky phone calls to his office and his home, questions about everything from a sudden fever to the advent of new and better insulin didn't ruffle his calm or his readiness to provide answers. When I married, Dr. Rubenstein came to the wedding to wish us well.

The diagnosis of peripheral and autonomic neuropathy did not herald a cure. I was apathetic to everything but the pain. I shivered constantly. The thermostat in my hospital room was set at ninety degrees, but I would lie under a mountain of comforters and shiver. During visits my mother would blanket my body with hers to keep me warm. It was the only thing that helped.

I was still unable to eat. My family suggested various foods, but to no avail. The day I woke with a desire for freshly squeezed orange juice, my parents brought a bag of oranges which my dad began to squeeze. Alas, the craving faded as suddenly as it had appeared.

I hadn't the strength to hold a book in my hands, so every day my father brought classic novels by Žemaitė and Krėvė-Mickevičius to read to me. I would labor up and down the hospital corridor for a few minutes, a parent on either side to support me.

"How long will the pains last?" I asked the doctors every day, and they would shrug.

"But you don't understand," I disagreed, "I cannot stand this pain."

They told me later that I had a "mild" case of neuropathy.

"You'll have to get used to it."

"Get used to it? You try a week of the nerves in your legs taking turns screaming in agony until you don't care to live and then tell me to get used to it."

Every time I saw my mother I cried because she was getting thinner and thinner, as I lost weight.

One afternoon my parents did not arrive at the hospital at two in the afternoon, the start of visiting hours. Twenty minutes later the nurse discovered me sobbing, "They don't love me anymore. It's the end. I can rot in the hospital."

A few minutes later my parents rushed in, apologizing for their lateness. "Somebody called just as we were leaving, then we had trouble finding a parking spot, so we're a little late, but here we are. How are you feeling? What did the doctor say?"

Gastroenteritis diabeticorum. Erosions of the stomach lining. Heart—okay. Lungs—okay. Eyes—retinopathy. Every day brought more x-rays, more tests.

Then one night, I called for a nurse to help me to the bathroom. One ring. Expectantly, I waited, a smile on my face. "Terribly sorry," I rehearsed my request, "but I need to..." Second ri-i-i-ing. "Would you help me to the bath...?" Nothing. Third ri-i-i-ing. Nothing. I was getting panicky. I had to go. Ri-i-i-ing. Nothing. "I'll go by myself." I pushed myself off the bed, stood for a moment, and blacked out, falling face forward and breaking off two front teeth.

As I lay on the floor, I thought, "Where is she, where is the nurse? I've been ringing that darn buzzer for a half hour. Where is she? Nobody's helping me, and I need help. My teeth, help me someone, my teeth!" Then I let loose. "He-e-elp! HE-E-E-ELP!" I yelled, adrenalin pumping to my brain. When the nurse finally came to help me up, she scolded, "What are you doing getting out of bed by yourself? You have to ring for the nurse and wait."

I was sitting straight up in bed, eyes flashing fire, nostrils dilated, when Dr. Rubenstein entered the room.

"If everyone was aware that I could not walk without help, why, for pity's sake, weren't the side rails of my bed up to prevent me from rolling off or getting out of it? I broke off two front teeth."

"Your teeth are not my primary concern. It's too bad this happened, but teeth can be crowned." Dr. Rubenstein was blunt. "What I care about is that you have decided to live again."

I was out of the hospital in a week.

I went home to my parents in East Chicago and lay around day and night, still unable to hold a book. Mother brought home a kitten abandoned in an alley in a rainstorm. Placed on my covers it frolicked trying to catch its tail, falling asleep in mid-leap. Admiring it was my main activity.

Slowly, month by month the nerve pains began to ease. I was able to sleep. As I got better, television began to grate on me, I felt stifled. There was nothing to do. I prowled the rooms and made decisions for myself again. I needed to get away to help myself recuperate, but where?

The situatuon called for a change of city. The doctor thought Uosis's apartment in Providence would be a fine place to convalesce. My parents acquiesced, Uosis issued an invitation, and I packed a bag. His apartment was unfamiliar, life in it proceeded on a different and more exciting schedule than my parents' settled existence. I still lounged around a lot of the time because the slightest exertion would tire me out.

Stopping by from work one late morning Uosis found me still in bed after my insulin injection.

"Look, I don't have time, I have to get back. Get up and eat breakfast."

But once he left the room, I just couldn't force myself to leave the bed. "I will, I will, in just a minute," I muttered, but torpor was making my body heavier and heavier. When he came back at lunchtime to see how I was doing, Uosis found me unconscious, and, angry that I hadn't listened, he grabbed some orange juice and poured it down my throat. Straight down the wrong tube. What followed was choking, aspiration, ambulance, hospital, pneumonia. As I began to convalesce, practicing my cough to the edification of my nurses morning, noon, and night, Uosis informed me that he had had it—he was sending me back to the parents.

After the pneumonia, I continued recovering from the neuropathy. The pain diminished. As I began to get up every day, to walk, to eat, to gain weight, to read, to sleep, I knew I had better think about my life. Though the parents tried to convince me to stay, I insisted on going back to the room in Chicago for which I had been paying rent all this time. I left home again.

"Who will take care of you?"

"Mama, I have to take care of myself, I have to live by myself, and be responsible for myself."

The day they brought me back to the address on Cornell, Liza, a graduate student and friend, renting the room next to mine on the third floor, was there. As Liza prepared lunch for both of us, I went up to my room twice to get something and sat down to wait for the meal. Liza later told me that in a few minutes I excused myself, went up to my room, and passed out. She thought I simply wasn't hungry.

Hours passed. A series of moans began to emanate from the upstairs bedroom. When Liza went up to see what was wrong, she found me unconscious and called an ambulance, but was annoyed by what she thought of as a deliberate action.

At the hospital someone injected glucose and I revived. My mom called my place a little later and asked for me. Liza told her I was lying down. Mother must have broken out in a cold sweat. "Please wake her," she ordered. What could

Liza do, but admit that I was in the hospital? My parents were at the Emergency Room in a half hour. To take me home. "No, Mama," I said, "It's okay. I have to persevere. I miscalculated the energy I would use climbing the stairs twice. I'll learn to adjust properly."

Against their better judgment they took me back to my room and left, unfairly but pointedly ignoring Liza. Relations were to worsen. While my parents were getting me from the hospital, my Aunt Lialė had talked to Liza, who said that, as she saw it, my unwillingness to take responsibility for myself and my too great dependence on my parents was partially their own doing.

My aunt repeated her version of the conversation to my stupefied mother.

I was instructed never to speak of Liza again.

## 8. Hollywood enters the picture, and a new set of friends appears. A fateful summer job materializes, and an offer is made.

In Chicago at the School of the Art Institute my eye caught a poster advertising classes of the Ted Liss Actor's Workshop.

"Should I? Dare I?" I scraped together enough courage to turn the doorknob and mutter "I want to be an actress." Ted had seen my kind before.

"Are you sure?"

"S-sort of," I stuttered.

"Ability comes with work. The more you do, the more you'll gain."

Once a week I attended classes, learning to breathe from the diaphragm and to project my voice to the person in the last row of the theater. I did voice exercises, prepared scenes from *A Streetcar Named Desire, Little Foxes,* monologues from *Cyrano de Bergerac* and *Electra*, and, no less important, made friends. In the beginning all our interactions took place in class. Then we began to meet on weekends to rehearse scenes and the ties of friendship strengthened. Once I had a third rehearsal scheduled at Ted's on a Saturday, and was astonished to find all of us "teddies" there after 7: 00 PM.

"Surprise! Happy Birthday!"

Ted pointed out our faults, drew skills from us that we were unaware we had. Our group dwindled and increased periodically. Some moved on to professional theater, a few switched to other schools, others dropped out, never to be heard of again, new hopefuls came. There were exhilarating moments when a student knew, just knew, that he or she had done well.

I spoke Lizzie's monologue from *The Rainmaker*, "There are all kinds of dreams. Mine are small ones, but they're real. So you can have yours and I'll have mine." My face glowed like a beacon, and when the light came on, I saw the reflection of that glow in my colleagues' faces.

"Less is more. Don't diagram. If you don't believe what you say, neither will the audience." Ted drummed these precepts into us. Stanislavsky's phrase "I don't believe you," spoken by Ted, hounded us through performances of scenes until genuine emotion erupted and was channeled into every role. Each achievement helped in ways we hadn't begun to understand.

I had opened the door to Ted Liss's studio pushed by a need, but blocked by fear that I was not good enough to act. I was sure I was barely average, if that. Praise had been rare at home. Criticism was considered a stimulus, while praise was bad for the character. It took time to attain a degree of self-worth, to accept that I had done things of which I could be proud. The acting classes were a lesson in self-confidence. When Ted's interest turned to commercial prospects, it was time to move on.

I had never considered diabetes an impediment to an acting career. I never had the feeling that the disease could stop me from doing anything I chose. Other factors could but as long as I would be able to control the illness, it would have no say.

\* \* \*

In late summer of 1970 Marija Smilga, a theater director, and I hitchhiked to California. It took us three rides to get from Chicago to Route 80 and one ride from an African-American professor to San Francisco.

In the mountain passes of Nevada fatigue began to affect our professor's driving. After his nap I curled up in the back seat of the VW and nodded off. I woke up shaking, unable to move or speak. I kept trying to form the Lithuanian word for cold, but Marija was chatting with the driver, the radio was blaring, and I couldn't make myself heard. Coming back from an insulin reaction without the aid of food, drink, or a glucose injection is a frightening experience because in the beginning nothing functions, not movement, not speech. Fear that I would be conscious of everything but unable to control the smallest movement ever again was overwhelming.

Marija, unaware that anything was wrong, draped a blanket over me. My blood sugar had been high for so long that I had friends who had never seen an insulin reaction. Only years later, when my care improved and toeing the line caused me to have hypoglycemic reactions more often, and wake up after long periods of insensibility, did I connect the process of regaining consciousness to that night in Nevada. In the VW I came to very slowly, and, because of my cramped position, the little finger of one hand stayed bloodless and numb until the next day.

We arrived in Haight-Ashbury at the apogee of the

flower-power movement. Dead-tired and unwashed, we had the telephone number of a Lithuanian medic, the friend of a friend.

"You don't know me," I began in Lithuanian. "My name is Eglė Juodvalkytė. Kristina Sabaliauskaitė gave me your name and number. I just hitchhiked here from Chicago with Marija Smilga—you don't know her either--but we need a place to stay. Would that be possible?"

"Sure, come on out. I'm working a double shift at the hospital, so I won't be home till evening, but I'll put the key under the mat."

The next day Marija and I roamed Golden Gate Park, where we encountered a man who played a stringed musical instrument neither of us had seen before. Owner of the Magic Mountain Workshop in Sausalito where dulcimers were made by hand, in San Francisco's cafes he coaxed gentle sounds from the Appalachian dulcimer in his lap.

With airplane tickets to Chicago in our pockets we spent a week on Fisherman's Wharf, in Golden Gate Park, going from one bookstore to another, at the theater, in cafes. Time was short, and we were due back for classes and work. We left the city as we had found it. *Oh, Calcutta!* was playing on stage with a naked cast, joints were being offered to strangers in San Francisco's airport. The whole city and Golden Gate Park in particular, reeked of grass and hash, and people wearing flowers in their hair were promising with Peter, Paul and Mary to "hammer out love between my brothers and my sisters all over this land."

\* \* \*

The second trip West took place in the summer of 1972

when Chris, an aspiring actress from Ted Liss's workshop, and I decided to go to Hollywood. We jumped in her VW Karmann Ghia and set out. By nightfall exhilaration had changed to irritation. By the time we reached Des Moines, Chris was ready to dump the car and fly to California.

"What are you yelling about? What's wrong? What's going on, Chris?"

"Nothing."

"Well, if there's nothing wrong, then what's the problem? Go to sleep. We'll be on the road early tomorrow."

"It's all right for you, but this trip is costing me too much."

"What are you talking about? We've both got jobs, we're splitting costs straight down the middle, the driving, gas, food, and hotel. Come on, what is it?"

"The problem is money. How am I going to make ends meet?" After a pause she confided, "I'm thinking of chucking my job and staying in Los Angeles. How about you, Eglė?"

"I thought our plan was only to assess the situation, check out possibilities for the future. I don't think I'm ready to dive blind off a cliff."

"I'm terrified. Hollywood, here I come," she smiled wanly. "What if it doesn't work? What if I can't get roles?"

In Hollywood we made a list of agents, had pictures taken, wrote resumes and began peddling them. I had chosen a stage name, as we had all been told that our real names just would not do. Only one agent asked to see me and exclaimed over my "Slavic" cheekbones that, he insisted, were popular that season. I restrained myself from pointing out that my cheekbones were not Slavic, but Baltic.

Chris tried to convince me to stay—she had decided

to throw caution to the proverbial winds and place herself with the agent who was willing to represent her, but I shilly-shallied. On the one hand, my aim was to devote myself to acting. On the other, I wanted to complete my education. One more year was all I had left and the commitment to my education was long-standing.

I flew back.

\* \* \*

Though I dropped out of Ted Liss's school, I didn't stop acting. Several one-acts were already behind me and I would audition for and win the plum role of Nora in a summer production of Ibsen's *A Doll's House* the summer after my graduation from the university.

That spring Liza, who had been seeing my brother since I had introduced them, moved to Uosis in Providence. At a Baltic conference in Chicago a Latvian professor from Southern Illinois University at Carbondale, Alfreds Straumanis, spoke enthusiastically about his Baltic Theater Project. I recognized a golden apple as fate dropped it into my lap. With a graduate assistantship in the Theater department in my pocket, I packed my bags.

I took the assistantship not just while it neatly packaged my two loves, Lithuania and theater, but also because it put the question of what to do with my life in temporary abeyance. In Carbondale I reverently leafed through grey, thumbed pamphlets helping to prepare a bibliography of Lithuanian plays published in America in the nineteenth and twentieth centuries, translated Kazys Saja's play *Devynbėdžiai* or The Village of Nine Woes into English and saw its publication in an anthology of Baltic plays,

*The Golden Steed*, as part of the government-funded Baltic Theatre Project.

Most fun that year was using mime to portray an eighty-year-old woman in a one-act play. I fought with lethargy, heat, water bugs, assisted guest director Arnie Kendall, and felt good.

I tried to stifle my disappointment when I did not get a speaking part in a play by Algirdas Landsbergis, *Five Posts in a Marketplace*. Assistant stage-manager was a poor substitute. Every time the girl playing the Soviet general came to grief in rehearsal was a balm to my heart. At the same time, I wanted the audience to sympathize with Lithuania's plight, so the actress had to do well. I stifled my egoistic feelings.

My disease would not let me off the hook. Sores began appearing on my calves, ugly, ulcerated wounds that itched and would not heal. For a while I ignored them but life with diabetes had taught me a lesson that I would have to relearn again and again. "Take care of the disease, don't wait." When I saw that the sores were spreading rather than healing, I took a bus up to Chicago to see Dr. Rubenstein. The dermatologists at the university clinics equipped me with a cream, swathed my calves in gauze from ankle to knee, reiterated that this too was a result of inadequate care of the disease, and sent me back to Southern Illinois. It took months for the wounds to crust over and heal. I was left with several slight, barely visible scars on each leg, like old tetanus vaccinations, but I was lucky—I healed.

Professor Straumanis called another Baltic Conference, this time in Carbondale. A member of the conference, Professor Landsbergis from City University of New York, was involved in preparing scripts for Radio Liberty's

Lithuanian Service. He asked if I'd be interested in writing and voicing reports on events that might be of interest to listeners in Lithuania. In addition, he offered me a summer job in the Big Apple.

I would be sharing the summer position with another woman, an ethnographer and former Saturday school classmate. Elena Bradūnas would be at the Radio the first part of the summer and I would take over from her. Before I started it was imperative to see Lithuania. Once I became a Radio employee, not only would I be considered *persona non grata* by the Soviets, but my employer would be just as loath to allow me to visit any communist country.

## 9. A chance appears and vanishes. Eglė's parents give her the present of a lifetime and the parameters of the gift encompass the present and the future.

The summer before the job offer I had applied to attend a six-week Lithuanian language course at the University of Vilnius. The Soviets denied me permission at the last second.

My parents offset the disappointment the following spring with the gift of a lifetime—my first visit to Lithuania.

It was a two-week excursion with stops in Helsinki, Leningrad, Vilnius, Riga, and Moscow. The Lithuanian segment of the trip would be a mere five days, but those were the Soviet rules. I was happy even with crumbs.

Preparations for the trip involved a number of things, among them quitting smoking. That had been a part of my life on and off since I was sixteen. I would try to quit at times, but halfheartedly; I didn't want to stop smoking. Doctors weren't as adamant about negative consequences as they are today, and I was young enough not to care anyway.

So I quit smoking again, but as soon as I settled into the airplane seat, my fingers reached for a cigarette. I'd bought several cartons to pass out to relatives in Lithuania and distributed packs throughout my luggage and shoulder bag. As soon as the no-smoking sign was turned off—hard to imagine today—I was puffing away on my "lifeline."

How would I recognize relatives seen only in photos? Would the gifts I was bringing be confiscated by customs? "Bribe the customs officer with bubble gum, ballpoint pens, cigarette lighters," said practiced fliers. But how? I'd never bribed anyone.

How would this trip alter the shape of the Lithuania I knew, the independent country of legends, which had existed only between the two world wars? Would I recognize it? Accept it?

Avoid female customs officers—this precept had been drummed into me, but I had no choice. I was directed into a line. In front of me a young man held out a Finnish passport to the hefty lady customs officer, who motioned to him to open his suitcase. She flicked, flicked, burrowed through his things, and I was preparing for my own ordeal, when she bellowed, "*A chto eto?*" The sentinel of the Soviet state was pointing at a small, white bag. She lifted it between forefinger and thumb, again demanding to know what it was. The guy reeled off a sentence in flawless Finnish, but the customs officer was not multilingual. "What's that?" she barked once more. The rest of the line sighed and leaned on suitcases. The official began to spew angry sentences, questions, commands in Russian, but the Finn didn't understand her nor she him. She departed to return bowing and scraping to a man clearly her superior.

He repeated the question; "*Chto eto?*" listened attentively to the reply in Finnish, untied the string around the bag, peeked in, sniffed, and turning to the woman with a look of withering contempt, distinctly pronounced, "*Syr*" (cheese).

The lady shoveled the man's clothes back into his suitcase—zip, zip, zip, and hurried him through.

The luggage of her next two victims—I was one—received a cursory glance. The official who checked our passports and hand luggage helped himself to an assortment of my ballpoint pens, chewing gum, and a disposable lighter or two. The bribery had taken place without my active participation. Our tour group was taken to its hotel in what was then still called Leningrad. The city had beauty and charm, the ballet dancers, who performed *Swan Lake*, did it beautifully, but my mind was on the next part of the trip.

We were taken to another airport for the Aeroflot flight to Vilnius. When we broke through the cloud layer, I got my first glimpse of Lithuania, though I would not be able to dwell on the enormity of the experience until my return to America. Now, if I blinked, I might miss something crucial. The problem of recognizing relatives did not arise. The moment they spied me in the doorway of the plane, a shout rang out, "Egluže!"

Tears, kisses. Hugs. My father's brother, Balys, stood, large drops inching down his cheeks. One of my cousins took matters in hand and introduced them all one by one. There were thirty.

The tour group's leader rounded up the twelve of us and told us we could take a relative on the bus to the hotel. I grabbed my cousin Stasys. On the way the leader clarified the rules. Permission was required for trips of more than 25 km. beyond the Vilnius city limits and for city, collective farm and factory tours. One tour was mandatory—the visit to the Ninth Fort in Kaunas. Not coming back to the hotel to sleep was forbidden.

"You may request permission to stay in Lithuania for five more days, rather than go to Latvia," our tour guide from Intourist told us, but only one father and his teenage daughter did. Permission was denied.

At the hotel my clan made plans for the next day. A cousin took me for a walk to avoid the hidden microphones. Other cousins and I would play tourists in Vilnius the next morning until we rendezvoused with another member of my extended family at a designated place. He would be driving a yellow Zhiguli. Destination—Zarasai, not quite a hundred miles away. On the way I would visit an aunt too old and sick to travel and be taken to see what was left of the farmhouse my father had built for his mother. After the Second World War my grandmother had been turned out, the building lifted from its foundations, transported to the village center, and turned into the office of a collective farm. I would kiss the earth of my grandparents' graves in Salakas. We did not request permission.

After breakfast in Vilnius two female cousins and I started out for the city center. We had progressed barely a step or two when one of them warned, "We're being followed by three men. One has a rolled-up newspaper under his arm." The back of my neck prickled, as though I could feel someone's glance. I shook myself. Why should they be following us? Were my cousins overly suspicious?

One of them took off to inform the rest of our party that we would meet them where Dzerzhinsky Street ended at the edge of the city and—lo and behold! One of our three "guardians" sloped off after her. The remaining cousin and I played tourists, our two "buddies" staying within ten paces.

We passed up a taxi whose driver had leaned out, asking if anyone wanted Dzerzhinsky Street, and got into another one. This driver began asking, "Dzerzhinsky Street? Why are you going there? Meeting someone?" Thoroughly uneasy my cousin asked him to drop us off sooner and we walked to where my relatives were standing next to a bright yellow car.

Ten minutes later, our driver dropped a brick, "We're being followed by two white Volgas." One passed us. A few minutes later a man in militia uniform flagged us down. He asked, in Russian, whether our car's turn signals were working. They were. "Destination?"

"We're going home."

"And who are all these people?" the militiaman waved a hand at the occupants of the car.

"My wife. My uncle. My cousins."

"Documents, please."

In the back seat my uncle began to mutter that it was nonsense, he had never needed to show a document to travel in his own country. The driver of our car laid his party card next to his identity card on the hood of the auto, but the officer didn't blink. Then he came to the sixth person in the car—me.

"And who is she?"

"My cousin."

"Where is she from?"

Well, that was it. The million-ruble question.

"America."

"Where is her permit?"

"Permit, what permit?"

"Her permit to travel outside the twenty-five kilometer zone."

"I had no idea that I need a permit to travel within Lithuania. I never had to in America."

My interlocutor was not interested in conversation.

"You others may continue your trip. We will return her to Vilnius."

"No, thank you, we'll take her back ourselves."

"Fine, but keep within a twenty-five kilometer radius of the Vilnius city limits.

He had written down every word I uttered in Lithuanian without translation, but asked his questions in Russian. I insisted on a translator.

What would happen? The idea that my trip would be cut short hung over us like a menacing cloud. In Vilnius, I immediately knocked on the door of the official Intourist representative, but it was locked. While waiting for him to return, we picked at a meal in a restaurant close by. Now we were followed blatantly. On his way to the bathroom one of my cousins passed a couple of the "guardians" and heard one complain, "What, eat again? But I just had dinner."

The Intourist representative inquired how he could be of service. No doubt he knew at least as much about the incident as I, but we both played our parts, lying with straight faces.

"I'm sorry," I apologized. "I seem to have inadvertently broken a law."

"Have you indeed?"

"Yes, I didn't realize I needed a special permit to pay my respects to my grandmother's grave in Zarasai."

"Oh, but of course you knew that," was the suave reply. "There was an announcement on the bus from the airport to the hotel."

"I was so moved meeting thirty relatives for the first time that I was in tears, incapable of hearing anything," I answered just as suavely.

"Ah," he said with narrowed eyes, "you might not have known." I exhaled a mental sigh of relief. "But your relatives certainly knew."

My stomach hit the floor and my back stiffened, as

the implication of his words sank in: I have caused trouble for my relations. I would be just fine, I held an American passport, what could they do to me, but cut my trip short? But my relatives were living here, had jobs, careers, children in school.

"They couldn't know, I'm their first guest from America," I stammered. He smiled. The smile did not reach his eyes.

"But let's talk about you. What shall we do with you? Take you to Moscow to wait for your group? You did break our laws."

He was enjoying his upper hand. I decided on insolence.

"Well, then," I said, wide-eyed and innocent, "if I need a permit, then please give me one now."

That took him aback.

"You break our laws and you want a permit?"

"That's how it is in America. If I were to break a law inadvertently, I'd be warned, nothing more. I could ask for and get a necessary permit."

This blatant lie issued from my lips without a single alarm going off, though the American maxim—ignorance of the law is no excuse—drummed in my ears.

"The Soviet Union is not America."

"I wanted to see my grandmother's grave."

"You will be informed tomorrow whether you will be allowed to continue your visit to Lithuania or will be sent to Moscow to await your group."

Before facing the unpleasant night, my relatives came up to my hotel room. When I related the conversation with Intourist, one of them, furious, began to badmouth the security forces. The others tried to calm him, pointing fearfully at ceiling and walls. At that, he yanked the radio out of the wall and uncovered a... microphone.

He blanched.

The night was interminable, the morning—anticlimactic. I would be allowed to stay but would have to pay a fine. Another cousin, holding a higher official position in the communist party, returned from a trip to Minsk, berated the family for its haste, paid the fine and tried to obtain a permit through "private channels," as was often done. No luck. No one would sign a permit after an official report had been filed.

My mother's clan was waiting for me Wednesday when our bus arrived in Kaunas, where Ona had spent her last years in Lithuania. We were taken on the only mandatory tour of the trip to see the Ninth Fort, a prison in which the victims of various political upheavals, including communism, had been incarcerated before the war.

After the tour, my relatives appropriated me for the rest of the day. Uncle Vytė shook his fist at the Volga that in Kaunas did not bother to hide its pursuit. Master of caustic speech and an incessant smoker, twirling a black cigarette holder in his fingers, Vytė took me to the cemetery where the remains of my maternal grandparents rest.

\* \* \*

It was 1963 in East Chicago when the doorbell rang. Mother put down her sewing and rose. She came back to the room, clutching a piece of paper, tears rolling down her cheeks.

"Mama, what's wrong?"

"My mother died."

The grandmother I had never seen had passed on. I would never know her touch, learn her wisdom, hear how

I was similar to or different from mother, listen to stories about members of my family. Five weeks later to the day and the hour my grandfather followed her.

* * *

In Lithuania I visited relatives, saw the gothic church of St. Anne, the cathedral in its Soviet guise of an art gallery, the tapestries of the University of Vilnius, and met with its rector Grigonis who encouraged me to send a few "writings" to him from Radio Liberty, some information they did not yet have. What would I like to do or see in Vilnius? It would all be arranged. No doubt. He must have thought I was just waiting to "cooperate" with the KGB, for which he worked. My wish to meet writers was fulfilled at an evening with Kazys Saja, whose play I had translated into English at the university in Carbondale. We were joined by Judita Vaičiūnaitė, a favorite poet, and myriad others. I went to the National Drama Theater, was taken on a personal tour of the Opera House. Sleep was limited to three hours a night.

There was much to understand. Some new acquaintances warned me against speaking about my future work at Radio Liberty and against writers I had met at the evening with them. The poet with whom I'd been exchanging letters from America was identified as working for the KGB.

When both clans saw me off at the airport in Vilnius, my mother's stepsister Kostusė, her hair white as snow, leaning against a pillar with a single red rose in her hand, the others piling bouquets of flowers, bags of strawberries, sausage, farmer's cheese into my arms, I wept and spent the next days in Riga, the capital of Latvia, in a daze. The Lithuanian Americans on the tour spent evenings in one of the hotel rooms, eating the perishables, drinking the alcoholic beverages we had been given, singing melancholy songs of an earlier time, and stifling sobs.

Moscow was the final stop of our journey through the Soviet Union. The metro, of which some locals are so proud, was stunning, gold-encrusted, like no other. It was built with the blood, sweat, and lives of political prisoners. I was ready to go back to America.

Customs at Sheremetyevo Airport was trouble free. Having been told that nothing that we wore would be inspected, I draped every amber necklace I had been given around my neck, bracelets on my arms to the elbows, and put rings on all my fingers. The customs inspectors laughed up their sleeves at the hordes of American Balts festooned in amber sway past, trying to look inconspicuous.

\* \* \*

The trip to Vilnius and Kaunas introduced me to food I had not tasted before: smoked eel, sorrel soup, mushroom delicacies of various kinds. Every family considered it a matter of honor to dine the guest from America in a grand manner, despite their straitened circumstances.

Both of my parents had written to their respective relatives, warning them that my diabetes would not allow me to drink and that food would be restricted. Some of my father's troops had a hard time with his injunction not to overfeed me, certain that their older brother was being overly strict. With no experience of diabetes, they assumed that rules were made to be broken.

I disliked strong drink and had no trouble being firm in my refusal of liquor, but victuals were another story. I ate with a hardyan disregard of consequences. There were repercussions. Count fat exchanges, which was a must for diabetics? Fat chance. I was unaware of the extent of my neuropathy. I had assumed that in time I would stand before my mirror in better shape than I had ever been.

Some time after the diagnosis of neuropathy and barely one year, since I had relearned living without constant pain, I still had not internalized that I would feel cold intensely, my body would not be able to digest quantities of fat without making a great fuss about it, areas of my legs would not differentiate between blunt and sharp again, that what I ate would sit around in my stomach and intestine, that my heart would be easily overburdened.

For the duration of my visit the family set feuds aside, held all disagreements in abeyance. When my father's eldest sister Ona pronounced in her broad *aukštaitė* dialect, that my voice was just like my father's, I knew I belonged. I was part of a multitudinous family on Antanas's side, though I had not met them till this trip. I had seen my mother's remaining siblings in Kaunas, though most of her immediate family was in America.

I filed what I could in my memory in those not quite five days that the Lithuanian part of the trip lasted: a hand pulling the curtain across a window lest some stranger's eye notice a fest; small Žilvinas, darting out shyly from behind his father for chewing gum; Vitalis, trading me a pack of Kastytis for a pack of Marlboros, each of us sure we'd gotten the better deal; ambling with Stasiukas through the narrow streets of Vilnius's Old Town in the rain and talking about dreams, theater, everything, nothing...

Some insignificant object, a conversation, song, voice can bring a flood of recollections—small but sweet strawberries from my uncle's patch, a sky the blue of rye flowers, a brass earring from a museum shop.

Other memories have not fallen through the holes of time, either: the surveillance, the attempts at intimidation, the distrust between ostensible friends, the lies, the fear, the bitterness of a people scarred by Russian and German occupations. In 1975 there was no end in sight, no faith in a better future, no belief that communism would crumble.

In Helsinki I was struck by the enjoyment visible on smiling faces. People were publicly chatting, guffawing, tittering, giggling, howling with laughter that was not bitter or furtive snickering at political jokes. This was heartfelt, nice-to-be-alive, pretty-day-isn't-it chortling, so different from what I heard in Soviet Russia.

As I walked in Helsinki and compared what I had seen in those two weeks to what I was seeing in Finland, I knew why I would work for Radio Liberty, why I could not, on a personal level, be indifferent to the misery, destruction, and neglect I had seen.

## 10. New York, New York! Joys, privations, delights. Eglė and the dog, Mother brings a telegram and agrees to her daughter's journey.

Two weeks after my return in the summer of 1975, firm of purpose, I was in New York ready to begin my summer job for the Lithuanian Service of Radio Liberty on 42nd Street between Madison and Fifth Avenue. The job was supposed to last two weeks but was extended to six. Through the intercession of Professor Landsbergis who had recruited me, his parents rented me a room in their Queens apartment for thirty dollars a month. Ideal landlords, they never complained about the hours I kept and left me to my own devices. A night owl, I often returned quite late. The house had one entrance, and the younger Landsbergis's family lived on the upper floors. Whenever I tried to sneak past their door well after midnight, Algirdas's wife Janė would call,

"Eglė? Chat a minute?"

"Love to!"

I'd get to bed very late and would have to be up very early to catch the J train into Manhattan, nodding through most of the ride. I worked unpaid overtime until half past seven in the evening. Then, New York was mine!

An Estonian-American buddy from the Theater

department's graduate school in Carbondale, Jan, could conjure up seats at the Met like a magician. He took me there every other day. "Hey, Tom, how are you tonight?" Jan would nod to the doorman and slip a dollar for each of us into his palm. Tom would slide open the door and we would join the throng of standees at the back of the third balcony until the lights went down. Then we nonchalantly stepped to the empty seats in the fifth row of the parquet that we had spotted from above.

An ominous throat clearing and a pair of tickets waving in our faces would cause us to rise, apologize, and depart at speed, but this happened rarely and most times Jan would pull his opera glasses out of his pocket for a closer perusal of the singers.

When I wasn't at the Met, I was at the cinema. Going back to Queens and out to the city again would have taken several hours, so I worked until show time, scouring the archives for poems, choosing music from records and tapes. I covered Lithuanian conferences in different cities. I felt like Nancy Drew, Girl Reporter. From time to time a word of appreciation would filter down from the Chief of the Lithuanian Service in Munich. I got along with my fellow Balts and the directors of the New York office. Life was good.

As the end of August approached I began to plan my return to Carbondale. I was clearing the poetry I'd jotted down on old memos and tape boxes from desk drawers when the phone rang. I was wanted in the Director's office.

"Have a seat, won't you," Mr. Kratch smiled at me. "You know Aušra and Jonas Jurašas are coming from Munich to take over the Lithuanian section here when you leave. Well, there's a bureaucratic snafu. The Germans are holding up their documents."

"Right," I said.

"The Lithuanian Desk won't have anybody here. The Service Chief in Munich is in a bind. Could you possibly stay on?"

"For how long?"

"January, maybe longer."

"I have another semester beginning in January. I'd have to go back for it."

He sighed with relief.

"Aušra will probably be here by then."

I called Carbondale, arranged for my belongings to be packed and stored in the attic of the off-campus student housing where I was living. I would be away four months.

I stayed on, queen of the castle, for my direct supervisor was in Munich. There were mishaps, of course. Once I sent a voiced program for broadcast, using a verse of the Lithuanian National Anthem. Little did I know that the anthem must always be broadcast entire. The piece could not be used. Another time disaster struck, but not at work.

A colleague asked me to dog-sit for a friend of hers, a Baroness, who had a place in Manhattan. Would I look after the dog for two weeks in exchange for the use of her apartment? I was eager to avoid the daily commute to and from Queens. Problem was, I was not a great dog lover, but we were sure to survive so brief a period.

The brute and I snarled at each other on sight.

As the owner patted the small, spindly creature goodbye, she looked dubious, but what could she do?

My role as food provider should have done wonders

for the animal's disposition. Something about not biting the hand that feeds.

For the first three days it refused to consume anything I put in its dish. When I left the little darling a newspaper and food in a closed bedroom, it ripped the pillows to shreds. When it succumbed to hunger, we growled at each other from opposite parts of the room till the end of my sojourn.

I was not asked to dog-sit for the Baroness again.

* * *

Close friendships were hard to form in New York City, where life and people dashed by, intent on one thing-- getting ahead. But though six weeks of restaurants, opera, ballet, films, and work were fine, six months of the same were wearing. An older Lithuanian couple helped me acclimate to New York, introduced me to bialys—those scrumptious boiled-in-oil bagels for which my fat-addicted European gut yearned. Low blood sugars, high blood sugars, I paid minimal attention, but survived.

As January approached and I began to tie up loose ends, I felt exhausted all the time and my back began to hurt. A mean pain got worse until I could barely walk, dragging myself up the subway steps with the help of the railings. The pain became constant. I saw a doctor.

"There's nothing the matter with you," he said hearteningly, ran no tests, and sent me away telling me to, "Get some rest."

I tried. The pain got worse. I looked up a second doctor who thought I might have pulled a muscle.

"You'll be fine."

I left New York in that condition and dropped in

on my parents before heading south to Carbondale and the university I had deserted for work in New York. By now I was in constant pain and vomiting. I turned to Dr. Rubenstein.

"Chronic urinary tract infection."

"Chronic? I never had it before."

"Yes, but it became chronic because nothing was done about it for so long,"

"But I went to a doctor..."

"Any physician could have diagnosed it. A urine test was all that was needed."

He prescribed a strong antibiotic. I was better within days.

When I returned to Carbondale at the end of January, things did not go smoothly. Friends had packed up my room, but through "attrition" a number of the boxes had disappeared—some kitchen stuff, a book about Tallulah Bankhead from my cousin Rimvydas with his inscription, a grey Munich beer mug from the trip to Europe—things not worth much to anyone, but me.

That spring I played a ninety-year-old woman in a one-act play based heavily on mime and received an award for the part. The director, a mime himself, had learned his art from Marcel Marceau in Paris. Director Takis Mouzenides came from Greece to lead a workshop in the rudiments of Greek acting. Jonas Jurašas, a former director of Lithuania's National Theater in Kaunas, arrived from Europe and came out to Carbondale to teach a weekend workshop in plasticity. When Arnie Kendall came from Texas to direct a play at Southern Illinois University, I was his assistant.

A small truck stop, famous up and down Carbondale for its cobblers—blueberry, boysenberry, peach, cherry, hot and heaped with whipped cream, played havoc with this glutton's diabetes. There should have been a skull and crossbones on the door of it and a warning sign—Poison for Diabetics!

\* \* \*

At the end of that semester I had chosen the members of my master's thesis committee and had my outline approved. I was writing on the women in the plays of Kazys Saja, a contemporary Lithuanian playwright I had seen in Vilnius. He had given me tickets to see the play I was translating into English—*Devynbėdžiai* or The Village of Nine Woes.

January, February, March, one thought preyed on my mind—how could I be useful to Lithuania? I had felt useful, while I worked in New York. In a letter to Juozas Laučka, the Director of the Lithuanian Service at Radio Liberty Munich, I offered to drop anything I was involved in, work or school, for a chance to join the Service. The heavens opened and manna dropped from the skies: the Munich Office wanted me. The heavens closed: a hiring freeze was in effect.

I sublet a furnished apartment in Carbondale for the summer, worked on my thesis, did yoga for a month, saw friends, sang, and felt great. I stopped playing games with my diabetes. At the end of the summer I moved back to Chicago. No news had come from the Radio as yet, and it was time to make decisions, but I dragged my feet.

When the doorbell rang, Mama went to the door and then was calling, "Eglė, Eglė ..." It was a telegram with the longed-for job offer. In three weeks I was expected in Munich.

The movers packed pots, pans, the large yellow mixing bowl from my mother's kichen, my bronze dinner plates, salad bowls selected by my mother, a mixer, a potato masher, garlic press, flatware that I had acquired living away from home, cups, Lithuanian books that my parents let me take from their library. Mama made sure that l had a selection of sheets, pillowcases, several quilts, eight towels. Father selected tools for a toolbox no one should live without: claw hammer, socket wrench, flathead and Phillips screwdrivers, pliers, awl, scissors, tape measure, and handfuls of different length nails, screws, tacks.

I spent a last weekend at the annual Santara-Šviesa Congress, which was a meeting of liberals, conservatives and others with open minds willing to think creatively. I read my poetry, parted from friends, and in September 1976 set off, my father's warning ringing in my ears, "God forbid you bring me back a German!" Father had no idea what trials his daughter would put him through!

A last look in the mirror before the trip showed me a young woman in rolled-up jeans and a wide, black-and-white Marimekko shirt casually draped over them. "I'm not making a fashion statement," I thought, "but I'm comfortable, and who cares anyway?"

\* \* \*

With old-fashioned courtesy the entire Lithuanian Service trooped out to the airport with flowers. After all my fellow passengers had disembarked from the plane, collected their baggage, and departed, a man approached me,

"Eglė?"

"Yes," I answered, turning.

Silence. A party of six and I eyed one another warily. Then words of welcome were spoken, and a bouquet was proffered. Most of the broadcasters scuttled back to work. Later I was informed that the thought uppermost in everyone's mind was, "Just our luck, in three months she'll be taking maternity leave!"

The man I was to share a room with at work so forgot himself that he neglected to hand me the posies he was holding behind his back until someone nudged him. The Chief stuttered in embarrassment.

The next day I wore an empire-waist dress to work. Personnel informed me about housing and stressed *Kindergeld,* a monthly allowance the German government paid for each child. A crib would be brought to my apartment.

"I have no need of a crib," I pointed out gently.

"But you will—anyone can see that you're expecting."

"Not at all."

"Well then," she reprimanded me. "You should wear a belt."

Years passed.

\* \* \*

When Gorbachev came to power, the word perestroika became part of many languages and life became less constrained, I tried to obtain a visa to visit my parents' homeland. "You will get it," I was assured by the Soviet Lithuanian Foreign Ministry, "but it can only be issued in Bonn. Send your passport to the Soviet Embassy there."

Lithuania's government sent me an official invitation, but the idea of getting a visa by mail did not sit well with me. I was fond of my passport—what if it got lost? I girded my loins, asked for a day off, and went to Bonn by overnight train.

I found the Soviet Embassy, and was second in line when it opened. Contrary to the visa ritual in most embassies, in the Soviet one suppliants spoke through an opaque one-way glass. The clerks saw everyone, but the petitioners—no one. A disembodied voice asked questions, requested documents, and returned a passport the same way, with or without a visa. After a few minutes my passport was pushed back to me.

"Request denied."

"But that's not possible."

"Denied," the voice repeated.

"I want to speak to a consul."

"Step away from the window. There are other people in line."

"I will not. The Soviet Lithuanian Foreign Ministry informed me that I would get a visa. What's going on?" I raised my voice.

A pause ensued. I didn't move from my spot.

"A consul will speak with you," pronounced the voice after several minutes of Russian conversation with someone. I moved from the window. Some time later, a man in a natty suit entered the room.

"Are you Frau Ju-od-val-kis?" he asked in German. "I'm sorry. We would like to give you a visa, but the decisions are made in Moscow." He turned some pages in the ledger he was carrying. "We received a telegram to the effect that entrance to the Soviet Union for Frau Eglė Juodvalkis is *strengstens verboten*."

That was the German equivalent of "no way, José." He

showed me an official Russian document from Moscow. It stated unequivocally that I was barred from entering the USSR.

I took the next train back to Munich. The grassroots movement *Sąjūdis* took hold in Lithuania. Masses of people demonstrated in squares, the city center, stadiums, and parks. A poet, Sigitas Geda, spoke veiled phrases about dwarfs toppling giants. Gorbachev visited the Soviet republic and offered a plan, which would allow it to petition Moscow for secession in five years.

Lithuanians refused to wait.

On March 11, 1990, Lithuania declared that it was restoring its independence.

Less than a year later on January 13, 1991, Soviet tanks rolled against a crowd in Vilnius. Fourteen people died, several under tank treads, others beaten by the butts of soldiers' guns or despatched by bullets. The jolt reverberated throughout the country.

As if that were not enough, on August 29, 1991, came the news of the century, declared in a column heading on the front page of the International Herald Tribune: "SOVIET UNION IS NO LONGER."

Radio employees walked around elated, dazed, and suspicious by turns. No Soviet Union! After seventy-four years of death, misery, and pain, communism had failed! What would follow?

Six years later historians published the *Black Book of Communism*, the first global study of the victims of one of the two totalitarian systems of the twentieth century. It turned out that altogether communism had already claimed between 85 and 100 million lives. The Nazis were responsible for "only" 25 million deaths.

My second trip to Lithuania took place in October of the same year, when the country was able to decide for itself who could enter its territory.

The flight was from Munich to Berlin where I changed airports and boarded a plane from West to East. In nine emotionally packed days I found time to visit the parliament, read my poetry in Kaunas and Vilnius, visit relatives in three cities, call on an old school chum of my mother's, and pay respects to some family graves.

During the visit my cousin Vytas took me to his summer house, a short ride outside the Vilnius city limits. On our way back we happened on a driver weaving into the lane of oncoming traffic. "Under the influence," muttered Vytas, passed him, and forced the car to a stop. Vytas, as a concerned citizen, took the man's car keys and left him to sober up. But that was not the end of the story. Vytas's family objected to his actions on humanitarian grounds.

"Look, Dad, the man's house keys are on the ring. He can't get into his house even if he gets home. Besides, the man could die of exposure in the cold night air."

Vytas's family didn't let up, so he went to the police, explained the incident, and handed over the key ring.

"Sign a complaint, buddy. You sign, we'll get him." The police urged Vytas.

"No, I won't do it. I did my job—I stopped him from driving. Now you do yours and rescue him. I've told you where the car is."

Vytas left the keys on the counter and came back to the house fuming. Another discussion ensued. In the end, his wife and son went by taxi to make sure the drunk was all right. Police were there when they arrived.

* * *

After 1990 Radio Free Europe's Lithuanian Service sent me several times to work six and seven week stretches in its Vilnius bureau. The Radio rented a furnished apartment for its correspondents in the ravaged historical Old Town. Henryk joined me during those stays, and while I was taping interviews with people and editing the tapes at work, he wandered through the narrow streets and alleyways of *Senamiestis* with an expert, my cousin Vilija, who had visited us in Munich and was soon to wed an American Lithuanian, Kazys. After their wedding he would carry her off to New England.

In the eighties I hadn't a hope of seeing the city again, of hearing my native language spoken around me in a free and independent country. Now I sang hundred-year-old folksongs, as I floated to work every morning on a cloud of happiness down Basanavičius Street. The worry on faces around me kept bringing home the knowledge that the average passerby could not call on a salary like mine to see him or her through hard times.

Nothing bothered me—not the water that ran cold and brown from Old Town faucets, though under duress the Radio did equip the apartment with a water heater, not the buses, overflowing with standing, pushing, shoving bodies, nor the lack of those amenities that ease our lives in the States. I was happy to subsist on cottage cheese dumplings, or buy fat, squat boletus mushrooms in the marketplace to fry in butter and eat with sour cream. Real sour cream!

I was living an ephemeral idea called Lithuania and had the best of both worlds—the economic support of America and an assignment, though temporary, in Vilnius, but the dream was finite: my gold carriage would turn into an airplane that would deposit me back in Munich before the first snow.

# 11. Eglė visits Poland thrice—with Henryk and others, imbibes vodka, reaches Paweł's manor in Sieradz, and sees the Golden City of Prague.

In the spring of 1990 Henryk and I went to Poland for Easter. My mother-in-law, Stanisława, had visited us in Munich after the death of Henryk's father, Zdzisław, but a large part of my extended family, my sister-in-law, Ewa, and her husband, Andrzej, both doctors, and their son, Tomasz, were unknown to me. I would see them for the first time in Łódź. I already knew them "by phone," for whenever Henryk and I needed medical information to calm us, we called Ewa or Andrzej.

In 1988 a medication drove my blood pressure so low that I could barely walk and had a blasting headache. A hydraulic drill was applied to my left temple for three days straight. I wanted to take prescription medicine to counteract the drug I had been told never to skip. Henryk insisted on using the Łódź-Munich "emergency line." Ewa, who forbade my counter drug, favors conventional medicine, but made an exception after I repeatedly moaned into the receiver.

She told me about strong black coffee with lemon. I was dubious, but willing. For three days I had tried every over-the-counter medication and had applied ice, darkened the room, but nothing lessened the throbbing pain. I scooped five tablespoons of ground coffee into the Bodum pot, brewed myself a cup that would make my hair stand on end, squeezed half of a lemon into it, closed my eyes, and drank.

Not horrible, my mind registered.

I downed it a gulp at a time to the last drop, leaned back and waited. Five minutes passed, then ten. The pounding was still sledgehammer power. Ten more minutes passed. Were the blows to the sides of my head easing? Another ten minutes and I was sure. Within an hour I was pulling Henryk by the elbow and asking him to call Ewa to thank her. I was a functional human being again.

Now I would see Ewa. Henryk and I traveled by dilapidated Polish train whose dingy upholstery symbolized the legacy of communism. We passed through badly polluted and run-down areas of East Germany and Poland in stark contrast to the neat, brightly painted, well-kept houses and farms of West Germany.

Łódź, a sizeable city, was just beginning to awaken from the torpor that had consumed it under communism and the first signs of private enterprise were still sparse. When I visited this city again five months later, storefronts were being decorated at speed, new stores were opening, and pink cobblestones were being laid. Poland was on its way up. Piotrkowska street became a pedestrian zone, its buildings, turn of the century Art Nouveau, refurbished and repainted in pastel colors, preened like Southern belles at an eighteenth-century ball.

By 1994 Warszawa, once leveled to the ground by Germans, had stepped into the lineup of European capitals, swiftly acquiring many Western attributes, not all positive, as life was hurled pell-mell into the age of convenience.

111

Hamburger joints, pizza parlors, lavish, but intellectually impoverished Hollywood movies became part of the landscape.

Kraków held out against the lure of the dollar by refusing to allow McDonald's into its marketplace—Rynek, spurning the hamburger giant's offer to hide behind a historic facade.

On the next trip to Poland in August of the same year, we were four—Ed, a Polish American from the Radio, driving down to Kraków for a few days, Judy, visiting me from New York, Henryk, and I. Ed was the only one equipped with a Polish visa, indispensable then for American passport holders, even for my Polish-born husband who had renounced his Polish citizenship because he wanted to sever all ties with the communist regime when he became an American citizen before we married.

We stayed overnight in Vienna and drove to the Polish consulate in Bratislava the following morning. Henryk and Judy got their visas. Then the official, an appointee of the old regime, turned to me.

"I'm sorry," he was contrite, "but I cannot give the lady a visa because she does not have enough space in her passport and the visa needs a full page."

We looked at each other in consternation. Then the official brightened, said, "If madame doesn't mind, I will stamp it on this page," and indicated the page marked "Amendments and Endorsements." Doubtful I nodded.

In a second the new visa was gracing the clearly wrong page of my passport. Still, it was sufficient to get me in and out of Poland with no questions asked, and it still adorns the amendments and endorsements page of what is now a historic document.

Though Henryk and I were married, Judy and Ed had just met, so the women and the men were sleeping in separate rooms. We headed to Kraków. Its castle houses the remains of many of the Polish-Lithuanian Commonwealth's rulers as well as the Lithuanian founder of Poland's royal dynasty, Jogaila.

We arrived in pouring rain and tried to call a friend Henryk and I had visited before, Consul Algis Avižienis, at the American Consulate, but couldn't reach him. We took a hotel in the center of town and traipsed off to the Wierzynek in the square to eat a five-course meal for what was a minimal cost at the time.

Before leaving the hotel, draped in a garment with no pockets, I had passed all my money to Henryk who tucked it into his wallet.

Attesting to our healthy appetites we gorged on various delectables and imbibed bottles of Żubrówka. As we sat blissfully satiated, buttons popping and belts straining, our waiter, clucking sadly, muttered under his breath, *"Państwo tak mało jedli."* "The ladies and gents ate so little."

The summer night was mild, our mood—light, Judy and I warbled old Gershwin melodies. The men bought some beer at our hotel and we separated for the night. Judy and I wakened to pounding on our door.

"Did I give you my wallet before I went to bed?" Henryk asked.

"Nope. I gave you all of my money."

"It's gone. I thought maybe I dropped the wallet on the stairs after I paid for the beer, but then I remembered putting it on the table between the two beds before I went to sleep. I checked the bathroom."

"Wouldn't it be funny if I couldn't find my wallet?" Ed

grinned. We didn't laugh and with reason. It too was gone—with credit cards and money.

Henryk spent the morning reporting our loss to the police and trying to reconstruct what had happened.

Both men half woke to the sound of the door closing in the early morning at different times. Assuming the other guy had gone to the toilet, each turned over and went back to sleep.

"Any chance of catching the thieves?"

"None," the officer shook his head. "The victims are almost always Americans."

Henryk figured that the security forces of the old regime had duplicate keys to the rooms. Both of our gents had locked the door behind them, put their wallets on the same bedside table, and had lost them apparently to the same thief.

When we reached Algis at the consulate, he offered us the use of his house for the weekend and lent us cash to cover the rest of the trip.

Since Judy and I wanted to see Prague as much as Kraków, Ed drove back to Munich through the Golden City of Europe. It took us two hours at a brisk pace to walk through the center.

"All done," Ed assured us. "Nothing more to see. You don't need to come back."

"But the architecture, the Baroque, Gothic, Rococo, Classical, and Neoclassical churches, Prague Castle, and Charles Bridge! If only we had at least a week to view it," Judy and I chorused.

The Czech Republic's capital had escaped bombing during World War II and beneath the ravages of the totalitarian system the city as it might have been had it had

114

the wherewithal for its upkeep was visible. The East German Trabi, a tin lizzie hoisted above the heads of tourists on four elephant legs in Prague's Old Town, a comment put up after the Velvet Revolution brought down the communist government, had disappeared by the time Henryk and I revisited Prague the following spring. Later still, we found out it had been moved to another section of the city.

As the four of us meandered through the narrow streets of the twelfth century Old Town and fourteenth century New Town we worked up a thirst and stopped in one of the bars for a famous Czech Pils.

"No chicken—no beer," was the curt answer when we tried to order beer only. We weren't hungry, but prices were so minimal that we were willing to order chicken and not eat it. Henryk had the idea of telling them we would pay for the chicken, but they could eat it themselves. This was taken as such an affront that we had to leave precipitously, our thirst unquenched.

I had miscalculated what the brisk walk would do to my blood glucose and began to feel a reaction coming on, so we stopped and I measured. Forty. As normal was then around one hundred twenty, I was quickly approaching unconsciousness. Something had to be done fast. We slipped into a bar and were able to order orange juice, which was precisely what I needed.

\* \* \*

Larry, then Deputy Director of Radio Liberty, joined Henryk and me for my third trip to Poland the following April. On the train from Łódź to Warszawa we struck up a conversation with a Japanese political science professor who was doing research on Polish caricaturist Arthur Szyk, who had operated with pen and paper just as the world teetered on the brink of World War II. As the train chugged along, Rinjiro Sadei of Hosei University showed us some of the artist's works of persons then in the center of world politics. On arrival in Warsaw we planned to meet for dinner.

Henryk, who knew a decent restaurant, Bazyliszek, in the city's Old Town, suggested we dine there. He and Larry went to reserve a table. A few minutes later they were back. Henryk spoke Polish to request a table at a window for four, but the headwaiter hesitated, then said that the tables looking out on the plaza were reserved. Henryk left without making the reservation

"Where we sit isn't important," I assured him. "We'll take any table, won't we?"

"But they're lying," Henryk resisted.

"Granted, but we do want to eat."

This time Henryk was told that every table was reserved.

In the evening we rendezvoused with Professor Sadei at the Forum Hotel. He had the hotel receptionist call a restaurant which turned out to be the same Bazyliszek to reserve a table for four American journalists. No problem. When we arrived at the restaurant, the professor and I went in to ask for our table.

"Sadei, Sadei, sorry, no reservation in this name."

"Impossible. The hotel called," I insisted.

"There is no reservation. Please, here is the list."

"It was made in my presence. Party of four."

The headwaiter disappeared to confer with someone, returned, and with a forced smile led us to a table.

As if on cue, the rest of our group trooped in and sat down.

We emptied four different bottles of vodka with our meal before professor Sadei ordered a beverage from the menu—Black Death, labeled as a California product, its logo, a skull and crossbones.

After drinking most of the bottle, Rinjiro rose every few minutes and shrieked, "Hai! Hai! Hai! Hai!"

Every eye was on us. We were cheerfully continuing when Henryk discovered that his sister's Japanese classmate from her Polish secondary school was a friend of our professor.

"We must visit him. At once," Sadei crowed with delight at this splendid idea.

"At this hour?" My enthusiasm was not great, but I was overridden.

A half-hour before midnight we trundled off to Yashiko Umeda's house. Larry and I refused to leave the taxi.

"Listen, Larry, the last train to Łódź is at 11:50 PM and, if we all go in, not even the police will extricate us in time."

Ten minutes went by.

Larry disappeared through the door, while I waited in the cab, counting passing minutes.

Nothing.

I had lost all hope, when Larry reappeared with both recalcitrants in tow, relieving Umeda, who waved wearily as we drove away.

Rinjiro, Larry, Henryk and I reached the train station, three of us jumped on the train to Łódź, calling, "In Tokyo next time!" to Professor Sadei, weaving forlornly on the platform.

But our week in Poland was by no means over. One of Henryk's friends from Paris, sculptor Paweł Jocz, had bought a rundown manor in Poland and had begun to restore it. The manor holds special significance in the history of the Polish-Lithuanian Commonwealth. It was not just a residence for landowners, but a stronghold of national identity. Having invited us down for a visit, Paweł picked us up in the train station of the village of Sieradz and drove us the rest of the way. As we entered the manor, I had a premonition that all would not end well.

Everything relating to our visit seemed anecdotal. The repair work had been completed on only two of the rooms. The rest of the building was in the throes of reconstruction.

Larry glanced around and sighed deeply. So did I. Paweł had a space heater in the dining room and one at each bed in the other room. He took a hare from the freezer and tossed it into a pot of boiling water, busying himself with its preparation, while a neighbor brought potato pancakes for the "master" and his guests. Larry looked at the hare, shuddered, and politely declined. Henryk and I fell to with the appetites of loggers. Drink was proffered profusely. Larry and I refrained. English, Polish, and French rang in the air. With Paweł's inebriation, Larry's fervent hope of leaving the manor that very night faded into nothing.

Larry and I had noticed that every window had thick cobwebs and a resident spider. He could not keep from checking on them every few minutes, muttering, "Did you see them? They're huge."

When it was time to think about sleep, the two of us went to view the accommodations, while Henryk kept Paweł company.

Larry, Henryk, and I were sleeping in a large room with one double and one single bed. I sat down on the queen-sized bed to test the mattress, when Larry, who knows my fear, said in a strangled voice, "Don't turn around. Stand up and walk toward me."

I followed instructions.

"I've never seen a spider that size."

My screams brought my husband running. "There!" I pointed over my shoulder.

Henryk, a bit tipsy, said, "My God, it's immense," slipped off his shoe, sidled up to the beast, praying that it not skitter away.

It is said that all of God's creatures, large and small, have an equal right to coexist in this world. But the world is big, and I occupy a very small part of it. Any bug that values its life has a lot of world to choose from, but if it ventures into my space, I give it fair warning, I will do my best to kill it or to have it killed. I turn gray and start whimpering, my eyes cross and shudders run up and down my spine as soon as I see a six, eight, or more legged creature. I did not open my pantry window in Munich for three years when I saw that a huge spider was caught between the double glass. I would just periodically make sure the corpse was still there.

After Henryk the Exterminator did away with this beast, we went to bed. I slept, trusting and safe next to him. Larry sat up all night in his clothes, suitcase clutched to his side, unwilling to close his eyes lest an uninvited many-legged guest pay him a visit.

Next morning Larry and I were in the car before Pawel finished extending his hospitality to us for a future time.

\* \* \*

By May 1991 Henryk and I were ready to go to Prague again, this time for a long weekend. Hotel prices had soared, but we got a room in a private home through a member of the

Czech Service at the Radio. The apartment was in a socialist high-rise, a monstrous cement block on the outskirts of the city. Public transport was available by subway and bus or by tram, but the latter was out of service.

Though between us Henryk and I spoke more than ten languages, some fluently, some haltingly, Czech was not one of them. Henryk did fine. Using a mixture of Polish, Russian, and body language he was able to make himself understood and could even hold a conversation. My case was worse. None of the languages I speak could be twisted into any semblance of Czech. My Russian had disappeared after many years of non-use, and Lithuanian, not being Slavic, was not helpful.

At the apartment, whose paper-thin walls allowed us to be—rumble, rumble, woosh—serenaded by every toilet in the house—rumble, rumble, woosh—after our landlady unlocked the three locks that were intended to protect her from robbery, Henryk communicated with her on some level. He ascertained that English, German, French, and Russian were not among her languages.

"Other languages?" he asked without much hope.

"Greek."

"*Milao ligaki ellinika. Eimaste proti fora stin Praga,*" I perked up.

"*Katalaveno.*"

Not only could she speak the language—she was Greek.

My vocabulary was greater because she had not spoken the language for forty years. Diabetes—in Greek *diaviti,* was clear, but "kidney transplant," which I knew as *"metamosxeusi nefroú,"* was a puzzle. There had been no name for a procedure that had not existed forty years ago. After the Hellenic Civil War Stalin had ordered its satellites as well as the Soviet Union itself, to accept Greek communists. She had been among children sent unaccompanied to Czechoslovakia. Later she had not resumed contact with relatives in Greece and did not seem eager for a renewal even now.

## 12. Eglė bids farewell to a childhood friend, Judy takes her mother to Greece, and our protagonist goes to Hydra to retrieve a suitcase. Uosis and Liza invite her to their wedding.

The first two years in Munich I paid as little attention to my diabetes as I could. My boss later told me, I seemed to be doing great because I was not being carted off to the hospital unconscious every time someone turned around. My blood sugar was way too high, but only I knew that. I didn't even register at a diabetes clinic, though Munich has an excellent one. Life kept rolling along. Twice a year I would visit my parents in Chicago and get a once-over from Dr. Rubenstein.

A pleasant surprise was waiting when I began to work in Munich. Five people comprised the Lithuanian service in 1976. One of them was a childhood friend who had kicked sand in my face on the Michigan dunes—Vytas Nakas, a singer. We planned a traditional twelve course, no meat, no milk dishes, Lithuanian Christmas Eve dinner for two radio colleagues, Judy and Katama. Vytas had brought me his mother's recipe for *baravykai* soup, which would begin a dinner of herring, fish, vegetable salads, mushroom and blueberry dumplings, as well as *kisielius*.

"Pickles, don't forget pickles, they count as a dish, too,"

Vytas pointed out.

"Only if you're desperate. Same for bread. Are we desperate?"

"Not yet. Depends on how many ways we're going to prepare the carp and the herring."

"There'll be too much food. We're going to overdo it."

"It's Christmas Eve."

He and I were to tape the Lithuanian Service's Christmas program on December 23, but at lunchtime he came back from swimming in the Hilton pool, complained of pain in his chest, went down to the company doctor, took off his shirt, turned blue, and died.

His aorta had burst. Vytas had been lucky to live to twenty-eight. Judy and I packed his clothes, his books, sent them home to Chicago, and sold his piano. I was twenty-six, and until then death had touched only older people around me. 1976 saw no celebration at Christmas.

The next summer Judy took her mother to Greece, fell in love, and, ripe for a change, decided to leave the Radio and live on the island of Hydra. Undoubtedly, the quickest way to learn Greek before going was to hang out at Greek restaurants in Munich if she could find "a partner in crime." Katama and Jackie were fans neither of loud Greek music, nor of the ambience of a Greek taverna, where waiters sing along with the band, smash plates, and dance on the shards. That left me. From the first time I stepped into a Greek restaurant, I loved it. To me Greece with its raucous and hospitable people was the antithesis of Germany.

I learned to lean my fork tines down on the edge of the plate so the waiter wouldn't whisk it away before I was done, my fingers tapped the retsina glass in time to the melody, and bouzouki music made my soul sing and dance.

The Greek language stuck to me, its complex grammar, its odd expressions, even the gestures that accompany speech.

Once Judy had dragged me to my first Greek meal accompanied by ear-splitting music, I almost ended up outdoing her in attachment to melodies like "*Sineuiasmeni kyriaki*" or "*Frangosyriani,*" food like *moussaka, feta, taramosalata,* and *retsina.* The Aegean Sea, poets Cavafy and Sappho, heroes like Odysseus and goddesses like Aphrodite, historical events like the Siege of Rhodes, and the Ottoman occupation fascinated me.

When she packed her things for the move in March 1977, I lent Judy a suitcase and saw her off, standing on the train platform, tears cascading down my cheeks. Three months later I landed in Athens and took a boat to Hydra. Judith was waiting with open arms. She looked terrific—thinner, tan, hair streaming down her shoulders, barefoot, white teeth gleaming—a Greek nymph, exuding health and beauty!

I was ready to jump into the briny blue of the Aegean, if I would come out looking and feeling like that.

"Are you happy?" was my first question.

"Ye-e-s."

Greece was wonderful, but there were difficulties in her relationship with Lefteris. The culture shock of moving from New York to Munich had been minimal, but that of transferring from Munich to Hydra—immense. Over seven days I heard the ins and outs, what was acceptable, and what frowned upon in Greek society. I carried a complex tale back to Munich, but through Judy I fell in love with Greece for good and all.

Diabetes affected my place of residence because it and its complications limited my choices. I had to live where health care was better than good, at least if I wanted to survive. So my dreams of Greece, and Lithuania, and Portugal, and Moorea were confined to weeks or months.

Not quite a year after I arrived in Munich and started working for Radio Liberty's Lithuanian service came a signal event in my life. Liza and Uosis decided to marry. I foraged through racks of dresses in Munich to find one that would do honor to the occasion.

On my way to America, I stopped overnight at the Lithuanian Gymnasium in Hüettenfeld. A Lithuanian-run secondary school recognized by the German government, housed in a castle, it took in student boarders. A Lithuanian American poet, Marija Stankus-Saulaitė, was overseeing the girls' dorm, imparting a mixture of understanding, warmth, compassion, humanity, critical insight, and authority—just what growing girls need. Though they did not happen often enough, trips helped to alleviate the culture shock of my transfer to Germany.

At Schloss Rennhof I leaped down a pebble path in the dark in my open-toed sandals, slipped and scraped my left big toe. I bandaged and forgot it. The next morning I showered and got on the plane. By the time I looked at the wound again, it had begun to fester. I hadn't thought to change the wet bandage before drawing nylon pantyhose over it. After a car ride to Boston where Uosis picked me up, I pointed to the red streak running up my leg from the wound.

"Hey, Uosis, you think later I could show this to a doctor? I'd feel more comfortable," I said.

Uosis was no fool.

"Let's go now," he said.

I didn't argue. The doctors sat me on a bed, took one

look and ordered, "Hospital. Immediately."

"Can't be done," I answered. "My brother's getting married."

"Blood poisoning," came the reply.

By that time Liza was at the hospital too, lots of doctors were talking to me, to them, separately, together. And the gist of the whole thing was—hospital.

"No," I said, and we were back at square one.

"Do you understand what we're telling you? You have to stay in the hospital at least three weeks and even then we're not making any promises that the foot can be saved."

"I'm not staying."

"You have to choose—your brother's wedding or your leg."

"My brother's wedding."

They couldn't move me. I had just scraped my toe and forgotten to change the wet Band-Aid, for heaven's sake.

Besides, I had only one brother.

He was going to get married once and nothing—NOTHING—would prevent me from attending the wedding.

In the end I agreed to compromise.

"You can hospitalize me—the wedding's still days away—and let me out of the hospital to attend the ceremony. Someone will take me there and bring me back to Miriam."

"If you want to leave, it will be against our better judgment and on your own recognizance." Even that was capitulation for them.

"Fine. Could I at least leave my things in the room?"

"No. Everything must be packed up and moved out. What if an emergency occurred, and the room was needed?"

The reason was clear. If they let me out, and my leg had to be amputated, I might bring a lawsuit against the whole kit and caboodle for malpractice.

There I was, hospitalized. My parents were on their way from Chicago. I was not looking forward to their arrival. Scared, I lay in bed, foot elevated, staring at my big toe and willing the red streak away. Nurses would bathe the toe two or three times a day in a hydrogen peroxide solution. Nothing at all was put on the wound.

Days passed. There was nothing—no healing, no worsening. I had time to think about what I had done wrong, how my parents would react to my hospitalization, whether the blood poisoning would get better, and how long it would take to go in whichever direction.

When my father strode into the hospital room after my aunt tried to prepare me for his visit, he thundered a furious accusation at me,

"You have never taken proper care of yourself."

"If that's all you can say, then get out," I screamed at him in response, shaking. And burst into tears.

Aunt Dozė tried to calm both parties. My father stood, glowering out the window with his back to me. I was sobbing and hiccupping, my blood sugar must have been soaring. All I wanted him to say was, "Poor kid! Really did it to yourself this time, didn't you?"

It would take me time to realize how afraid he was that I might do irreparable damage to myself. How else could he show that, other than by yelling at me for not doing a better job! How would I learn to fend for myself in a cutthroat world if at the age of twenty-eight I still did everything wrong? Oh sure, it would have been nice to get sympathy, but that would be forthcoming from other sources. He must have felt abashed as well because he definitely lowered his voice an octave, though the flint in it didn't soften. Still, he came to the hospital every day. Then, aunt, mother, sister-in-law-to-be soothed ruffled feelings and we both softened just enough.

The suspense was equivalent to that of an old thriller: will I attend the wedding or will I succumb to the villain? The day before the wedding dawned, and I forced myself to consume the requisite number of carbohydrates to avoid low blood sugar, as I waited for the doctors to make their rounds. Once they had all filed into my room, I asked the million dollar question. "May I go and come back with your permission, yes or no?"

I waited, heart in mouth.

"We're going to discuss it after the morning rounds and get back to you."

Lunch, never a great culinary experience, was straw and cardboard in my mouth. The decision came mid-afternoon.

"No, we will not let you out for the day: yes, we think it too dangerous, no, we cannot be responsible for what might happen. No."

"Well, what are my options?" I asked.

I was not as brave as I pretended and to leave the hospital for several hours with the doctors' approval or at least agreement would have been preferable, but sit the wedding out? Wait for a visit from the bridal couple, as they left for the ceremony or came back, brushing rice and rose petals out of their hair, after it?

"How can I leave and come back?"

"You can sign yourself out on your own recognizance," came the stern reply, one I had heard before. "Or stay here."

I politely opted for the first choice, but again requested

permission to leave my things in the room, since I would be returning to it in several hours.

Not a chance.

Next morning I signed the sheet of paper, stating that I was doing this against the doctors' advice, decked myself out in the dress I had brought from Munich for the wedding, took the crutches, had my big toe swathed in white bandages until I looked like the victim of a skiing accident, and was driven to Newport by my family.

The wedding was outdoors. There was a minimum of stumbling around for me on my crutches. I received a lot of sympathy, most people murmuring condolences on my bad luck skiing, but I lost no time in setting them straight. "Just an infection of my left great toe," I would grin.

"That's too bad," they would murmur, moving on to somebody they could understand.

My brother and Liza made sure someone found me a chair so I wouldn't have to stand. I sat even as I read the part of the ceremony chosen for me, since holding the text and steadying my crutches comprised a feat I was unwilling to undertake. It was a double ceremony, Catholic and Jewish. For the latter, four of Liza's brothers held the wedding canopy over the couple.

Before the religious ceremony there was a puppet show by friends of the bride and groom that related the story of two puppets, Liza and Uosis, who met, fell in love, and decided to marry. Separate scenes showing each father's dissatisfaction with the prospective son-in-law or daughter-in-law were depicted, but the puppet couple reached the altar and wedding canopy. American perseverance prevailed.

I kept an eye on my father, as the show was played out, because I did not think he would find it amusing. I was hoping he wouldn't understand his role in the story. About three-quarters of the way through he turned on his heel and left, muttering angrily under his breath. I thought it was all over. But he was upset that this puppet "masquerade" was destroying the solemnity of the occasion.

He allowed himself to be soothed and led back. The very-laid-back friends of the bridal couple had put a lot of love into the portrayal of their story. They would have understood neither my father's anger, nor his feeling that they had "cheapened and ridiculed" the wedding. After the rites we retired to an inn for the wedding supper. I was particularly careful, not wanting to return to the hospital with blood sugar soaring, and afraid to interfere in the healing process.

The foot survived my escapade, the hospital accorded me a different room when I arrived, and, after a week there, I came out, though I still had to stay at my brother's for another two weeks to heal the foot completely before I returned to Germany.

## 13. The Radio mission. Life alone. Laura comes to Munich. Some physicians try thinking "outside the box." Health insurance in Germany.

I was now working full-time for the Radio in Munich but my duties were as different from those I had performed in New York as Swiss chard is from chives—the green is the same, but how disparate their shapes and flavors! Had I known the difference in advance, would I have taken the job in Munich? Probably, though the disappointment would in large part have been diminished, if not eliminated.

I chose this work because I believed in our mission—to disseminate information from and about the Soviet Union back into all of its segments, beaming facts, not propaganda, behind the Iron Curtain in the many languages of the Soviet Union and its republics, its communist satellites and the occupied Baltic States.

I arrived in Germany without a word of its language, for in high school I dabbled in French and Spanish and at the university concentrated on Lithuanian and added Russian. German had never attracted me, so of course, a German-speaking country was my fate.

Service members were required to be native speakers in their broadcast language and fluent in English. The first requirement was cast in iron, the second? A handful of

Radio staffers were polyglots, still fewer were native in two or three languages. Some were less than sure of English. Much of the material from which a broadcast could be hammered was provided in that language. Daily life called for some knowledge of German. One could point at rolls and sausages in the supermarket only so long.

My first months in Munich I was still thrilled with the work I had been doing for Radio Liberty in New York: being the only full-time member of the Lithuanian Service, I had taken responsibility to heart, worked like one possessed and loved it. I could choose the subjects of my scripts, tape poetry for special broadcasts, interview people, like Nobel poetry prize laureate-to-be Czesław Miłosz, who was translating the Bible and wanted to know more about the feminist movement, which, he said, he could not understand. The Service director in Munich had me cover American Lithuanian Community and American Lithuanian Council conferences in Cleveland, Detroit, Chicago, as they planned strategy to keep members of the U. S. Congress informed about Lithuanian issues. In the New York office the stage was mine alone and I hurried to learn my role and perform it without stumbling over lines.

The position in Munich was a bit part, a nice one, but definitely not top billing. I found myself one of five at the beginning and one of eleven at the end. I was just a translator of political articles from American newspapers. I had to swallow some disappointment as the work was more mundane than that in New York.

In the eighties our Lithuanian service relied both on Radio analysts, who reacted to events in the Soviet Union or Central Europe at a moment's notice—while a handful of services breathed down their necks at any given time, and on syndicated newspaper columnists, like William Pfaff.

The man who had hired me was kind. It was not his fault that my expectations had been raised too high. When they fell, they did so with an audible thud. Not expected to show initiative, I didn't. I cranked out first one, then two translations a day.

Once a year there was an academic Week of European Lithuanian Studies somewhere in Europe and I was often sent to cover it, but what about the other fifty-one weeks? The Lithuanian secondary school near Heidelberg was the center of some activity, but it was far. A dance group met on Thursdays in Munich to practice folk dances and swill beer, but—oh heresy!—I did not like beer and had already danced my fill in the States. Several times a year there were celebrations—Independence Day, Mother's Day. I spoke, read poetry, but that was the end of it. So, I had a problem. The work was very different and I felt I was in a cultural void, though I was speaking my native language daily.

Before coming to Germany and from then on, I lived alone. The Radio provided housing. For a diabetic being alone was significant, I had to relearn being responsible for and to myself. I had noticed an unpleasant tendency in myself to lean on the closest shoulder with all my weight. In the absence of a post, I stood up straight, so the experience of living on my own was not just a preference or an indulgence. It was good for me, despite the negative opinions of family, friends, physicians, an exercise in self-reliance.

After I had settled down in my host country and felt comfortable, a letter arrived from Storrs, Connecticut. A fellow member of Santara-Šviesa, Professor Benediktas Mačiuika, was teaching Soviet politics and history. Through his lectures he had provided me with an inside look at the functioning of the Soviet system and its effects on Lithuania. His daughter would be coming to Freiburg. Could she stay with me on a visit to Munich? "As often and for as long as she likes," I wrote back.

My policy with guests was simple: I provided a place to sleep, a key to the apartment, a map of Munich, and a rule that Lithuanian speakers spoke only that language with me.

Laura arrived, and our friendship was sealed.

When she came to Austria to teach German for a year, she stopped by more often. After visiting Lithuania at the height of the burgeoning movement for freedom, she stopped by Munich to share her impressions with Henryk and me. I listened with envy. The thaw had begun there, but I was still barred from entering. While Laura was studying at Harvard for her doctorate, her trips to Europe became a rarity, so whenever I would get home leave or some time to visit family and friends, I camped out on her futon in Boston.

\* \* \*

Two years after I made Germany a home of sorts, the diabetes, silent and low-key for several years, began to pipe up again.

In 1978, after two relatively hypoglycemic-episode-free years in Munich, I had an insulin reaction that required hospitalization. The doctors inquired about my diabetes care and, in shock because I was not under medical supervision, recommended Dr. Mehnert's Diabetes Clinic at the Schwabinger Krankenhaus. Diabetics were seen at the clinic either by appointment or on a first-come, first-serve basis one morning a week. In the beginning I saw any doctor, knowing nothing about them. All were proponents of the theory that a diabetic must conform to the physician's concept of how he or she should live. I was beyond that. I had had a doctor in America who had not needed to chop off my toes and shave my heels to fit my foot into the diabetic slipper. I had learned that a doctor could and should help ease the life of a patient. Give would be required on both sides.

I distilled my attitude to this: a doctor should not consider rules more important than people nor the disease a cage that impedes movement through the air. It was my intention to fly, figuratively. It took time to find a medic who could match Dr. Arthur Rubenstein in the requisite ways. When I did, the physician was a woman and diabetic herself, a warm, loving, understanding person. The combination was unbeatable. Until I met Dr. Kraus, German physicians I ran into were horrified by my way of life, while my own eyebrows were constantly raised at their ideas of how I should live.

The easiest change from the American to the German way of controlling diabetes was the diet. I was used to exchange lists—fruit, milk, meat, fat, vegetable, and starch exchanges and combinations of these for every meal. The German method was based on a bread unit made up of twelve grams of carbohydrate. Fruit, grain, pasta, potato, vegetable portions were calculated in bread units. All I needed was a portable scale to retrain my eye. Protein could be approximated--one gram per kilogram of body weight, all of it as low in fat as possible. Fat grams had to be counted.

The insurance situation was different. As everyone working under German labor law, I was entitled to national health insurance AOK or DAK, which paid 100%

for doctors and hospitalizations. It covered prescribed medication with a then minimal co-pay. Pharmacists dealt with the insurance companies, not the insured! Private plans had smaller premiums and paid for such luxuries as private rooms, but they were not available to the chronically ill. My Deutsche Angestellten Krankenkasse, allowed no frills, but did not skimp on necessities. In Schwabing Hospital at which I guested more often than I'd like to remember, I shared a room with four or more convalescents. There were no curtains for privacy. When doctors examined patients, the others would simply look away. But these "privations" were a lesser evil. In Germany I was fully insured at all times, whether employed or not.

Because I did not have private insurance, some doctors could or would not take part in my care while I was in the hospital. Hospital staff physicians did that. Since the diabetes clinic I went to was affiliated with the hospital to which I was delivered by ambulance and my doctor was on the staff there, she was able to oversee my care.

Once I was hospitalized, the protocol of doctors' visits was quite different from that of America. A slew of physicians, interns and nurses would enter my room together, chorus a greeting at the bedside, to which I, the patient, was allowed to respond. That was pretty much the last time the "sickie" was expected to speak. Then someone would lay a chart on the bed, the "staff sergeant" would run down a brief history of the illness for the "general." No one else would give voice to thoughts. After the staff sergeant summarized the problem, all of the physicians exchanged a few words among themselves and turned to the next bed. This was the moment to leap in with questions. My first was always, "When can I go home?"

Sick leave was unlimited by law. Hospital stays were incomparably less expensive than in America, and physicians did not tend to cut them short. Sick pay was provided by both the employer and the insurance company. The Radio required an employee to provide a doctor's note on the third day of an absence for illness. An employer had to allow employees company time to see doctors and dentists.

Adapting to a global economy has forced Germany to limit the services it provides, but the physical and mental health of its society, not just the profit motive, is still one of its major concerns.

## 14. The Radio breathes its last in Munich. Prague enters with oxygen. Eglė and Henryk turn about face and set their sights on the States.

The Radio was an odd creature—a private, non-profit organization, funded by the American Congress and overseen by an entity created for that purpose—the Board for International Broadcasting. Until 1992 Radio Free Europe broadcast to Poland, Bulgaria, Hungary, Czechoslovakia, Romania, Lithuania, Latvia, and Estonia. In 1992, when Czechoslovakia split into two separate nations, the Czech service followed suit becoming the Czech Republic and Slovakia. In 1993-1994 Poland, Hungary, and the Czech Republic were considered the countries most solidly set on the road to democracy of any of the Eastern and Central European nations, so when the budget of the Radio was cut by two-thirds and the call came to cut expenses by an equal amount or have the Radio suffer an untoward fate, the Polish, Hungarian and Czech services were the first to go.

At the outset the possibility that the Radio would be closed altogether loomed large, but finally the Czech Republic's offer to house it in Prague's Federal Building was accepted, and wheels began to turn to effect the transfer. The remaining services got ready to move.

The Lithuanian Service had not always been a part of

Radio Free Europe. When I arrived in Munich in 1976, the two Radios—Free Europe and Liberty—had only recently united, severing their links with the Central Intelligence Agency, and receiving congressional funding. The Baltic Services were fledglings, initiated hardly more than a year earlier. Several years after my arrival at the Radio, the three Baltic States were shifted from Radio Liberty to Radio Free Europe. The reason? To reflect the policy of the U.S. government—nonrecognition of the occupation of the Baltic States by the Soviet Union!

In Munich the Radio was a beehive of foreign languages. Many of their owners held American passports, but had not lived in the States. This was possible because of a law that extended the privilege of citizenship to those working for RFE/RL. Stories circulated of how well members of various services did on the US citizenship exam. One Russian had memorized the answers to the questions his friend had been asked at the Immigration Service. The first one had been, "When was America discovered?" This time, however, the immigration officer asked, "Who is the president of the United States?" The Russian answered, "One thousand four hundred and ninety-two."

The Radio building on Öttingen Strasse in Munich was huge. It lay on the edge of the seventeen kilometer English Garden, the largest park within the territorial limits of a European city. The Chinese Tower, a beer garden and a landmark in Munich, quite close to the Radio, allowed employees to slip out in the summer for a *Weißwurst* and a *Weizenbier*.

When I came to the Radio, the building stood in unprotected splendor with only a wire fence separating it from the English Garden in the back and on one side. A bomb detonated under the windows of the Czechoslovak Service on a Saturday in 1981 resulted in a thick wall being built and security increased. No one liked the barrier, the guards, the checking of bags, but all of us understood the necessity.

After several years, when nothing of the sort was repeated, security got lax again. That seems to be how an employee of one of the services brought an ax into the Radio in a paper bag. A version of the story ran like this:

A programmer, George, was criticized by his superior Ivan. (The names have been changed to protect the guilty.) George was responsible for the program.

He percolated like a coffee pot. All night blips ran across his screen, he rose, he paced, he was filled with thoughts of revenge. His ancestors, brave men whose rawhide whips spurred their mounts and curbed the lowly masses, would be ashamed of him if he sat like a sack of potatoes and allowed that son of a thief to spit in his face. But what could he do? At dawn his bleary eye lit on an ax he had used to chop a piano into firewood. Ivan would regret what he had said. George put the axe in a paper bag, grabbed his briefcase, and carried both into the Radio past the security guards,

"*Guten Morgen, guten Morgen,*" smiling as he went.

"*Was hat er im Sack, meinst Du?*" "What do you think he's got in the bag?" said one guard to the other.

"*Nichts besonderes, Mittagessen wahrscheinlich.*" "Probably lunch," came the answer.

George turned a corner, pulled the ax out of the bag, and brandished it in Ivan's face.

"George? What's the matter? George, put that down, man, you've been working too hard."

"My program is a good one. I work hard. Take back what

you said yesterday or..."

"Petya, you're a friend. Tell him to take it easy."

"George, some healthy criticism between friends..." Petya did his best.

"Take the day off, you're tired. Take a week, go home, relax. No, no, don't worry about the ax. Petya will take good care of it."

The wet spot on the back of Ivan's shirt spread from armpit to armpit.

It could have happened that way and maybe it did. All I know is the skeleton of the story—boss criticizes program, employee brings ax and threatens to decapitate boss.

Then there was the member of a Soviet Asian republic, who caused a minor contretemps at the copy machine. He was copying a book—a favorite pastime of radio employees—and a colleague needed a copy of a script, as he was on his way to record a program. According to Radio etiquette, the man going to the studio should have been given precedence—the book could wait, the recording studio could not. However, the compatriot at the copier was not willing to interrupt his work, so the colleague in a hurry pulled out a knife and added force to his argument.

The book copier was taken to the hospital.

Another employee with a sarcastic way of speaking that rubbed someone the wrong way was about to plop down on her chair when she noticed that someone had dotted the seat of it with pins—points up. Her expensive fur-lined boots became a casualty of the next assault. Someone, and rumour had it that it was a rather flamboyant and coarse-mouthed lady from Russia, had emptied a bottle of glue into them...

Such was life at the Radio.

In many services desk members split into factions, some religious, some regional, some political. Most famous for their vituperative comments were members of the Russian Service. The Poles—rungs higher on civilization's ladder— were less vile. At any given moment the Radio was rife with rumor. Scuttlebutt made its way down corridors, slithered like a snake under office doors, turned corners, shedding one skin for another, taking on new forms until its initiators passed the refurbished tidbits of gossip on as absolutely new. "Did you hear? Well, let me tell you..."

And then there was the Lithuanian Service. Like the Estonians and Latvians, the Lithuanians were a happier mixture than many. Ours was still a young desk, and for the first few years after its inception only simple disagreements occurred. Then small dissatisfactions swelled, and two factions formed, one that supported the director of the Service and one working to get him dismissed. Successfully. The rift that then appeared lasted through the next four years. Certain members of the service did not speak to each other beyond a barely civil greeting, but that was the extent of it—no fisticuffs, no knives, no axes.

Juozas Laučka came out of retirement from Voice of America's Lithuanian Service to head that of Radio Liberty for three years. He hired me. Kajetonas Čeginskas succeeded him from Sweden and was my roommate till he moved to the Director's chair. Old-fashioned, courteous, pleasant, intelligent, learned, sometimes a trifle long-winded, he was a dear person. We sat facing one another, our desks pushed together and sharing a window to the outside. I appreciated the chance to share that window a second time with him for several years before he retired. He was succeeded by another

American Lithuanian, Kęstutis Girnius, who initiated close ties with Lithuania, once they became possible.

Some colleagues on the Service were good friends: Saulius Kubilius, whose wedding in Vatican City to Jūratė from Munich I witnessed. I lost sight of them when they moved to Rome; Edvardas Tuskenis from Chicago, who acted in the Lithuanian amateur satirical theater group Antras kaimas (Second Village) a decade after I had, and passed his U.S. Civil Service exam after departing from the Radio; Mykolas Drunga of Chicago, an expert in Vivaldi's and Čiurlionis's music, with whom I had rubbed shoulders at countless Lithuanian events over the years and who would complete his Doctorate of Philosophy at Vytautas Magnus University in Kaunas. Others qualified as better or worse office buddies—Gintaras Aleknonis, the first colleague brought from a freshly independent Lithuania and four émigrés—theater director Jonas Jurašas, his wife Aušra, entrepreneur Aleksandras Kacas, and writer Saulius Kondrotas who cooked a mighty Polish *bigos* with a Georgian touch.

I made other friends at the Radio as well, some of whom have withstood the test of time and changes of place. Yale graduate Judy Vale, who left Broadcast Analysis for a Greek island and later changed Hydra for Wall Street, Sallie Wise from Ohio, who left Audience Research for marriage to François Marc Chaballier in Paris, Stephan Kellar, native speaker in four languages and master of innumerable others, who was promoted from cutting articles out of newspapers step by step to Personnel Director of the Radio, Californian Larry Sherwin, who from drudging with Stephan became Deputy Director of Radio Liberty, and Katama Bonthron from New England, a research editor who played a cello and stayed in Germany after the Radio transferred to Prague.

There was a time when it seemed to me that there could be no life after the Radio, but this—surprise, surprise—turned out not to be the case.

## 15. Greece comes on stage with *bouzoukia*, Sotiria Bellou, and *zeimbekika*. Hypoglycemia stops giving warnings. Kristina and Eglė twirl from Kavala to Easter with Judy on Hydra.

Greek songs made me want to raise my arms, extend them, twirl, fly. As soon as the *bouzouksi* started fingering chords, I would smile, tap the wine glass in time to the sounds, and forget the world. I learned Greek as I sang along with the singers, a habit that, fortunately for those around me, the loudness of the music drowned out. I neither knew what I was singing nor was I able to figure out where the words began or ended.

"Eureka!" I shrieked years later, when I realized that "teeny" was not one word but two "*einai*." No wonder the dictionary had been no help! I felt no embarrassment singing along. A foreigner singing Greek appealed to the Greek spirit.

As my dance mentor I chose Bobby, a German retiree, who led dances and had invited me to her table after I had appeared at the Akropolis a number of times alone.

The Greeks I met in Munich were approving and supportive of efforts to learn their ways. But they showed no reciprocal interest in other languages or cultures. Lithuanian was noted and then ignored.

Visiting friends on Euboea one summer, I did meet a writer, an older man helping out in a hotel store.

"You speak Greek," he commented in English.

This was a standard remark to foreigners, not said in Greek.

"*Ligaki.*"

"Where do you come from, what do you do?"

This was asked in Greek.

"I'm Lithuanian, work for Radio Free Europe, and write poetry," I responded in Greek.

"*Malista.*"

We talked about Lithuania, he inquired about its literature, the themes with which it deals, the difficulties writers encounter. Yianni Papareskou gave me his short story in Greek concerning a woman about to give birth who spends much time pondering the sex of her unborn child because her husband wants a son.

"This attitude—that a boy is better than a girl—is still prevalent in many parts of Greece and," he went on, "literature does not treat it adequately."

In 1978 I was spending my Friday and Saturday nights in the restaurant Akropolis, eating *choriatiki* salads, watching the dancers, and imbibing *retsina*, that wonderfully potable cousin of furniture polish which immediately elicits either undying affection or utter abhorrence.

The dancer surrounds himself or herself with a crowd of loyal friends who show their approval by smashing plates and bellowing for rounds of drinks as they kneel and clap and slap the floor with their palms. The dancer steps, turns, twists, twirls ecstatically, lost in himself, fingers snapping, outstretched hands at shoulder height. He's dancing the *zeimbekiko.*

I call it the "wounded bird dance," while Judy terms it—the "dance of the dying swan." Old men dancing didn't preen or glance around to see who was watching. Taking small steps, they were intent on the dance, lost in their thoughts. Young men—*palikaria*—told me they practiced their steps in front of a mirror and danced, not lost in an inner ecstasy, but showing off their acrobatic prowess.

Historically, the dance was imbued with the mysticism of another culture. My view of it was colored by knowledge of the origins of the *rembetika*, sung and danced in the opium dens of Piraeus in the 1920's and 1930's by refugees from Asia Minor.

Eight months I watched before daring to step out on the dance floor, to dance my first *zeimbekiko*. It hadn't taken me that long to try the line dances. They seemed much safer, especially between two experienced dancers, head up, back straight. Others could sing and laugh, but for me—one glance to the side and my feet would tangle, lose rhythm and step, until my eyes found a mentor again. Non-Greeks had a tendency to move every part of the body—hips, back, hands, head that Hellenes kept still. Foreigners would bend and sway, while Greeks moved straight-backed. Some guests improvised movements "as the spirit moved them," paying no attention to the steps of the dance. Folk dance practitioners were the few who did not gallop or prance or boogaloo while Greeks were sidestepping.

\* \* \*

Funnily enough, when I started caring for my illness under the supervision of the team at the Mehnert Diabetes Clinic in Munich, hypoglycemic reactions or low blood sugars became a problem. Because I had had the illness for so long, I stopped feeling the warning signs leading to unconsciousness. One late morning I woke up in my undies, shaking with cold beneath my kitchen table, having lain there fourteen hours. That particular horror happened only once, but I have no memory of the events that led up to it, no idea how I ended up on the floor, when or how I bit my tongue until it swelled like a wet sponge to fill my mouth. I must have taken long-acting insulin when my blood sugar was already very low, without noticing the onset of the reaction.

Lisa Rech, a German colleague at the Radio, and I had begun to take yoga lessons from Liga, a Latvian co-worker who had taught it on the Canary Islands. We would rotate having the lessons in our respective apartments. On the Sunday, when my turn came round, Lisa rang my doorbell, but I did not respond. She peered into the ground-floor apartment and was just able to make out my body crumpled at the foot of the bed. She called the police, who climbed in through a partly open window and administered first aid before taking me to the hospital for the night— hypoglycemic reaction.

Another time I was on the phone with a Lithuanian friend, Kristina, when she noticed that my speech was slowing like a top winding down.

"What's wrong?"

"Nothing, nothing."

"Do you understand what I'm saying to you?"

"Yes, I meant to, but went to, though the sun where..."

"Say a complete sentence or I'm going to get help."

"I... I'm... but... no..."

Kristina hung up and called my boss who lived one

floor above me. The doorbell roused me. As I pulled myself upright, the phone that was still in my hand fell to the floor.

Swaying, I reached the door and flung it open. Ebba, my superior's Estonian wife, spoke apologetically, "Kristina called me and..."

"Go away!" my voice shook with anger, as I tried to slam the door in Ebba's face.

As quickly as my brother when we were small and he was on the warpath, she thrust her foot between the door and the jamb and yelled to her daughter to call an ambulance.

Once again I had cause to be grateful, this time for the "Baltic connection."

On a tram to the city center once, I regained consciousness in a hospital far from my intended destination, was treated for hypoglycemia, and released. Dressing to go, I found a scrap of paper in my pocket, but had no recollection of having put it there: a forty German mark fine levied for riding public transport without a ticket. In the same pocket was my canceled ticket.

In Munich the honor system still functioned, but with a safeguard. Inspectors in civilian clothes did, and as far as I know still do, spot checks on various trams, busses, and metros. Who knew when a fellow in a jeans jacket or a middle-aged woman in glasses would flash an ID card and ask to see your ticket, "*Fahrkarten, bitte.*" Since I remembered nothing like this, I must have been barely conscious. Nevertheless, the fine was assessed and pressed into my hand. At the last stop the driver of the tram discovered my unconscious body and alerted the police and an ambulance.

I asked the hospital doctor for a note stating that

because of severe hypoglycemia I should not be considered a malingerer and sent it in with the reminder to pay the fine. I thought the matter closed. A few weeks later a second demand graced my mailbox. It did concede something to my illness—now I was to pay a five mark reduced fine.

"Can fining a person suffering an attack of a debilitating illness be considered harassment?" I scribbled on the notice in my ungrammatical German. That was the end of the matter.

One evening I regained consciousness in a hospital to see someone's face leaning over mine, an insistent voice asking: "What drugs did you swallow?" Drugs? I was not quite conscious yet, in pain and unaware why, the realization that here-I-am-again was slowly dawning, and the question being hammered into my consciousness was the wrong one. I shook my head to clear it. An orderly grabbed me by the shoulders, "What drugs did you take, tell us." Drugs, what drugs? I finally got an answer out in what was still my broken German, "But I didn't take any drugs. Why does my stomach hurt?"

"Why are you here then? Did you have an argument with someone?"

"Why am I here? I had an insulin reaction."

"Is that the only reason?"

"But what else could there be?"

I was slow to understand, I admit it. Blame it on the insulin reaction. By that time I had identified Dr. Kraus as my physician, who was on the staff of the hospital, and related the circumstances of the insulin reaction, praising my friend, Dana, for calling an ambulance, instead of leaving me to revive and survive as best I could.

Only then was I told that the Emergency Room doctors

had pumped my stomach. Despite the medical bracelet on my wrist which I subsequently stopped wearing, despite Dana's statement that I was diabetic, the hospital staff had concluded that two foreigners had had an argument, one of them had taken sleeping pills in an attempt to end her life, and, at the sight of her unconscious body, struck by fear and remorse the other, Dana, had called an ambulance and concocted an explanation.

When I finally realized, with painful nudges from my tortured stomach, what the hospital staff had thought, I lost my ability to see the comic side. I was furious. The incident became evidence of what can happen to an unconscious diabetic.

Dr. Kraus presented me to other doctors as "the one whose stomach was pumped."

\* \* \*

In 1979 Kristina and I traveled through mainland Greece for ten days, stopping in Salonika, Kavala, Thassos, and then going to Judy on Hydra for Orthodox Easter. In Kavala we stopped in a taverna for a late lunch. We were the only customers. At the back some Greek waiters and their friends were congregating at a table. I was able to speak and understand Greek. Kristina and I were conversing in Lithuanian. The waiter brushed the tables next to ours clean of crumbs, and when he brought us water, asked me, "Are you girls German?"

"No, we're not" I replied in Greek.

"Swedish?"

I shook my head.

"Norwegian? Swiss?"

"*Ohi*," was my answer to each new attempt.

Running out of plausible possibilities, he blurted out, "*Ti isaste?*"

"*Lithuanezes.*"

"But where from?"

"Lithuania."

He nodded sagaciously and walked to the back where the other waiters crowded around him, "Well, well, are they American? Scandinavian?"

"No, no, no."

Not wanting to keep them in suspense, preening a little, he told them, "*Lithuanezes.*"

"From where?"

"Lithuania."

"Where's that?" chorused the occupants of the back table.

He eyed them smugly, before answering what any fool knows,

"*Stin Afriki.*"

* * *

On the island of Hydra Judy's ersatz family gathered us into its fold, set us to turning the spit with the lamb entrails roasting to just the right crispness, and took us to church at midnight to bring home burning candles, as worshippers kissed and greeted one other with "*Christos anesti!*" We answered, "He has truly risen," took our places at the table laden with lamb, *kokoretsi*, spinach and cheese pies, *melitsanes*, goat, *kolokithakia*, *tarama*, *tzadziki*, and the sweet *tsourekia*, *koulouria*. We each got a red egg and a plate of *mayeritsa*—Easter soup made of lamb entrails, spinach, and an egg-lemon base.

Afterwards, Kristina and I moved on to Crete, where an untimely squall prevented her from making her return flight from Athens to Munich. I stayed in Crete another week, traveling up and down the coast by bus: Rethymnon to Ierapetra. The buses were modern, though not air-conditioned, and the times, about which Judy had been told, when local Greeks would travel to market with chickens clucking under their seats, were long gone.

I took the old road that ran along the edge of the sea. The new roads were farther inland and quicker, but less picturesque. Many of the old roads were carved out of rock face—on one side was the plunge to an Aegean so blue that it drew every eye like a magnet, on the other side rose cliffs. Crete was barren and breathtaking in the blinding light of the spring sun. The Cretans suffered under the whip of Turkish occupation from 1669 to 1913 and periodically made valiant attempts to rid themselves of their shackles.

*Eleutheria*. Freedom. No idle word.

The way the island had taken to tourism was daunting even when I was there. Small wonder. It promised relief from a hard life, too often one of poverty, of eking out a living growing grain.

\* \* \*

Every two years the Radio would extend to me the privilege of a month's home leave in addition to my vacation, which was four to five weeks a year. During home leave, which I spent with my parents, I would drop into the University of Chicago clinics. In September 1979 I made an appointment with Dr. Rubenstein.

"Your kidneys are showing signs of end-stage renal

disease. You have two options—dialysis or a transplant."

I had been reading the diabetic magazine *Forecast* for years. There must have been articles about this complication of diabetes. Had I ignored them? Read and erased the memory of them? It was as if I had never heard of diabetic kidney problems. Amputation, skin ulcers, retinopathy, autonomic and peripheral neuropathy, heart disease, blindness—yes, but nephropathy must have seemed so remote a threat that I had not internalized the information.

Doctor Rubenstein took the time to tell me what to expect. I felt calm, but detached. The import of what he had said had not begun to sink in. Kidney failure as my future wouldn't penetrate the brain for a while, and I would learn a lot about myself before it did. Creatinine, till then a meaningless number on the laboratory report of my blood tests, now glowed like a neon light. An indicator of kidney function, it had risen to over 1.0. Normal range—0.4 to 1.4. There was still room for hope. "How long do I have?" The thought of peritoneal dialysis, a hospital procedure by which a machine removed the blood from my body, filtered it of the impurities the kidneys were no longer capable of removing, and pumped it back into the body in a four-hour process twice or three times a week, was daunting. I wanted the other option. Dr. Rubenstein hazarded a guess, "Three years."

My kidneys lasted four.

Where does one get a kidney for transplant? There are two possibilities—a living donor or a cadaver. Who can be a living donor? In 1979 only immediate family—parents, brothers, sisters, in other words, the genetically closest— were even tested for the best match. Blood type, cell tissue and much more must match to provide the best chance for the kidney not be rejected. How dangerous is the operation? What percentage of kidney transplants fail? What are my chances?

I was given several handouts to read for information and encouraged to send lists of questions to Dr. Rubenstein from Germany during the next few years. The one-year success rate of a kidney graft at the time was close to 90% for living donors, a good 10 or 15% lower for cadaver kidneys.

Was the operation dangerous to the donor? As much as any operation, though the donor has a more painful time of it physically. What would happen, if the donor should need his or her second kidney in the future? He or she would need a transplant. Is only one kidney transplanted into the recipient? Yes.

Are both of my kidneys sick onto death? It was a comfort to be told that humans have been lavished with more kidney than they need: a third of a functioning kidney does the necessary work. People with two have one kidney to fall back on. Are the ailing kidneys removed? No, they remain in the body and shrivel over time. They are rarely removed. Cadaver kidneys, I was told, come from the bodies of brain-dead accident victims with the kindness and foresight to declare themselves organ donors.

After the transplant, the body dislikes foreign objects and tries to expel them, along the lines of "this is not me, get it out of here!" I have discovered that not just run-of-the-mill individuals, but even medical professionals, who don't deal with transplants directly, labor under the misconception that in time the body acclimates to the new organ. Not so. Five days or so of leaving immune-suppressive drugs on the shelf and the landlord evicts the intruder. As if that were not enough, the body can reject the kidney after a month, a year, five, or ten without provocation. At any time a black day might dawn and the recipient of the transplanted organ returns to being kidney-less and on dialysis.

What keeps the kidney in place? Medicine. The patient takes drugs that suppress the immune system twice a day till the end of life. Medicine is making such strides that, by the time I publish this, I expect kidneys to come in refrigerate-after-opening packages of five and a patient with end-stage renal disease will just velcro a new one into his or her body once a month, together with, if he or she is diabetic, a detachable, disposable pancreas. But that is only a writer's imagination at work.

I'm jumping the gun. I didn't learn all this in the hour I spent with Dr. Rubenstein on that portentous day. I gleaned the information from various sources in the next four years as the inevitable day neared.

Uosis, who was home on a visit from Providence, drove me to the clinic and back the day of the fateful announcement. After the doctor and lab work, I quietly slid into the car and said, "Uosis, listen, I'm going to need a kidney transplant." He answered, "It's okay. I'll give you mine".

Still, I decided to take my chances with a cadaver kidney. A new anti-rejection medication, cyclosporine A, was being tested in Illinois. If I lasted until FDA approval, it would considerably improve my chances of keeping the new kidney.

I went back to work that autumn. Within three months I was sending Dr. Rubenstein the first questions. Could I continue to travel? I was planning a trip to Crete with Liza, my sister-in-law, who was pregnant with Rebecca. Would there be a problem? The doctor okayed the trip and in April 1980 I was once again looking at the sites of Phaestos and its surrounding plains and Knossos with its Daedalus designed labyrinth beneath the palace.

Mythology came alive in Knossos under the same strong Mediterranean sun that sent Icarus to his doom. The son of Daedalus strapped feather wings partially held together by wax to his shoulders and, forgetting himself in the exhilaration of flying, soared too close to the blazing orb in an ecstasy similar to that of modern Cretan dancers.

I spent most of my vacations in Greece, soaking up sun and ancient history. Once, when my destination was Crete, I landed in Iraklion airport, ensconced myself in the city bus by a half-open window. Cicadas vibrated shrilly, as the metal frame shimmered in the heat. High school girls on the bus giggled in piercing voices. An old woman hauled her black-clad body up one step of the bus and glared at the driver, who was turning up the volume of a Ksilouris song. "*Avta ta kokina simadia bori na 'nai ki'apo aima...*" He jumped to give her a hand. A whiskered taxi driver, leaning against the whitewashed airport wall, aimed and spat at a rock in the red dust.

The bus started up and we rattled past auto dealerships, body shops, stores. A motorcycle slowed to a crawl. At the handlebars a girl in shorts and a blue and silver helmet flirted with our driver and sped away. The bus passed a lush green park with crimson flowers and palm trees and then we were in the center of the city.

Around one side of the *Plateia Eleutheriou* were five or six cafes, serving Ouzo, Metaxa, *mezedes,* the waiters sprawling on wooden chairs as business slowed after the noon rush. There were rows of small tables with chairs untidily pushed back or to the side. I sank into one, ordered "*ena frappé sketo, me galla,*" pulled out a map, and got my bearings.

Soon I was heading up the street to seek help for tourists. "Good day. Perhaps you know where I can find an inexpensive hotel?" The official in a sweaty uniform eyed this foreigner with surprise.

"*Milate ellinika?*"

I turned to the Tourist Police for help in finding an appropriate place to stay in every Greek city. They gave me maps, lists of attractions, local bus schedules, inter-city transport, advice and information.

I had trouble locating accommodations only once. My travel agent had sold me a cheap round trip flight Munich—Athens—Munich in mid-April. I was overjoyed, but there was a catch. The plane would land in Athens at close to midnight Saturday, minutes away from Greek Orthodox Easter morning. Should I or shouldn't I take the flight??

Instinct said that going alone on a major holiday to a city where I knew no one might be like *tzatziki* without the cucumber. My mother had taught me parsimony, which now goaded me to use an opportunity to save money. Parsimony won. I landed in Athens close to midnight. The airport was deserted with only one discontented girl working at the Olympic Air ticket counter.

"Where is the stop for the bus into Athens, please?"

"What do you want?" The question was followed by the answer, "Outside, in front." The girl pointed one red-lacquered fingernail toward the entrance.

"How often do buses run?" I was not finished.

"From six in the morning until midnight every half hour. Except today."

"Where can I find a taxi?"

"Taxi?" She was beginning to enjoy herself. "Tomorrow

morning."

"How can that be?" And after a pause, "Well, is it far to the city?" I hoisted my bag to my shoulder. The answer gave her immense satisfaction.

"Quite far, and the road is not very good."

After standing for several minutes in the chilly night air, I retraced my steps to the counter and roused the attendant, now deep in a magazine.

"Is there an airport hotel?"

"To the right when you walk outside and again to the right at the first crossing. About five hundred meters." She sank back into languid perusal of the latest Parisian fashions.

Having overpaid for a bed, I fell asleep, only to be roused minutes later by the protracted howling of a dog. He shared his misery all night, as airplanes landed and rose, landed and rose.

* * *

A jug of retsina, a hunk of Greek *psomaki*, a plate of tomatoes in olive oil, a little sun and the Aegean—who could ask for more? Continental breakfast? Not for me. From the time I was able to fend for myself, I ate odd meals. Soup for breakfast? Of course. Leftover pizza? With pleasure. Salad in the morning? Sure. A sweet roll? Jam? No, no, no. Couldn't face it at that hour, even if I had not been diabetic, even in my "baddest" phases.

I would convince hotel owners to give me a thick slice of feta cheese instead of jam. Feta looks so lonely on a white plate that often the owner would garnish it with a few olives, pour on a spoonful of olive oil, and sprinkle it with some aromatic *rigani*. This was bliss. Even day old bread tastes delicious dunked in olive oil.

On the second day of a stay in Heraklion I ventured out to the market street so narrow that two couples going in opposite directions could barely navigate it. Shelled and unshelled walnuts, salted pistachios, pumpkin seeds; plump, gleaming, purplish black Kalamata olives, and tiny, wrinkled ones, their plump, green cousins, all jostled for space inside the stores and out; peaches, grapes, apricots, apples spilled over the edges of wooden crates; on a barrel in the shade juicy slices of watermelon dripped redly; squares and rectangles of fresh white feta rested in saltwater, rounds of *kefalotiri, kasseri* graced counters, fresh sheep and goat yoghurt in barrels waited to be ladled into bowls. All stores, even butcher shops, were open to the air, slabs of lamb, plucked chickens hanging from vertical poles, horseflies darting from one to the other, the butchers themselves in white aprons, indolently swinging cleavers—that was the market.

Interspersed between the food stores, were clothing shops, souvenir stores, a *kafenion* or two, a general store, a restaurant, serving *patsas* for those suffering the effects of the night before. All were small, some owned by families for generations.

Lunch, a production of hot and cold dishes, potato, meats, vegetables, salads, dessert, usually consisted of tomatoes with a bit of feta and a few olives swimming in olive oil for me. I didn't worry about fat. I have since discovered that payment is exacted for everything one does and even for what one does not do.

Maybe the diabetes would not have brought so many complications had I followed the rules. What if it had, anyway? What if I had ended up with eye, kidney, heart and heaven-knows-what other problems and hadn't broken rules right and left? To feel I had deprived myself of the enjoyment of living and suffered anyway would be harder to bear.

It was not my intention to provoke the inhabitants of Mount Olympus. I loved *barbouni, sardelles, ntomates,* olive oil, *retsina*—the epitome of simple, everyday Hellas, with its leather-faced old men, incessantly playing cards and smoking, and old women in perpetual mourning, embroidering tablecloth after tablecloth, as they kept a sharp eye on the street. *Retsina* tasted of good things— hospitality, political discussions, compassion, simplicity.

I had not asked a doctor how that wine was counted in the diabetic diet. I simply assumed that, though resinated, it was reckoned like any dry white wine. My eyes were opened many years later, when a medical practitioner warned me to avoid it, as inappropriate for diabetics—too much sugar.

When I began going to Greek restaurants in Munich, consuming alcoholic beverages, *retsina* and *metaxa,* there were few guidelines for the diabetic who enjoyed imbibing, even moderately. Yes, I did find alcohol in food exchange lists in Jeanne Jones's *The Calculating Cook, a Gourmet Cookbook for Diabetics and Dieters* and was grateful for that knowledge, but either not much research on the effect of alcohol consumption on the diabetic had yet been carried out, or it was thought that information of this kind would be tantamount to encouraging drinking. In any case, it wasn't available. So, I decided to gather my own evidence.

It did not take me long to notice that correcting a high blood sugar in the evening would almost guarantee an insulin reaction the next morning, but much time passed before I got it into my head that there was a direct correlation between these two things. I was keeping a record of my blood sugars and insulin dosages, but still could not picture everything clearly enough. So, I graphed it.

After six weekends I ascertained that if my blood sugar was in the 300 range at bedtime, for me early in the morning on Greek nights, it was safer not to correct it at all. Often a perfectly lovely blood sugar value would plummet into a hypoglycemic reaction by noon or a relatively high one would come down to normal.

Sometimes everything reversed. Either I had consumed more carbohydrate and sugar than even the alcohol could cancel out, or I had not danced as much, or had not tested before I sank into bed and the blood sugar had been very high, or, and this was always the key, my body was doing something unexpected. When I made my charts with the red lines arrowing into danger zones and pastel-colored target areas, I saw total inconsistencies.

## 16. Mama comes to Munich and traipses off with Eglė to Greece where the latter runs foul of the diabetes. Before Mother goes home, Eglė comes to some realizations about herself.

Mama flung open the door of my apartment in Munich, suitcase in hand, ready for adventure!

Having left my father to look after himself, my mother, aged 74, had slipped on her magic slippers—comfortable walking shoes—closed her eyes, turned on her heel three times, and wished herself in Munich. There I took over and transported her to Crete and to Rome.

In Heraklion I deposited Mother in a café in *Plateia Eleutheriou* and marched off to find us a place to stay. A small, clean, quiet guest house on a winding street offered all of the requisite amenities, so I collected *Mamytė* and, carrying both bags, led the way back to the pension. Yawning prodigiously and barely able to lift suddenly leaden feet, I sank down on the bed for a nap under my mother's disapproving eye. "You should sleep too, Mother," I muttered drowsily, as I drifted into unconsciousness. Literally.

"Almost everyone in Greece speaks English," I had assured her in response to certain objections about the projected trip. Now I was in no condition to argue the point.

"My daughter needs..." she approached first a cleaning

163

woman, then a guest.

"*Dhen milao anglika. Dhen katalaveno,*" both pushed the air in front of them with the palms of both hands, denying any knowledge of English. Time was passing. Mother was frantic.

Finally, a child sped off to fetch a man with a plate of sugar and a teaspoon, but I was too far gone.

"Ambulance. Hospital. My daughter must be taken to a hospital," my mother kept insisting.

"No, no. It is better to wait. Tomorrow she will walk to the hospital herself. Yes, much better to wait."

"No," Mother was adamant, "right now. Taxi." They shrugged and called a cab.

After standard intravenous glucose therapy, I revived speaking Greek to doctors who spoke English back.

"*Pou eimai pali?*"

"You are in the hosptal."

"*An eimai kala tora mboro na pao spiti?*"

"Are you alone? Perhaps you should stay overnight."

"*I mana mou einai mazi mou.*"

After ascertaining that a hypoglycemic reaction was the extent of my problem, the doctors ordered me wheeled to a room and given tepid milk and dry bread crusts—hardly what I had looked forward to as my first meal in Greece.

Used to what is now the American way of "no pay, no heal," we worried about the bill, but were not asked to pay anything, and I was released from the hospital as soon as I felt better. We went home and out to dinner, Mama making sure I stuffed myself adequately. Next day we headed northeast to Sitia by bus. The rest of the two weeks rolled by without diabetic incident.

In Sitia we flagged down a cab at the bus station. "*Apo*

*pou isaste? Pou pate?*" The driver waited until I had seated my mother before he began to ask questions. "Do you have a hotel?"

"Please take us to the wharf. Are there big hotels there?"

Sitia was unknown to me, and I was wary of falling into traps. The driver, mustached like many Cretans, turned his head and, indicating my traveling companion with his chin, asked, "You are friends?"

"My mother."

It was magic. He smiled approvingly, nodded at my mama, and told us he knew a perfect place for a mother and daughter. He was a good-natured Greek, well into his sixties, who knew about Lithuania, as he had fought against the Germans in the last war. He screened his fares for prospective tenants, because the room turned out to be in his own house. We were charmed—It was clean, comfortable and inexpensive. We stayed long enough to explore the town, try the tavernas, enjoy the sun and the palm-shaded sand beach at Vai for five days before traveling again.

Though the Greeks who drive the buses between cities on the coast road are experienced, for a nervous lady they can seem more than reckless. The view from the window may be breathtakingly beautiful, but looking down is a little like standing on the edge of a precipice and teetering back and forth. I kept my mother in aisle seats.

In Rethymnon I suggested a trip to the monastery at Arkadi, so we booked a half-day tour. The countryside was spectacular, as we wound up and up the spiral road through one village after another. We were in good spirits.

The monastery was a historical site. On November 7, 1866, as villagers and monks were trying to fight off Turks and losing ground, they blew themselves up rather than fall into the hands of the enemy and took numerous assailants with them. A grotto houses the skulls of the monastery's defenders.

The cloister was still in use and monks distilled and sold their own *cipro,* a potent alcoholic beverage loved on Crete. I caught sight of our bus driver, downing one shot of *cipro* after another with great gusto. I steered my mother in the opposite direction, but the sight didn't instill confidence. When we got back on the bus, I made sure Mother had an aisle seat and explained the odd whoops and cries coming from the front of the bus saying that Cretans were very fond of singing. Mother responded to this in the traditional Greek gesture of negation—by raising her eyebrows, but she accepted my assertion, though she found the driving a bit idiosyncratic and the "singing" odd. She did not see how close we came to tumbling down the mountainside as the *cipro*-happy driver whipped around corners, honking his horn and bellowing.

\* \* \*

"Mama, I still have a few days of vacation left. France, Spain, Italy, Portugal, Austria—name your heart's desire."

"Rome. The Catacombs and the Vatican."

Rome it was. I booked us a first-class sleeping compartment on a train to the Eternal City, and we started out. I slept, but the rattle of the wheels and the knowledge that trains to Italy were notorious ground for thieves kept Mama alert.

On my way from Munich to Verona for a weekend the summer before, I had closed my eyes in a sleeper for six, purse under pillow, and had woken to the sound of my door closing. I groped for the bag and was awake and out of bed in seconds. I pulled the unlocked door open, yelling, "Hey, you!"

In the morning it was as quiet as it gets on a train. We were not nearing a stop. The train car, a sleeper, was locked for the night—no coming in, no going out. Sheepishly, the young thief retraced his footsteps and pushed my bag into my hands, putting his finger to his lips.

He gave it back intact and took to his heels.

Tell the conductor?

"*Signorina parla italiano? Non? Io non parlo inglese.*" and I would have stood, kneading my bag with my fingers, speechless. I had been lucky, but it was not a story to tell my mother.

Roma Termini.

The Casa Lituanica, run by German-speaking nuns, provided food and shelter for a minimal fee. As my mother repeatedly told me, I was a *tešlinė* who loved flour in all of its varied forms—spaetzle, dumplings, wontons, tacos, enchiladas, blini, pierogi, macaroni, spaghetti, virtiniai, naleśniki, pancakes, crepes, cookies, breads, cakes, pies. We had arrived in pasta heaven. I drooled. My mother had no fondness for flour beyond plump loaves of rye and bricks of pumpernickel. The food in Casa Lituanica evoked visions of Germany rather than Rome. Mama was happy. Our home away from home closed its doors at midnight, but we retired at ten, though I did it unwillingly, to the distant sounds of a city just beginning to wake from its afternoon torpor. Days were devoted to the Vatican, the Coliseum, and the Catacombs. We made the traditional discoveries of the wheel, exclaiming over the Trevi Fountain, St. Peter's

Basilica, the Spanish Steps, evenings soaking our bodies in a tub.

* * *

Back in Munich I was at a loss. How could I occupy my mother while I was at the Radio? She had ideas, sure, but they all involved work—scrubbing, dusting, organizing, cataloging. That wasn't my idea of a vacation.

Mama could not spend ten days with her hands folded in her lap. Since I can be oblivious to everything around me, and was so obsessed with choosing where I would take her and which pieces of Munich's architectural topography I would show her, days passed before it dawned on me—something in my living quarters had changed. By then Mama had alphabetized and grouped several shelves of books. The project was immense because at the time I had about eight hundred volumes in five languages, all thrown on shelves higgledy-piggledy, reference books next to poetry, history flirting with gymnastics, yoga leaning on a collection of rembetika songs.

So this was what she had been doing with her days when I thought she was busily rediscovering Munich! I scolded her, though I was glad for the much-needed push toward order.

When I gave her a farewell hug at the airport and watched her show her passport to the official in the booth, I turned away with physical pain, the pain of separation. It wore off, as everyday life returned to its pre-mother routines, but renewed itself each time I told her or my father goodbye, a wrenching pain as palpable as a smarting tooth.

## 17. Kidney failure and its ramifications—one of the black spots in Eglė's knowledge of diabetes, its complications, and herself. THE TRANSPLANT. Back to work.

Systolic, diastolic, hypertension, hypotension, elevated, low, orthostatic—terms I had never been aware of increased my vocabulary as my kidneys headed toward failure. Equipped with a manual blood pressure monitor, I was recording readings and graphing jumps and plunges. They were making no one happy—neither my kidney specialist, nor me.

I applied myself to cutting down on salt, an essential ingredient of the food I enjoyed. A liberal sprinkling preceded the tasting of most main courses and then I added more. Theory has it that salt blankets the real taste of food, that the exquisite taste of saltless food, enhanced with epicurean spices, is equally delicious and satisfying. If that is the rule, I'm afraid I'm the exception. Though the variety of saltless, as well as sugarless foods in Germany was great, the first bite of smoked saltless cheese made me gag.

For inveterate salt-users there was, of course, ersatz salt, but it had to be used with a light hand or its perfidy would become evident. I did find an American brand of a potassium-based substitute whose presence could barely be detected, and since then No-Salt shared equal space on my shelf with the real thing. I trained myself to like boiled eggs and tomatoes without the seasoning. Two years I struggled to adapt to a lack of sodium chloride and failed. There was no happier news after my transplant than that I could return salt to my diet, though it wasn't recommended.

In November 1982 Chicago hosted a Lithuanian Science and Art Symposium. Professionals from various continents milled about, united by a common language and heritage. I had timed my home leave for this weekend and was now trying to locate a paper on radiology which I had been told would be read by a great specialist in the field and attended by multitudes of physicians.

Not that I was a particular fan of radiology. The author of the paper, however, was another matter. Eugene Gedgaudas, chairman of the Department of Radiology at the University of Minnesota, now professor emeritus, was a relative, my mother's first cousin, one I had not met. I can't remember the room or the color of the walls, but something did leave an indelible imprint.

Apparently as pleased to make my acquaintance as I was to make his, Professor Gedgaudas continued our conversation for some minutes.

"How's your health?" he inquired.

"My kidneys are failing. I'll be getting a transplant."

"Could I be of help? Where will the transplant be done? Are you happy with your doctors? We do transplants at the University of Minnesota, if..."

I assured him that I was under the best of care at the University of Chicago. Then he pulled a folded piece of paper from his breast pocket and handed it to me, saying that I should know what kind of friends I have. Marija, the poet I had become so close to in Germany, had offered me her kidney some weeks before and asked that I find out if the transfer could be done. I told her that living donors were limited to close relations. Apprehensive that I was fudging and would simply not relay her offer to the medics, she had penned a note explaining what she wanted to do and given it to Dr. Gedgaudas. She was going over my head, as it were.

A year after the Symposium my world shattered and re-formed. My kidney function had perceptibly deteriorated. The previous year had been a watershed year. The three years Dr. Rubenstein had given my kidneys had come and gone. Maybe I could stave off D-Day *ad infinitum*; maybe the kidneys would just keep waddling along.

Not a chance. In the fourth year I was told that I would soon need dialysis. I could picture the apparatus which would suck my blood, filtering out impurities that poison the body, and spew it back into the veins. I pictured my veins, the shunt that would be permanently inserted in one of my arms so dialysis could be done over and over, I imagined the scars, the food limitations, no salt, limited liquids, weight loss, fatigue.

All of this flashed through my mind as I sat listening to Dr. Rubenstein in Chicago. Impassive exterior, inner shudders. How would I feel about signing up for a kidney transplant, without waiting for the debilitating process of dialysis to begin? Pause. Think. Would this not be a cleaner, less tiring choice? The end result could not be altered—the kidneys would fail, but the possibility of avoiding dialysis was suddenly real. I grabbed that chance to have a transplant before my kidney failed completely.

Immediate tests followed—heart function, blood and tissue samples, X-rays, blood-clotting. I couldn't be put on the waiting list until I decided when I would come to America and begin the wait of two, three, six, or more months or years.

I chose November. The first month would count as home leave, and then we would see. Radio Free Europe would allow me to continue waiting in America on some kind of leave—sick leave, emergency leave, or unpaid leave.

I returned to Munich to work until then. I talked about my disease. I always have, considering it no more than a misfortune I could do nothing about, not something to be ashamed of or hide.

When asked if I was afraid of the operation, I said no. What could I fear? Dying? But then life with all its problems and worries would be over. "If I die, I die." Not that this was "a consummation devoutly to be wished," but if it occurred...

I continued work and extracurricular activities: dancing on weekends in Greek restaurants with Kristina and Bobby, retiring late, reading a lot, writing poetry.

Then an odd thing happened. I became nervous. I had not been. Hot-tempered, yes, quick to ignite and after a sulk, quick to forgive, yes. Being late for work, for plays, for operas, for flights, annoyed me. But now I became a bundle of nerves. In the middle of chats with colleagues I would say, "Excuse me, I hope you don't mind, but I'm going to walk to the door and come right back. Then we can continue." And that, to the amazement of my conversationalists, was all. I would walk to the door, wheel around, come back to the table and talk. I could neither sit nor stand in one place for more than a few minutes.

But I couldn't ignore the change in me when one night at a Greek restaurant I did an unprecedented thing. We were dancing a line dance. The restaurant felt stifling. I slid out from between Kristina and Bobby, whispering that I needed a walk, and escaped. I flew around the block and came back to continue dancing.

After midnight, as I was kicking off my shoes in the car, Kristina, a psychologist, asked me again, "Are you sure you're not afraid of the transplant? I'd be terrified, if I were you," she dropped me off, waving goodbye.

Had I been lying to myself? Did I think I would die? No. Was I afraid I would? No. But if I did, would that be a great tragedy? Seriously? A tragedy for humankind? No, no. Not a calamitous tragedy. A small-scale tragedy? A one-person disaster. A tragedy for whom? For me? But how could that be? I wouldn't even be here anymore. Here? Wouldn't I? Be? If I weren't here then where would I be? What else is there? Heaven? Hell? Purgatory? A good place or a bad place after death. What else did I believe? What else had I been taught? That those who had the opportunity to believe and chose not to would be damned. Choice. Had I made a choice? Had I damned myself with my choice? Would I be damned forever? Was that what I was afraid of? Damnation? Eternal damnation?

Oh dear...

I fell asleep.


The next day at work passed without incident. I did not interrupt any of my conversations to walk to the door and come back. I was no longer nervous.

Having reached Chicago in November and registered for a cadaver kidney, I spent some weeks with my parents then packed a bag and descended on Judy in New York City, where she had gone after Hydra. The second evening as I expounded to her on the length and breadth of the waiting process, the phone rang. It was my mother. "The hospital just called. They want you there tonight. The operation is scheduled for the morning." I was packed and back in Chicago as fast as I could spell t-r-a-n-s-p-l-a-n-t.

The hospital allotted me a room, I showered and slept. It wasn't even dawn when a light woke me. The nurses shaved my groin, removed my glasses and gave me a pill to relax, then settled me on a wheeled cot. I waved cheerfully to my parents and Marija in a nearsighted haze, and the next thing I knew I was in the operating room. The anesthetist told a joke and as I began to giggle the curtain came down.

I was not the only kidney transplant scheduled. The donor had two healthy kidneys—one for me and one for another girl who wasn't as lucky. On dialysis for years she contracted a venereal disease from blood transfusions and her body battled the new kidney before accepting it.

The operation performed by Dr. Frank P. Stuart lasted three hours. I woke in grave pain. That was all I could think of. I moaned, groaned, whimpered, and called for the nurse over and over, then I sat straight up in bed and hollered. The nurse came running. I got an injection and drowsed off again.

The next time I opened my eyes, my mother was smiling down at me, my father and Marija just beyond.

I had been waiting for the Food and Drug Administration to approve a new immuno-suppressive medication to maximize the chances of avoiding rejection of the new organ. Approval came in November 1983. Three of us who were transplanted on the second of December were the first three patients in Illinois to be treated with the new drug—cyclosporine A (Sandimmune). In addition we were given daily doses of Prednisone and weeklong injections of another drug whose name I have forgotten. After six months I was weaned from the Prednisone and lost my hated moon-face caused by it. Drug therapy was reduced to the cyclosporine.

After our operations all of the "transplantees" on the floor would sit around waiting for our daily creatinine levels. I received my kidney when my creatinine test level had reached 4.6. Normality lies under 1.4. After the transplant I clocked in at 0.8 for a brief, thrilling moment. I was like one of those Mylar balloons that rise to the ceiling and don't come down for weeks. The doctors tried to let a little bit of the helium out to restrain my enthusiasm and warned me that the creatinine would rise and then level off at a more "reasonable" level, when the drug's "therapeutic window" was reached, but I was floating ecstatically out of reach.

Sandimmune had only a small dosage opening that was therapeutic—it kept the body from rejecting a kidney transplant. Too much Sandimmune would kill the kidney, too little would let the body reject it. The key phrase was "just enough."

On the subject of medication the doctors told me about people who had lost their kidneys because of stupidity, pigheadedness, or disbelief. One guy took his medicine diligently for sixteen months before he decided—enough. A week later—no more kidney. He waited years before his luck kicked in and he was transplanted again.

My hospital stay was seventeen days. Today the time can be less than a week, barring complications. I was lucky or blessed. No setbacks. No rejection episodes. What it meant was—no problems. There were first daily, then three times weekly trips back to the hospital for blood tests to determine the creatinine level, then I was allowed to have them done twice a week at a hospital closer to home. All was well. After two months of pestering my American doctors for permission to return to Munich, I received it.

The German doctors at the Transplant Clinic at Grosshadern, then in West Germany, suggested I wait a while before returning to work. Six months was the period normally allotted to transplant patients for convalescence, but I was going stir crazy.

In America an employee learns not to abuse sick leave. In theory the situation was different in Germany, but I was unwilling to put it to the test. The physicians shrugged their shoulders and gave in. "You want to work? Go ahead." Three months after my transplant I was sitting at the microphone again. "This is Radio Free Europe. Eglė Juodvalkė at the mike." In Lithuanian, of course.

## 18. Eglė begins to write poetry in two languages. Geometry competes with verses. Publishing differs in Chicago and in Vilnius.

In 1966 Washington High School's geometry teacher wrote a problem on the blackboard, and twenty-five seniors bent diligently to the task of solving it. I scribbled hastily, but my mind was not on geometry.

Beneath the sheet on which I was wrestling with the dissection of parallelograms was another of lined paper. I was working on the fourth line of a stanza and trying to find a rhyme for "hand:"

> *Come to me at blackest midnight, Death,*
> *And close my eyes forever with your hand.*
> *Let me expire, taking one last breath—*

The last line had to carry the thought. "Sand" would rhyme with "hand." Now, could I use it to convey the meaning of "end?" Let me see. Totally involved, I wrote:

Spilling the final grain of sand.

"Hrrumph."

I heard a throat being cleared, but ignored it.

"Hrrumph."

A little loud. I slid the page with the problem over the poem and looked up. The teacher, who had been walking up and down between the rows of desks, checking his students' work and correcting obvious errors, was looming over my desk, I attacked the geometry problem vigorously. A pencil rolled and fell to the floor. He picked it up, straightened and said, as I held my breath,

"Having a hard time?"

"No, sir, not at all, no," I stammered.

"If the problem is not difficult, why haven't you solved it yet?" And he picked up the top sheet between two fingers, leaving the poem exposed.

"See me after class."

"Sir."

"And bring that," his forefinger tapped the poem.

The ten minutes until recess I sat with my stomach in my heels. The rest of the class was snickering. Would my grade, balancing at A level, slide down to B? Would my parents be informed?

The bell rang.

I rose from my desk and dragging my feet, made my way to his table to stand, rubbing my right toe on my left ankle.

"I don't mind you writing poetry, but please don't do it in class. This is geometry, not creative writing."

"No, sir, I won't," I let out my breath and quickly turned to go.

"Just a minute."

I froze.

"So, you write poetry."

"Yes, sir, I do."

"Good. That's good."

Long pause. I fidgeted.

"Would you mind my reading it?"

"Well, I just write for myself. It's not worth showing."

"I'll be the judge of that. Type the rest and bring them in. I'll return this tomorrow."

"Thanks a lot."

I walked out in a daze. Did he really want to read my poetry? Would he be disappointed?

From then on, I showed my math teacher every English poem I wrote and he penned short comments in the margins. "Grownups don't rhyme" had the greatest effect.

I never wrote rhyming poetry again in any language.

By this time I had sent two poems in Lithuanian to a Catholic Youth magazine *Ateitis*. The editors published them. Five years later, in 1972, my first volume of Lithuanian poems appeared, a thin blue covered paperback, followed by a second book eleven years later. I didn't see that one before I was rolled into the operating room for my first kidney, but my parents laid the volume on my bed two days after the transplant.

There had been a few mishaps before actual publication. One day in early summer 1983 the phone rang at my parents' house in Chicago. Would I stop in to see the typesetter's copy of my book before I flew back to Germany?

The editor, poet Kazys Bradūnas, whose work I read avidly, handed me the book. I was floored, since I had not been sent any proofs to check. At home I noticed a few typos, then a misplaced line, a space where there shouldn't be one. I took my manuscript and began to compare. Twenty mistakes comprised the list, which I took to the editor. He tsk-tsk-d and expressed sympathy, but said, opening his palms, "Nothing we can do. The book has already been typeset and is about to be run off."

For a while we sat in silence.

"A page of errata can be printed and put in each book," I came up with a solution.

"No one will put them in. No one will read them," he tried to dissuade me, but I was adamant. A page of errors there would be, and I would insert them into the books myself.

And so it went.

* * *

When I was asked to explain my poetic credo to a friend, I was stymied. What did I think free verse consisted of? Was I writing free verse? Blank verse? Slam? Classical? Sonnets? Did it matter what I called it? Was the study of the Grand Old Men and Women of poetry a prerequisite for the writing of it? How does one learn to read poetry? Could a person just muddle through? I mulled these questions over periodically to find that my view was inconsistent.

To make a poem come alive the reader delves into images and emotions that the author's words elicit. The reader internalizes the poem and gives it personal meaning, which may, but not necessarily must, differ from the author's. The words of the poem are constant. They remain inviolate, while the thoughts they evoke can have many meanings.

A course of Lithuanian language and literature at the University of Illinois included some of my poetry. As a guest "living author," I was asked to arbitrate a heated argument between two proponents of two different interpretations of one of my poems.

"So, which is the correct version? You're the author, tell

us," the students begged. I shook my head.

"Take the poem apart line by line. If nothing in the poem conflicts with your interpretation, it's correct. If a word or line doesn't quite fit, something is wrong. If you have to remove words or, heaven help you, change thoughts, then no, that interpretation is far from the correct one. Look, you might not like the poem once you have an interpretation of the words. Too bad. Look for a poem that conforms, or think about what the poem actually says and why you don't like it. Poetry's not a closed field. It has lots of space, lots of leeway. Two requirements are honesty and openness. After that, there's a lot to say and innumerable ways of saying it."

I thought some more and continued, "Don't be afraid to read poems again and again. Quick comprehension is not a measure of the worth of poem or reader or writer. Many verses might require repeated reading before they unfold their inner meaning."

* * *

Several signal events had marked a four-month period of my life, as 1983 turned into 1984. I had managed to have a second book of poetry published while I was still around to enjoy it. I had survived a kidney transplant and was managing to make the new organ feel wanted and loved. I had enjoyed autographing copies of my book and presenting one to Dr. Rubenstein. At the end of January I had turned thirty-four.

Seven years later, in October 1991, after Lithuania had declared that it was reinstating its independence, I flew to Vilnius.

* * *

As I tumbled into my cousin Vytas's waiting car, I announced, "*Vaga* wants to publish my poetry."

"If we receive your manuscript by the middle of December, we will publish it next year," the director's last words rang in my ears. We had shaken hands and I had had no warning premonition.

The end of November came and went. When I awoke from my torpor in December, there was no possibility of getting the manuscript to *Vaga* in time, especially since the post was less than reliable.

"What's the problem? Give it to someone to take," Audrius Siaurusevičius, one of our freelancers from Vilnius temporarily in Munich, responded through the clouds of smoke that trailed him everywhere.

"I don't know anyone who's going before then," I moaned.

"I'm booked on a flight tomorrow. If you bring it to work in the morning, I'll take it," said Audrius.

I was happy, until I realized that the manuscript was not ready. The poems existed, but in which drawer, hidden in what stack of papers, scribbled on what envelopes or dinner napkins were they? I had to get started. I rushed home, assembled the book, named the chapters and worked on the title. In the morning I had two copies of the whole thing and placed the original securely in my colleague's hands.

The director of *Vaga* was silent. Myriad versions of one gloomy idea chased through my mind for weeks.

The projected publication date came and went. I still did not know if my manuscript had reached *Vaga*. Other problems presented themselves and pushed the book to the back burner of my mind. A year later my pot boiled over.

I picked up the phone.

"The director is not in," drawled his secretary in May.

"The director is unavailable," she informed me in June.

"The director is on vacation," she barked in July.

"Please call next week," I heard in August.

In September my boss told me to pack my bags and go to Vilnius for two months of on-the-spot reporting. Complaining in the Radio office in the Lithuanian capital one day that I didn't so much as know if my manuscript had arrived, I heard one of our freelancers say, "My brother designed the cover for a book of your poetry."

"But I haven't even signed a contract!"

At *Vaga* the director was absent, but the editor of my book showed me the cover. There was only one thing wrong: my name was in larger letters than the title.

"Please change it."

"But it will affect the composition. We are preparing to publish the book. In any case, you must speak to the director."

The editor promised to speak to the director about the contract and the correction of the size of my name.

Time passed. The summer of 1994 I was again in Vilnius. This time the director was there, all apologies.

"Yes, we've been having financial problems, but things are going all right now, your book will be out very soon. We'll see about the cover, though, in my opinion, you're better known for your work at Radio Free Europe than for your poetry. We haven't had a chance to read much of your verse. Your name is what would attract attention..."

"Nevertheless."

"Let's have a look at the cover right now."

"Great."

He pushed a bell for his secretary.

"Ask one of the editors to come in and bring Eglė Juodvalkė's manuscript." In a few minutes he continued, "Could you show us the Juodvalkė book?

The editor stood stammering in embarrassment.

"We, we certainly don't have it here. As a matter of fact, I have never seen it. Are you sure we have it?" he asked, turning to me.

The director intervened, as I said, "Not only is it here, I had the book and cover in my hands a year ago."

"Well, it's certainly not in the building. Maybe at the printer's."

"I do hope you find it," I turned to the director.

"Of course, of course," he said and ushered me out.

Another year of one-sided phone calls passed: no letters, no contract, no book. Fall of 1995 I was in Lithuania on vacation. Back I trudged, up the stairs, to find my book's editor gone and the manuscript still somewhere, no one knew where, though everyone had seen it.

"Don't worry, we'll find it. By December, at the latest January of next year, we'll know whether your book will be out by mid-year."

I listened, but did not believe.

I was right. December 1995 and January 1996 came and went. In February my patience ran out, and I demanded my manuscript back. In answer I received an unexpected letter from *Vaga*—with a contract. There had been major administrative changes. A new man had replaced the former director. The publishing house was sorry. If I would allow it, my book would see printer's ink by Christmas.

I signed the contract. This time sooner than promised

my third book of poetry was in my hands and I was in Vilnius autographing copies.

## 19. Weekends in Paris with Sallie. Henryk comes to rue Guersant late one evening. His and Eglė's dance stretches into forever. Paris and herring.

I was back at work after the transplant when a colleague whispered in my ear that there were changes at the Lithuanian Service. My absence from work may have been causing some dissatisfaction to my employers, perhaps even my colleagues. If I qualified as a person with a disability I would be protected from being fired without cause. In Germany an employer had to have a certain number of workers with disabilities on the staff or pay a fine.

Professor Rüdiger Landgraf provided my medical history to the West German State Board and I was given a disability grade of 80% for the transplanted organ and diabetes. If I were unable to do my work for reasons of health, the Radio would have to transfer me to some other position. My ability to do the work was not in question.

For a year after the transplant I curtailed my trips abroad. As care of the new organ became more routine I began to move out of Munich on weekends. Short jaunts to Paris were on the agenda. I would clamber on the Orient Express at just before nine in the evening in Munich and wake up as the train announced its arrival at the Gare de l'Est with a whistle at just before seven the next morning.

"Good morning, Paris," I would mumble into my *café au lait*, savor a warm croissant, and watch the city come alive, as cafe owners set out their round tables and wicker chairs. I could have spent my two days going from cafe to cafe, but time would be moving, and by nine I would wander to a public phone to rouse my hostess.

Sallie usually picked up the instrument groggily, but in a moment the fog would lift.

"Where are you? Come on over."

"Half an hour."

I would swing my bag up over one shoulder and leap down the stairs to the Metro. From the Champs Élysée I would saunter down narrow streets that flowed like ribbons, breathing air a touch warmer, a bit more caressing than Munich. Paris! Every time was a discovery, every season had its delights. I would spin down the street, singing as I walked.

"Come visit in March. Paris is wonderful in March. Come the weekend of the fourth. I'm having a party," Sallie had urged.

How could I resist? Besides, I wanted to interview Pranas Gailius for the Radio. He was exhibiting his work in a gallery not far from Sallie, who suggested, "If he looks interesting, invite him." Delighted by him, his art, the woman he was sharing his life with, I threw open Sallie's portals, figuratively speaking, to both of them. Rima Puniška, a member of the Lithuanian community in Canada, had moved to Paris, was working at the Canadian Embassy, and writing poetry.

Pranas left Lithuania at seventeen. He fled from the second Soviet occupation and was given sanctuary in France. He studied painting with Fernand Leger, lithography at

Beaux-Arts, and exhibited in Geneva, Toronto, Toulouse, Berlin, Tokyo, New York, to name a few places. His embossed and colored graphics, acryllics, watercolors and limited edition books were distinctive, impregnated with his childhood in Samogitia.

He pointed to a vivid blue slash in one of his paintings and told me that since he left Lithuania he has been trying to recapture the feeling of fishing in the stream that ran along the border of his father's farm or the texture of the grass under his bare feet as he raced through the meadow. His speech was colored with French exclamations as he hurtled through sentences. An energetic man fond of food and drink, he spent much of his time in Provence, palette in hand, returning to Paris for a few months in the winter.

"Have I your permission to turn a poem of yours into graphic art?"

"I'd be delighted. And come to Sallie's this evening, you and Rima."

\* \* \*

Sallie was in a state. She was certain the refreshments would not be ready in time, the apartment would be in no condition to receive guests, and no one would come. Whether the food would be good was not a question. The preparation of the feast was nerve-wracking for Sallie and any loiterers. She was tearing her hair out when I returned.

I developed a strategy. There are people who would not believe my contention that I am a calm person. Henryk would be the first to remind me of the way I get ready for work, starting out relaxed, even laid back, almost lazy, but then revving up and dashing from place to place, while he watches, bemused. If something is not to hand when I need it and I, of course, need it and only it desperately, be it my Mexican socks, my aboriginal earrings, or the piece of cheddar that I swear I hid yesterday behind the jar of beets in the refrigerator, I am an emotional wreck, ranting and raving. Nevertheless, as soon as Sallie began to approach hurricane status, I acquired the calm at the eye of the storm.

Recognizing the futility of disagreeing with anything, I did not obtrude into the cooking process. I only offered to drudge. "Let me peel the carrots, wash the lettuce, slice the potatoes, chop the avocado. And please show me how you want it done."

It worked! As she completed her tasks, Sallie's hurricane winds died down. I can't say that she reached a state of blessed calm before the guests arrived, but the food was prepared, Sallie was dressed and able to put on the face, not mask, of a charming hostess.

"Wine and snacks in the living room, coats in the bedroom, this is Eglė from Munich, let me get you a glass of wine."

Most of the guests milled about, drifting from this threesome to that twosome. I filled my plate with guacamole, eggplant salad, salmon dip, spicy walnut cheese rounds and ensconced myself in a chair.

Before Pranas and Rima came, I exchanged a few words with Kathy, a half-Irish, half-Polish American who alluded to the purported amicable relations of the Lithuanians and Poles. This was waving a red rag at a bull. I lowered my horns and charged, "Bad relations between Lithuanians and Poles date back centuries."

One look at my flashing eyes and the smoke pouring out of my ears, and Kathy backed up a step, "But all that's history, the past."

"Is it? A Lithuanian who spent half of his life in Soviet concentration camps told me just last week that a Russian Pole interrogator was known for his cruelty!"

The argument was specious, but Kathy retreated. Several hours later she came up to me with a guy in tow.

"I wanted you to meet a Pole who's different."

I must have looked incredulous because first he said, "Vilnius is undoubtedly the capital of Lithuania."

I began to look at this man with a bit of interest. Admittedly, he was not bad to look at. Then he opened his mouth a second time, "There can be no doubt that Lithuanians suffered culturally from the Poles."

"That's a start," was my answer, as I looked into two brilliant blue lakes and promptly forgot my rule about keeping my feet on the ground and my head above water. I went under once.

"What do you do?"

"I write. What about you?"

"I write. Poetry?"

"No, prose."

"I write poetry."

"Must be hard to survive."

"I work for Radio Free Europe, too."

"I did that, but in New York. I had a desk next to the Lithuanian Service."

"I worked in the New York office too, but before Munich. It gives me a chance to do something for Lithuania. How did you get out of Poland?"

"I'm a political refugee."

"Where did you learn English?"

"In America. First New York, then I worked in

Washington for the Voice of America. Then California. Then I came here. You like Paris?"

"Love it. What do you do here? Do you speak French?"

"I do. How about you?"

"Nope. Wish I did. Wait a minute, you didn't answer—what do you do?"

"I'm writing a book, a novel about bohemia."

I went down a second time.

"I have a kidney transplant, and I'm diabetic."

That first evening we discovered that on the subject of politics, except for my inherited distrust of Poles, we could pretty much see eye to eye. He asked me to dance. I went down for the third time. Drowning was very pleasant. I lost all desire to surface. One of our fellow guests, Misha, knelt with a centimeter to measure how much we were moving and came up with zero. We were oblivious. By the time Henryk and I stopped dancing, all the guests had left, Sallie had gone to bed, and day was about to dawn.

Though I didn't want him to go, and he didn't want to go, it was time. I buried my face in the pillow as dawn broke. He called five hours later, as promised. Sallie stumbled to the phone. "It's for you," she said.

Henryk wanted me to come over, gave detailed instructions, which I carefully wrote down.

"Sallie, I don't know what to do."

"Do you want to see him?"

"Yes, but..."

"If you don't want to go there, invite him here." Then she turned over and went back to sleep. "Open the door when he gets here."

I nodded, a bit dazed, and went to call Henryk.

"I'll be there in an hour."

We were together all day. When we said goodbye, I was afraid to think. No expectations, no disappointments. I was supposed to return to Paris in three weeks for the opening of the Baltic House, but, I knew that if Henryk did not get in touch, I wouldn't. To this day he shakes his head in disgust, when I tell him I wouldn't have written him, had he not written first, but, sad as this is, I know it's true. My answer and my actions would be different today, I think, but it's humbling to admit that thirty-five years had not imparted to me the courage of my convictions about male/ female relationships. I was sure that if I wanted to see Henryk again I would not wait for him to take the initiative.

Henryk's first letter, though not precisely a love letter, was written and mailed on the day I left Paris. Back in Munich, I promptly came down with the worst case of flu I could remember having. Bedridden for a solid week, I alternated between sweating and freezing. A basket case, I could barely compute my new insulin dosage, dictated by disease: less, because I wasn't eating, more, because of the infection. Henryk's letter came in the midst of this and read like a continuation of our conversation in Paris. He would be waiting for me in March.

A poem by Yeats, "The Song of Wandering Aengus," the motto of the book Henryk was working on, was included.

It could have been just his favorite poem or one that he was fond of at the moment, but I read everything into it, as people in love are wont to do. On the back of his letter I penned a note in Lithuanian: "Letter, four poems, biography. Sent 1985.III.17." It took a week to get well from the flu but the letter sure hastened the healing. In the first letter he had asked for some poetry and a short biography for a Polish publication. Four days later he mailed me a second letter, confirming my coming visit, warning me to prepare for a new Polish invasion of Lithuania, and enclosing another poem by Yeats, already "according to tradition."

As I got off the train, clutching an overnight bag and a tape recorder, and examining faces as nonchalantly as possible, I felt panicky. What if he didn't come?

I was grown up, I had his address, but maybe I'd just wake Sallie and discuss it with her first. My train had left Munich in two parts, each with a separate engine. What if Henryk was racing up and down the track looking for me in the other railroad cars? We would never find each other again, I thought, certain there was no point in even trying. I reached the front of the train and looked around, feeling abandoned.

There he was, rooted to a spot that people detraining from either train segment would have to pass. He had been standing off to the side. At that moment I would not have impressed anyone as the self-contained, self-sufficient, self-confident woman I thought myself. Pathetic was how I characterized myself at the moment. Vulnerable would have described me more accurately.

Henryk did not seem plagued with similar doubts. He took me to the apartment he shared with Woytek, another Pole, at l'Asile Popincourt in the eleventh arrondissement. Later, he and Sallie accompanied me to a Paris suburb for the opening of the Baltic House that was being run jointly by an Australian Lithuanian woman, whose deep and sonorous singing voice wrapped itself around a listener like a cashmere shawl, and her Estonian companion. After a program of Baltic songs, piano and flute music, the Lithuanians, though greatly outnumbered by Latvians, tried to out-sing them.

Henryk's and my eyes, drawn to each other like positive and negative cells, produced sparks whenever they met. Sallie told me later that being around us was dangerous.

Back in Paris, Henryk invited Sallie and me for margaritas at the Studio in rue du Temple. He and I laughed our way to the Orient Express that would return me to Munich. Before I was lulled to sleep by the chug of the train wheels, I thought—this might be serious. Something is certainly brewing.

I turned my sights on America in April, as the Easter holiday promised extra days off from work. The mailman brought a postcard from Henryk to my parents' address, and a letter greeted me in Munich when I came home. At the end of April Henryk came to Munich for a four-day visit of walking, talking, making the rounds of my friends.

A long period followed during which we didn't see each other at all, since he was in the States. Mail and an occasional telephone call were our only contact. Twenty-two postcards and twenty-six letters dated March to December 1985 reached me in Munich from Cleveland, Chicago, Buffalo, New York, Seattle, San Francisco, St. Petersburg, Denver, Salinas, Phoenix, Monterey, Kansas City, finally Paris again. In America Henryk was on the move, seeing people and speaking at meetings to gather support for activities against the communist government, like sending forbidden literature disguised as cans of food, or instructions how to construct homemade printing presses.

He passed through Providence to meet Uosis and New York to look up Judy. Some members of my family began asking questions.

"He travels so much. Is he dependable?" asked one relative.

"Does Henryk work for American Intelligence? How can he travel so much? And appear to be surviving without a settled job?" inquired another aunt.

He wasn't doing anything of the sort. My wanderer was trying to help communism self-destruct. He was being paid for writing scripts at the Voice of America, Radio Free Europe, and later working as an instructor at the Defense Language Institute. I wanted my parents and relatives to know how responsible and trustworthy he was.

From Cleveland he sent me the first of a series of T.S. Eliot cat poems, this one called "Growaltiger's Last Stand." He sent a "SPECIAL SMILE FOR YOU! This evening I'm going to read all your letters once again," from Highland Park, Illinois. We rendezvoused in San Francisco in September.

At the end of November he was again in Paris, writing, "Every feeling is a mixture of fear, hope and happiness. My nature is not different from yours. I'm smiling when I'm happy, and I'm despairing, if something goes wrong. I'm weeping just now because I can't find my jeans."

Everything was in the letters: humor, poetry, intellect, emotions. This was the first man I had met who was not afraid to express his feelings openly. I would hug myself after reading his letters and dance around the room until I came to my senses.

He invited me to Paris for Christmas. I took a vacation and went for two weeks. I counted on having something figured out by the end of that time.

I did not see much of the city on this visit, though I did insist on our breakfasting no later than mid-afternoon.

Henryk would pick up a few *croissants, pain au raisin, baguette, pâte forestière, mousse au canard, choucroute, rillettes,* hams, cheeses, a few tomatoes, pickles, and anything else that appealed to his eye. He had a Japanese knack for arranging cold meals on a platter for taste, appearance, color.

After breakfast we would sally forth to work. Henryk was writing a novel in English that would later be submitted to Faber & Faber. We would take the text and dictionaries and find ourselves a cafe to sit in, consume tea and argue about words, meanings and their possibilities.

"You can't say that in English. It sounds odd."

"Why not? You can't say it in Polish either, but I did. It's innovative."

"Maybe in Polish, but not in English. You have to trust me or get someone else to help you."

"I trust you, I trust you. I just wonder what you would have done to James Joyce.

## 20. Problems with the diabetes in Paris and in Munich. A life change. Eglė witnesses a colleague's wedding in the Lithuanian Chapel of St. Peter's Basilica in Vatican City.

There were days in Paris, when Henryk and I would be walking and I would interrupt him mid sentence.

"I think I'm having an insulin reaction."

"We need to sit down and get you some orange juice."

"I'm sorry."

"Why should you be sorry?"

"I just have to sit for a few minutes and drink."

Time passed and I'd say,

"We can go now."

Later that afternoon as we'd be working on the book, "Henryk, I think... low..."

"*Monsieur, jus d'orange pressé, s'il vous plaît.*"

"But it's not... possible..."

"We'll talk later."

And in ten minutes with my head in my hands, I'd wonder, "But how could that happen? Twice in one day! I didn't take too much insulin, and we haven't been walking a lot. Oh, rats! I can't figure it out. I hate that."

I was inclined to think my irregular eating habits were at fault, but the number and frequency of the insulin reactions were just too great: almost daily, sometimes several times a day. I expected my diabetes to return to normal in Munich, but when I counted seventeen reactions in two weeks I turned to my doctor for help.

Professor Landgraf hospitalized me.

I lucked out. The professor was Chief of Endocrinology and specialized in treating diabetics at the University hospital in Munich. He had his own ward there. The doctors were competent, but I did not leave the hospital for two and a half months. The problem lay in the inexplicable highs and lows of my diabetes, which, as I told them at the outset, was in a chaotic state. It is one thing to eat a hot fudge sundae, as I undoubtedly have done, and have the blood sugar shoot up, quite another to eat a slice of cheese and a pickle, both with nonexistent carbohydrate values, or to eat nothing at all, and have the blood glucose level jump sky-high. There were days when I would lie in bed twelve hours and watch the blood sugar level fall to 34 one day, stay the same the next, and climb the third, all the while consuming measured quantities of diabetic hospital food.

Another part of the problem, at least in the beginning, was that the doctors did not quite believe me when I used the word "chaotic" to describe my condition. That hospital's staff had not seen me before and thus could not judge the extent of my knowledge and my veracity. Was I lying to them or keeping something from them, not unknown with diabetics? Was I eating on the sly? For three weeks they tried to ascertain what was wrong by having me adhere to a rigid schedule of diet and insulin. At the end of that time they threw up their hands and admitted failure.

"Now what?" I asked and waited. Prof. Landgraf oversaw three more weeks of tests, trying out one theory after another. Nothing. At the end of the second month he tossed into the ring the idea that I might be allergic to pork or beef insulin.

Bingo!

After countless injections of first pork, then beef insulin for thirty some years, I had developed an allergic reaction and was manufacturing insulin antibodies, which prevented me from processing the hormone in a normal way. I was put on human insulin and told never, but never, to use animal insulin again. But that wasn't all.

"*Fräulein* Juodvalkis, have you ever heard of the insulin pump?"

"I know it's considered the best tool available for achieving near normal blood sugar levels," I said evenly, but my hackles began to rise.

"Have you considered a pump for yourself?"

"Sure. And I rejected the idea."

"Perhaps we could dispel your doubts."

"I read an article in the *American Diabetes Forecast* that the pump was not recommended for anyone living alone who has difficulties recognizing the symptoms of a reaction. My case. The pump is programmed to continue injecting insulin until it is turned off. If unconsciousness occurs before the person can turn the pump off, then insulin will continue flowing into the unconscious body and the diabetic will die."

"What we'd like to offer you is the possibility of trying it in controlled surroundings. We think that in your particular case, it would be very helpful and would give you a more flexible lifestyle. Try it for five days. If you still don't want it, fine."

What could I lose? They would hardly let me die on the premises: bad for business, worse for professional reputation.

I had already been in the hospital more than two months, a period scarcely conceivable for Americans, as United States insurance company policy on hospital stays is "get 'em in, get 'em out." Three weeks is considered a lifetime.

Not so in Germany at the time I was there. Sick leave was doled out at the doctor's, not the employer's or the insurer's, discretion. Bills were a fraction of the amount American hospitals charge.

I was lucky enough to be in the new wing of an old building. For humanitarian reasons, it had no more than three beds to a room even for patients without private insurance like me. What did I do with myself for over two months? There was no television. I was not confined-to-bed sick, I was just diabetic. Roaming the building's corridors trying to approximate my life outside quickly palled.

The nurses pretended not to notice when certain patients, and I was one of them, disappeared for hours at a time in the afternoon, particularly on weekends. Patients were not tagged on arrival, as they are in the States, where medical personnel are paralyzed by the possibility of being sued. Many "sickies" were encouraged to dress in outdoor clothing and walk in the hospital grounds. Diabetics were supposed to stay active, as that made the transition from hospital to home smoother.

I was able to get changes of clothing, books, and other necessities myself. What a pleasure it was to walk into my apartment the first time! My knees were shaking. I washed my socks, collected my reading glasses and running shoes, watered the plants, and trudged back to the hospital. At first, I played hooky circumspectly, later I took time off as I needed. Nurses warned me of planned X-rays or doctors' visits, and I could schedule my outings around them. A short subway ride took me home, to Marienplatz, or to a bookstore. Fear accompanied me whenever and wherever I went, for had anything happened while I was out gallivanting, I would have forfeited my health coverage.

The week with the pump I spent "on call." The doctors warned me to hang around the hospital, and I had no desire to experience pump failure by fading into oblivion alone on some park bench.

It took only a day for me to love the pump, although the needle had to be changed every two or three days. Attaching a new catheter required no doctors or nurses. From the moment I experienced the flexibility the insulin pump brought into my life, nothing would have separated me from it willingly, save a pancreas transplant or a cure.

I studied the pump, its liabilities and assets, parts and supplies, and most importantly, the calculation of the basal rate which keeps blood sugar level at all times. My Lilly Betatron could be programmed with up to four basal rates that would change automatically at four chosen times. Boluses, or short bursts of insulin, were administered by pushing a button at meal times to cover carbohydrates or at other times when the blood sugar rose abnormally high.

Theoretically it's possible to extrapolate a workable basal rate from the amount of insulin taken by injection, but in my case the absorption of both food and insulin varied. Even if I seemingly controlled all the variables, every day was a roller coaster. The discovery of my insulin allergy and the switch to human insulin helped, yet even after I ruled out a blocked catheter or stress, the problem, though less acute, remained.

After the new therapy my doctors reached a consensus. The switch to human insulin, the pump, and continued outpatient care comprised the best they could offer me. I packed a bag and went home, not unhappy with the results, which gave me a way to live with my diabetes.

The weekend before I returned to work I was planning a trip to Rome for the wedding of two close friends—Saulius and Jūratė. On one of my midday outings my glance landed on a strapless flowered turquoise dress with a jacket and a ribboned hat in which I felt lighthearted and charming. The two-month stay in the hospital with its low-fat food resulted in lost weight: I was sylphlike.

When I arrived in mid-April the day before the ceremony, I needed shoes to complete my outfit. The bride and I spent the afternoon ambling down cobbled narrow streets, warding off wildly gesticulating shopkeepers who tried to entice us, "*Signorine,* just try them on. You will see how perfect they are. And so inexpensive."

On the day of the wedding the sun, a round platter of solid gold, portended joy.

After the rites in the tiny Lithuanian chapel of St. Peter's Basilica, a single ray of sunlight illuminated the couple for a moment as they drifted through the cathedral—a favorable omen for the future of their union! We piled into cars, had the requisite small accident, common enough in Rome, stopped, stepped out of the car, and drank champagne while exchanging addresses, passing cars honked, passersby smiled and called, "Viva!"

For the wedding feast with its traditional customs we went to the episcopal see, east of Rome. Tivoli is the site of the emperor Hadrian's villa, a medieval castle built by Pope Pius II and the Villa d'Este's magnificent Renaissance fountains.

After ritual greetings with bread, wine and salt and

having bought the bridal couple's places at the table back from imposters, getting free passage for the groom by giving candy to children, amid singing and laughter, the matchmaker was sentenced to death by hanging for having lied to the bride about the virtues of the groom and misled the groom about the dowry of the bride.

After the sentence was commuted, the bouquet thrown, and all had eaten and drunk their fill, the wedded couple, I and several other members of the wedding party returned to Rome and home. There were, as usual, intrepid souls who enjoyed themselves until dawn.

My insulin reactions were limited to one in a restaurant before the wedding. Saulius ordered the necessary orange juice in rapid Italian and saw to it that it reached the table without delay. It was my first journey with the pump. I wore it in a pocket of my jeans the day before the wedding. For the ceremony my dress had no belt and I was unsure of where I would keep the machine, until I decided to cut off the bottom of one of the dress's pockets and stick it in from the bottom. A number of safety pins and voila! It was properly hidden, yet accessible. I found the pump extremely adaptable and continued carrying one for seven years, topping off with the Disetronic V model.

\* \* \*

Henryk left for the States to complete the last six months of his physical presence requirement for American citizenship. When the examiner, laying a hand on his book, insisted that five years of physical presence are required, Henryk pulled out his own book, also a U.S. Government publication, and showed the examiner chapter and verse. Being right cost Henryk an extra two months because the examiner resented being put on the spot. Had my beloved been wrong however it would have cost him more. Henryk applied to his congressman from Monterey, Leon Panetta, to clear the matter up.

In November 1986 I opened my door to a brand new American citizen. I had offered Henryk a roof in Munich so he could apply himself to his writing, and he had taken me up on the proposal, though he was not very eager to trade Paris for Munich.

My apartment, company housing, was oddly laid out: a very wide corridor with doors to a large kitchen, a bathroom and a bed-living room. It was actually the garden half of an apartment that had been split in two.

One corner of the kitchen was cut off, making the room pleasantly odd-shaped. The bed-living room was immense with French doors opening onto the tree-lined garden. Henryk and I did sit there some summer evenings, sipping wine and swatting mosquitoes.

We shared this apartment meant for one in almost perfect harmony. The "almost" refers to some adjusting that was needed after years of living alone and making solitary decisions, not compromising on anything. We were easygoing people, who quickly learned past what point it was safer not to push, nor to insist on our own way. Both of us accompany CD's of Pavarotti, Domingo, and Carreras at home with enthusiasm when they sing, "I did it my way," each claiming the song expresses our unique individuality.

Since the neuropathy, I'm extremely sensitive to cold and need warmer rooms. Henryk was willing to adjust. He suffers from winter blues; I don't. He would go for a week somewhere sunny and preferably historic, like Malta, or we would both take a winter break to the Canary Islands or South Africa. What fun it was to travel together. We found adapting to each other a natural and relatively painless process.

A raised voice––mine naturally ascends the scale and intensifies when I am excited no matter whether the excitement's cause be anger, sorrow, surprise, joy, or disgust, meant distress for Henryk. It took awhile for me to process this information.

"Please don't eat all the chocolate covered jellies and the five rolls of orange Pims, Henryk. You'll feel bad and you'll regret it tomorrow."

"Will you skip the ice cream and French almonds, Eglė? I will, if you will."

We relied on each other. He dealt with my reactions.

Love flourished.

In March 1986, several months after we'd been living together, Henryk's father, Zdzisław, a tenured professor of literature and a former participant of the Warsaw Uprising in 1944, died. Since Henryk was a political refugee, he had not seen his father after 1980, when he left communist Poland for the West with his parents' blessing and the knowledge that they might never see each other again. Henryk wrote his father, and later his mother, once a week from wherever he was. He was not even allowed to return for his father's funeral.

The loss was like the loss of a right arm.

# 21. Australia beckons, and Eglė answers the call to another youth congress. Christmas in Sydney. An egg-sized abscess. Return to Munich and Henryk's surprise.

Christmas 1987.

Australia fascinated Henryk and satisfied his yearning for adventure. It meant something different to me—isolation from dense European culture, unbearable distance, and intolerable heat.

I was going alone, in a sense "on business" for I had been invited to read a paper at the Sixth World Lithuanian Youth Congress, and the organizers had requested my presence for the entire three weeks. It would commence in Sydney just before Christmas, include study days in Canberra, various workshops—theater, history, handicrafts—in Adelaide, and would close in Melbourne.

A colleague had talked me into seeing the beauty of the Philippines, so I was stopping for a week in Manila before the Australian leg of the journey. My B-class hotel was acceptable—clean, quiet, in a secure area, it lacked nothing. On the contrary, when I pulled open first one drawer of the dresser and then a second, I found that I was not exactly alone in the room.

What was I to do? The management was sympathetic.

"They" would be eliminated. A teenager swept past me with a large spray can of DDT cradled in his arms and advised me to walk for an hour or two. I walked. When I got back, I checked the drawer—empty.

In the morning I pulled it open to see. Surprise! New tenants had moved in.

I called a five-star hotel, ascertained the availability and price of a room, then asked, "Do you have cockroaches?" The voice hesitated, then muttered, "Yes."

I stayed where I was.

That day, whenever I tested my blood sugar, the display flashed the highest figure my machine could show. It was the same when I measured on a bench in Manila's enchanting park and an inquisitive throng gathered to listen to my speech in English on the function and purpose of a blood glucose monitor. One of the teenagers crowding around me nodded sagely, "Ah, diabetes. My sister has it. But not such a machine, of course. How much does it cost in Germany?" They rolled their eyes and whistled at the price of the monitor, which was beyond their reach, though the technology was within their understanding; computers had arrived.

I made sure I could see the next bench before I forced myself into a standing position and lurched the few steps necessary to reach it. "Don't fall, don't fall," I hissed through clenched teeth, so tired I tottered, barely able to keep myself upright. I had eaten nothing and was constantly adding insulin with no desired effect. Back at the hotel I checked the obvious. No blood in the catheter of the pump, no redness or puffiness around the site of the needle. I felt like a corpse and was undoubtedly on the edge of a coma. What was wrong? I was very sensitive to insulin and had never needed much. I injected another six units and waited. No change. I pulled the needle out to check the catheter for blockage. That was it. A bolus of five units produced no drop from the plastic tubing.

The pump had not been transporting insulin into my body.

I had packed only fifteen disposable syringes to use in emergencies for the whole four and a half week trip. The necessity arising on the first day of the journey had been the last thing on my mind. What could the problem be? When I shook the insulin cartridge out of the pump, it was unexpectedly wet. Condensation or insulin?

The end of the catheter did not fit the cartridge snugly.

How could I pad the end of the cartridge? My first attempts resulted in curses, but, using manicure scissors and a roll of surgical tape, I cut a strip the right size, fattened up the end of the cartridge, and bolused ten units of insulin to the rescue. Within forty-five minutes the insulin was doing its work. I reached an acceptable blood glucose level in three hours. I was finally ready to enjoy Manila.

Marveling at the beauty of nature, I played tourist on excursions to the Pagsanyan Falls, to Taal volcano, over rapids. I strolled back to my hotel from a restaurant at midnight through deserted streets, and past shabby buildings. During daylight hours I was struck by the fat cats doddering through the opulence of the business district, the luxurious shopping centers, islands of abundance in a gigantic lake of misery.

* * *

R-i—n-g, r-i-n-g, r-i-i-i-n-g. No one picked up the phone.

People were all around me, clearly heading places. I, having arrived in Sydney from Manila, was going nowhere. After an hour I became aware of two young women, suitcases in hand, who were looking in my direction, taking a step or two, changing their minds and going through the process again. After another false start, one came up to me.

"Excuse me, are you Lithuanian?"

"Certainly. You too?"

"We saw the flag on your bag. Are you here for the Youth Congress?"

"Sure am. Are you being picked up? I haven't been able to reach the Center."

"We just got through. Someone will be here in an hour."

At the Center we were parceled out to local Lithuanian families for the duration of our stay in Sydney.

"Klarisė Bacevičiūtė," the call came over the mike, and a girl from Brazil rose to meet her hosts.

"Tauras Radvenis," this time a guy from Los Angeles responded to the call.

"Eglė Juodvalkė."

I made my way to the counter. Two older people clasped my hand in both of theirs and hugged me.

"Skoruliai," they introduced themselves. "You must be tired. We'll be on our way as soon as we have our second guest."

She was one of my two companions at the airport, Raimonda Schreifeld from Heidelberg. We would be billeted together in Sydney and in Melbourne.

Theater director Stasys Skorulis regaled us with stories of Lithuanian life in Australia and theatrical anecdotes.

Christmas Eve supper, traditionally spent in a close family circle, took on a somewhat different character as five hundred people, local Lithuanians and guests from eleven countries, took seats in the great hall in Sydney. Outside in the warm midsummer night rain was coming down in sheets; inside fir trees twinkled, Christmas Eve dishes graced the tables, carols echoed. Holiday spirit abounded as we shared Christmas Eve wafers, a Lithuanian tradition, and wished one another happiness for the coming year.

The next day, Christmas Day, involved a shock to the system: swimming in the ocean. This, an Australian tradition, was an unusual twist of events for inhabitants of cold climes. Nonetheless, we were willing.

In Canberra the delegates to the congress returned to the question of maintaining Lithuanian identity outside that country over and over. It was a central theme, many delegates for the first time openly confronting the question of survival as members of a Lithuanian community.

The morning of the Canberra march for freedom was devoted to preparations: blowing up forty-seven black balloons, symbolizing the years of Soviet occupation, lettering posters, twining barbed wire round a wreath draped with the Lithuanian national flag. As our demand that *Lietuva* be allowed to exercise its right of self-determination was read at the entrance of the Soviet embassy, an Australian TV crew caught the ambassador of the USSR on film, as he precipitously withdrew out the back door.

Not for him the fate of a predecessor. In 1966 at the First World Lithuanian Youth Congress the Soviet representative politely scratched his signature on the petition for Lithuania's freedom that a smiling Australian-Lithuanian girl presented to him.

Adelaide saw a week of arts and crafts workshops. Everywhere young people were weaving traditionally patterned bands or throwing earthenware pots.

In Melbourne my future sister-in-law Joanna and I met tête à tête for the first time. She invited me home for dinner, where I talked and talked.

The end of the trip was nearing. I was happy to have had no further pump problems. My duties were done. I had passed the halfway point without any more health mishaps. I was becoming complacent.

Mistake.

While changing the site of the catheter needle one morning, I saw red. Literally. A place on my belly, the former site of a needle, was an angry color, hard and painful to the touch. Since the weather in Adelaide was hot and sultry, day after day the red spot increased in length and breadth to the size of an ostrich egg and began to soften. There were no physicians in the camp, so I waited until Melbourne to ask for help. A Lithuanian doctor agreed to see me at his home on a Sunday.

"Abscess," he confirmed. "I'll give you an antibiotic and some poultices. The boil will either dry up or burst. If it opens, disinfect it and keep it clean."

Burst it did while I was celebrating the closing of the Congress in Melbourne's Lithuanian Center. Raimonda, a no-nonsense woman and a capable physical therapist with experience of the Amazonian jungle in Brazil, took matters in hand. The wound had to be disinfected. We ransacked obvious places in our hosts' home for rubbing alcohol. Nothing. "This will do nicely," Raimonda held up a bottle of the German lemon-scented *Kölnisch Wasser*, and dousing a handkerchief, began swabbing. I went to Hong Kong the next day with a bandage plastered on my stomach over a clean wound.

Tasting of China but looking like the West, Hong Kong was a stark contrast to the wide-open spaces of Australia—a city of tall, block buildings for business and shopping, efficient and pleasant. When I walked up the stairs to a silk-peddling establishment, a vast place between a warehouse and a store, I fingered racks of blouses, dresses, skirts, suits, all soft and yielding to the touch. Gently a salesgirl prodded me in the right direction.

"Would the lady care to try anything on?"

"Yes, but I'm not sure what..."

"Would you like to see a dress?" she pointed to shimmering gowns in solids, prints, stripes of all shades.

"No, I..."

"Perhaps a blouse?" She held up a swirling blue paisley print. "No? A skirt? Pants?"

Like magic a yellow and orange delicately patterned skirt appeared in her hand.

"A suit?"

A bordeaux and silver suit danced in her fingers.

"Yes!" I gasped. "Yes, I would like to try that on."

And that was the end of it.

I returned to my room, bag with suit and matching shoes, a final indulgence, in hand and happily spent a half hour smoothing out wrinkles after packing the silk into my suitcase for the trip home.

In Hong Kong I ate like an empress, savoring dim sum and other delicacies. I could not get my fill of various dishes, though I was approximating carbohydrates. The whole Philippines-Australia-Hong Kong trip from beginning to end was a rough estimate in the case of food and diabetes, sometimes more, sometimes less lucky.

The pump gave me flexibility and freedom. I shudder to

think what the results would have been had I played with food the same way on conventional insulin therapy.

I stepped off the plane in Munich the second week in January. The doors opened, the waiting crowd surged forward as I eagerly scanned faces. My eyes darting in an ever-widening circle, I began to feel puzzled. Then a familiar, sand-colored, Chicago mafia-type hat appeared in my line of vision, and we were in each other's arms. It had been a long time. Eyes, hands acted like magnets.

"I have a surprise for you," he said. "But you have to wait four days, till the nineteenth of January."

His name day.

"Oh, Henryk. I'm bad at waiting. Please tell me now, please."

Nothing would move him, not all my entreaties. Finally, Saturday rolled around. He took me to a French restaurant *Vis à vis*.

After dessert Henryk handed me an envelope. On it was typed "The Petition."

It was a proposal that we "regulate" our status, written in "our" language, the patois of Lithuanian, Polish, English, French, and invented words that we often spoke.

I had long ago decided that autonomy and independence were necessary to the human condition, whether of an individual or a state; that human beings could attach themselves more easily to others without losing their integrity by informal bonds than the official ones of marriage. My opinion had not changed. Henryk had espoused the same point of view more strongly than I. His about-face was unexpected. Was it time to reconsider?

When I suggested that we return to the matter after a time, his reply was terse—maybe we would, maybe we wouldn't.

## Story Within a Story or Trials and Tribulations With the Pump

April 22, 1988, Istanbul's newspaper *Günaydin* published an article on page 3 under the headline—***Macar turist kadin az daha aluyordu!***

Above the text—a full color, two-column photo of a woman in black jeans, on a stretcher, surrounded by doctors and journalists. "**Member of Hungarian tour group almost dies at airport.**"

The facts—I was the woman in the black jeans, neither Hungarian, nor a member of a tour group, nor, thank God, close to dying. I was undoubtedly in trouble, but still alive and kicking.

In the spring of 1988 Henryk and I went to Istanbul for a week, ready to be fascinated. We were but first something happened. After going through passport control, as we turned to get our luggage, I clutched Henryk's arm, dropped to the floor, and began thrashing in the throes of a major insulin reaction.

Henryk reached for the glucagon and injected it. Time passed. I did not revive. That was a first. Glucagon, which activates the stores of glucose in the liver, had never failed us before. He injected a second one. Nothing. Henryk was frantic. What would happen, if the glucagon simply did not work?

A paramedic arrived, dogged by a pack of photographers and reporters. I was hoisted onto a stretcher and injected with intravenous glucose. In the ambulance I opened my eyes to see tops of trees hurtling past the windows of the car, as the ambulance wheeled screeching toward the hospital.

I registered Istanbul and faded out again.

This time consciousness returned in the emergency room, as someone fished around in the crook of my left arm for a vein with a needle that felt like a grappling hook.

"I have none," I kept yelling, annoyed. No one paid attention. I could see Henryk a few feet away talking to a doctor in English and yelled, shaking my left arm, "I have none."

The doctor turned to Henryk, raising an eyebrow, "Is she a little—?" and tapped his forehead meaningfully. Henryk eyed me doubtfully, not sure what this insulin reaction had done.

"Could you explain?" he urged me.

"As soon as you get this guy away from my arm."

Henryk waited.

"Look," I was barely conscious and co-coordinating speech and thought was difficult. "I have terrible veins. They're thin, they roll. The one in my right arm can always be relied on. I thought I'd make it short and said, 'I have none.' Now do you understand?"

"Sure."

Blood was drawn from my right arm. The heartening results showed that the sugar level had risen to acceptable. I assured the physicians, who were both competent and friendly, that I was well enough to leave. This was my vacation, for heaven's sake, and I was ready to embark on it. At the door of the hospital some banished reporters still waited, cameras in hand, in hopes of scooping the news of my demise. We took a taxi back to the airport and, as we pulled up, I said to Henryk, "Oh Lord, here we go again."

Attendants helped me into the first-aid room and

Henryk administered another glucagon. This one worked. I came out of the reaction, we collected our suitcases, and went to the hotel.

The management was great. I had already become so known because of the article that it had given us the best room with a triple bay window. As we began to unpack, I thought it might be a good idea to see just how high my blood glucose had risen. 45! Very low and heading for disaster. No time to lose. We used the last glucagon, I crammed everything edible we had down my throat in record time: glucose, sugar, chocolate, bread.

Useless.

I was unconscious again, with an ambulance whirling me back to the same hospital I had come from not two hours ago. This time, when the doctors revived me, they insisted I stay overnight.

There were two beds in the room at Emergency. My roommate was male with heart problems. A tired and worried wife leaned on the end of his bed.

"Henryk, please. I don't think they feed patients here."

In twenty minutes he came back, carrying Turkish fast food wrapped in newspaper. The aromatic odors of spices and meat wafted through the room, reviving my neighbor and his wife.

The food smelled scrumptious, and I was ravenous.

"Please have some," Henryk offered the sick man and his wife a portion. Smiling and nodding their thanks, they took a taste. Then the wife ran out and returned with more food, offering me some.

Henryk took my glasses to the hotel with him when he left for the night to prevent me from seeing the cockroaches in the sink, standing in a corner of the room. I would have kept vigil all night. Instead, I disconnected the pump lest the cartridge malfunction and slept like a baby. The next day I demonstrated my insulin pump to a team of doctors who knew about them, but had neither seen, nor handled one till then.

After checking my blood sugar one final time, they let me go and we returned to the hotel.

What had happened? Would, could whatever it was happen again? We had no more glucagon and still didn't know what was wrong. When I examined the insulin pump, an extraordinary thing became clear. If I inverted it, insulin flowed uncontrollably through the catheter and out the needle. Because of some mechanical failure, an immense amount of insulin must have been released into my body. All questions were answered months later when the company informed pump owners that at high altitudes or during airplane landings, pressure built inside the pump and pressed on the plunger of the insulin cartridge, sending a large amount of insulin into the body.

In the meantime, there I was in Istanbul, my pump out of commission. I had only five disposable syringes for a week and no long-acting insulin. The second day I again had a hypoglycemic reaction, but the reason was different. This time it was exertion, or rather, overexertion. Exercise affects my blood sugar inordinately, though this, too, was something I determined years later.

Henryk and I had decided to test my blood sugar more often than usual. After walking through the Topkapi Palace and admiring the Blue Mosque from inside and out, I measured. Normal.

I measured again in a half hour. The result had plummeted. I stuffed the five pieces of sugar I had on me into my mouth. Henryk bought me the only thing we could see that was edible and sweet, a Turkish cake. No soft drinks in view. I measured again. Bad, very bad, on the verge of catastrophe.

We leaped into a taxi to speed back to our hotel, and as we careened past a fresh-pressed orange juice stand, Henryk yelled to the driver to stop and wait. One by one he brought four glasses of juice, which I drank as though my life depended on it.

The rest of the week passed uneventfully, except for the rumor of an earthquake, though we constantly had to be on alert.

Stumbling down narrow, cobblestone streets in an old section of Istanbul, we found the former home of Adam Mickiewicz. Born in Lithuania he became one of the greatest poets writing in Polish. He died in Istanbul, an inspiration to the volunteers gathering to fight together with Turks in their war against Russia. The house is a small museum. We wandered through its two floors down to the basement, where daily someone placed a wine-red rose to honor the poet.

We relished fresh, cooked halva made of semolina, and learned to enjoy chai, drunk ceremoniously from tiny urn-shaped glasses.

## End of Story Within a Story

## 22. Wedding plans for Paris and Chicago. The Berlin Wall collapses. Soviet tanks rampage in Vilnius. Lithuanians stand firm for democracy and freedom.

One December morning in Munich I woke up and thought, "I want to spend the rest of my life with this man." There was no reason to wait. I could not imagine existence without Henryk.

The man looked me in the eye and said he would have to think it over. I bit my lip and nodded.

The blessed "yes" came three days later.

We chose to marry in Paris, though there was a residency requirement of about six weeks. Henryk had an entourage of friends there, among them artists, people well versed in living, who enjoyed the finer and had an intimate knowledge of the baser aspects of life in many disguises. We both knew real people there, the genuine article, rich in spirit, experience, imagination and abilities.

Paweł Jocz, the sculptor Henryk had spent much time with in Paris, had offered his atelier for the reception. Not only was he Lithuanian himself, though non-speaking, his family living in the Vilnius region for generations, but he had married an American Lithuanian. Claire had been shot to death by a man who had fallen in love with her.

The bride and groom would wine and dine their friends among finished sculptures, works in progress, implements of the art. We were not planning a formal event. Indeed, our intention was to stuff ourselves on Parisian "soul" food—smoked duck, pâté, cheeses—and wash it down with some fine Médoc or Châteauneuf du Pape, not seated at long tables, but leaning against sculptures of Demosthenes or Beethoven if not sprawled at their feet.

Still, the question remained—how would we collect our friends, scattered on many continents, under one roof when most of them did not have the resources to join us in anything but heart and spirit?

The idea we considered brilliant hit us both at once: we would have two ceremonies, the civil and the church nuptials on different continents at different times.

September seemed a delightful month for a Parisian wedding, the major heat wave past, but the weather still good. We would have had the civil marriage on September first, but that was the day Germany invaded Poland in 1939, marking the beginning of the Second World War. It would have augured poorly for our continued joy, so we settled on the second of September, 1989.

That summer Henryk went to Paris again and again. One afternoon he went to file some official papers at the *mairie,* taking a French-speaking female friend with him. Beata was the antithesis of me in appearance—dark, straight hair, petite, compact, narrow face, planed features. Polish-born, she spoke fluent French. Henryk had my passport with him.

The official made the not unnatural assumption that the future bride and groom were sitting in front of her and proceeded to complete the papers accordingly. She took the passport, studied the photograph of a light-complected, broad-faced, potato-nosed, curly-haired woman, compared it to the mademoiselle sitting in the chair, closed it, and returned it to Henryk.

"*Le nom du père?*"

Beata looked questioningly at Henryk and asked him in Polish for my father's name.

"Antanas," answered Henryk.

"Antanas," repeated Beata.

"*Le nom de la mère?*"

"Ona," said Henryk.

"Ona," parroted Beata.

After several questions and answers the French official laid down her pen.

"*Bon, c'est tout,*" she smiled and held out her hand. Henryk and Beata walked out, completed documents filed and processed. They dropped in at the nearest café for a drink as a more careful look at the picture in the passport would have brought the mistake to light and could have prevented us from making our plans reality. Destiny was on our side.

In late August Henryk went to Paris a few days early to make final arrangements. We had reserved the wedding chamber of the Charles V in Marais for two nights.

Henryk met my plane the day before the wedding. In my purse I had more than a thousand dollars, my passport, our white gold wedding rings, my blood sugar monitor, insulin, and cyclosporine. I had one suitcase with the dress I had bought in Paris for the occasion and flat navy-blue shoes that have since become known as the " wedding shoes."

I was deliriously happy.

We waited for a shuttle to the train to take us into Paris,

the luggage on a cart. When the bus came, Henryk grabbed the overnight bag, and I followed him. The ride took less than ten minutes. As I descended from the bus, I reached to adjust my purse.

It wasn't there.

Did I leave it in the cart?

"*O Dieve, Dieve!*" (Oh God, God), I moaned. "*O Dieve, Dieve,*" again, in an undertone. I couldn't think yet, I only knew that we had a disaster on our hands.

In a crisis Henryk reacts quickly. One glance around was enough—no taxis. The bus was gone. There was not a moment to be lost. Henryk saw a private car with the motor running and leaped to the window. The woman behind the wheel listened to the story, understood the money he was waving in his fist, and agreed to take us back to the bus stop at the airport. Within another five minutes we were there. As we approached the stop, I sighted the cart standing forlorn and empty at the curb.

"We'd better report the theft," Henryk said in a dead voice.

"*O Dieve, Dieve,*" was my response. It was only then that I began to comprehend the enormity of the loss. There would be no wedding, I would need a new passport, my kidney medicine would have to be replaced, the money to pay for everything was gone, but beyond that were the wedding rings. Could there be a worse omen for a marriage than the bride losing the rings?

We entered the lobby and walked to the information counter. The woman was speaking into a loudspeaker. I had to wait. And then the import of what she was saying hit me. That was my name being mangled in French and that was my passport she was holding in her hand. And right in front of her was my leather purse gaping open where she had rummaged to find identification.

And everything was in it, including the rings.

I had been spared. The world was a wonderful place. An old man had turned it in. He had been standing next to us at the bus stop and had seen the empty cart with the purse nestling in it after the bus left. He accepted no money, but gave us his address. Eternally grateful we sent a gift from Munich, but the package and letter were returned unopened.

The danger past, the rest was glorious.

We celebrated with friends, ate smoked duck and pâté, drank Veuve Cliquot and Margaux, and were merry. Henryk gave me a velvety gray stuffed elephant with a red beret and the necessary scarf rakishly tied around his neck. I gave him a book on Corsica, home of his admired Napoleon. Four friends had witnessed our marriage with their signatures—Paweł's second wife, Christine, Pranas, the Lithuanian painter, Sallie, who had been instrumental in our meeting, and Alison, a New Zealander, who had joined us from Munich.

Paweł himself, who had espoused the idea of our marrying before we had any intention of doing so, had gone to Poland on business six weeks before the wedding, promising to return in good time. As the date drew closer, Paweł was still away and unreachable. When he called a week before the wedding, he still promised to come. He didn't. When the time came to put his Paweł Jocz to our marriage document, he was absent. Christine Jocz stepped in.

Paweł arrived that night around midnight, while we were partying in his atelier. He brought his brother, his dogs, apologies, and a Lithuanian wedding cake, *šakotis* from Puńsk, the Lithuanian-populated region of Poland that had belonged to Lithuania before WW II. The cake was a meter tall and incorporated sixty eggs.

I smiled, but remained unappeased.

Soon after the wedding we returned to Munich and continued on to Kos in Greece for our honeymoon. We were prepared to add a new experience to our store of common treasure.

"What are we going to do today?" I sang, as I tickled him, and he rolled over laughing on our bed at the hotel.

"We're off to Patmos, where apostle John wrote his Apocalypse," Henryk pinioned my arms and kissed the tip of my nose. "Say you're sorry for tickling me. Say you're sorry, or you'll regret it.

"No, don't tickle me, no, no," I writhed in his grasp. "Why are we going there? It must be horrible if it inspired those images of destruction."

"You've got to be joking!" Henryk was so astounded by my words that he let me go.

I leapt to the other side of the room.

"It is a Greek island, isn't it?" I danced out the door.

In apostle John's cave on Patmos I clutched Henryk's shoulder.

"Take a couple of steps back and look there," I said.

A vista stretched before us, the loveliness of which turned my thoughts to the Garden of Delights.

"Maybe it was a bleak, rainy winter," I mused. "Hallucinations? Did he want to conquer evil by intimidating the faithful?"

I fretted, while Henryk absorbed the peace of the sea and the sun.

That night in a cafe our thoughts were more

mundane.

"Where shall we go tomorrow?" I asked, swallowing a mouthful of silt without protest as punishment for not letting the coffee grounds settle before taking a sip.

"Let's explore Kos by bus."

"How will we know where to get off?"

"I don't think there are a lot of choices," Henryk emptied his Metaxa and stood up, "but we better get some sleep. We're starting out as early as possible to avoid the rest of the tourists."

When we hopped off the bus in Mastikhari, a burly pipe-smoker greeted us, waving his arms in the direction of a handful of motorbikes and scooters parked in front of a store.

"*Mikhanaki?*"

"After lunch!" we yelled and darted down the yellow brick road. We were back after lunch for a Vespa.

"I'll try it out first." Henryk rode up and over a hill, dust rising behind him. He came back in a few moments, grinning from ear to ear, and said, "Jump on!" and we chugged away on our scooter.

We picked a deserted side road parallel to the azure sea and rode for hours, the sun kissing our faces, as I kissed my Henryk's back.

Before we returned the Vespa, I had to drive it. I had never dared anything but riding behind the driver. Being alone and in control was a heady feeling, indeed. I forced myself to curb my wings and head back to where Henryk was waiting. The next day we took another bus to Kefalos.

"Look, more motorcycles!"

"Shall we? Let's!" and we fell pell-mell into a shop at the bottom of a hill.

"*Thelete ena Vespa?*" the owner showed us his scooters. "Where are you going?"

"Up there," we chorused, pointing to the hill.

"Be careful how you take the upper curve. The Vespa might not hold both of you. It's very steep."

I wrapped my arms around Henryk's waist, and we began to spiral up the road leading to the village at the top. As we rounded the upper curve, the scooter dipped and fell. Henryk tried to take the fall on his leg to save me from getting hurt. He succeeded.

Blood poured from the deep gash. A sportsman, he would probably have righted the bike, if I hadn't been on it.

He hobbled down the hill to a gas station with a first-aid kit.

"Don't touch me," he ground out.

I wanted to help staunch the blood and clean the wound, but he ordered me outside. "I'll call you when I'm done."

"Can't I watch?" I said in a small voice, but he was resolute.

The accident happened just days before our return to Germany where a tetanus shot, an antibiotic, and bandages waited for my wounded husband. The wound permanently left a bone in his knee jutting out slightly.

\* \* \*

After our return from Kos Henryk packed his bags and went to Poland for two weeks. The country had its first non-communist government, and Henryk was returning for the first time since he had left in 1980. The intervening years had seen political changes: *Solidarność* rose and declined, martial law was imposed and lifted, and societal pressure built slowly, but inexorably. It brought the end of the communist system in a Poland that had neither completely internalized, nor accepted it. It augured the end of communism in East and Central Europe.

To the delight of his mother and sister in the fall of 1989 with an American passport in his pocket, Henryk faced no more barriers to his return home.

The contrast between 1980 and 1989 was huge as mammoth socialist structures tottered and people began the process of learning to think for themselves, accept responsibility for their actions, and conquer their fear of innovation.

When he returned to Munich, Henryk recognized that the road would be, in the words of a popular song, "long with many a winding turn." We started to plan my first trip to my mother-in-law and Poland. The Radio had barred travel to communist states for fear of provocation while I was in its employ.

At the end of October we went to America on my home leave. I was in Chicago, and Henryk was bumming through Mexico with a gringo friend, Teddy Wojnicki, when East Germany crashed—the Berlin Wall came down, chunk by chunk, each piece torn out of the hated edifice by jubilant throngs.

A few weeks later—Czechoslovakia's "Velvet Revolution."

\* \* \*

In February of 1990 winter seemed interminable. Away, away, to sunlight and warmth! Where? The largest of the Canary Islands, Gran Canaria, for a week to experience something new, to see Las Palmas, where Christopher Columbus had stopped on his voyage in search of the West Indies.

We stayed in the resort area of Maspalomas, crowded with huge hotels looming above swimming pools, billboards and souvenir shops dotting every inch of road, numberless restaurants of every conceivable nationality crowding one another on the sidewalks. The swirling white dunes were a welcome relief from the hordes of other tourists.

Las Palmas, with its narrow streets, ancient balconies, and the old Church of San Antonio Abad where Columbus prayed in 1492, sweetened the sour taste left by excessive pandering to self-indulgent visitors who wanted only Big Macs, painted stones and postcards.

In May my eyes turned from politics to self again as I sewed my *gužė*, a Samogitian wedding wreath. The church union would take place at the University of Chicago's Bond Chapel, easily accessible to my parents, other relatives, and friends, on June 2, 1990. This would be a more formal occasion. Henryk agreed to submit to a tie, and I would wear the national costume made and worn by my mother. We ordered Renaissance music. A friend, Reverend Antanas Saulaitis SJ, would perform the rites.

Toward the end of the month we packed our bags and went to the States. We had to make arrangements for the reception in a restaurant in the middle of what was then still Lithuanian Marquette Park in Chicago.

An objection to ethnic food for the wedding supper came from my mother. Three of us were sitting in the kitchen—Mother, my Aunt Dozė, and I—looking at possible entrée choices at Seklyčia.

"Start with consommé, then beef and chicken. It's the

usual thing for weddings, and they prepare it quite well," smiled my mother, expecting agreement.

"But, Mama, the reason we're having the reception in Seklyčia is to have Lithuanian food. You know, *virtiniai*—mushroom and meat dumplings with butter and sour cream, sausage and sauerkraut, *šaltibarščiai*—cold beet borscht, *kugelis*.

"Henryk," I called to my husband who was trying to sneak something from the refrigerator, "don't we want ethnic food?"

"I leave the decision to you, Eglutė," he deserted the field, mumbling something about telephoning a friend.

"Teta Dozė," I called on my favorite aunt, who had already arrived from Toronto, to lend support. "Help me. I'm right, don't you think?"

"You two hash it out. I have no say in this," and Dozė bowed out, ostensibly to have a cigarette in the yard.

"Mama, listen. I don't like beef and I have chicken whenever I want it. A wedding is supposed to be special. I love Lithuanian food, and that's what I want."

"You have to think about other people as well. How will it look? What about your American friends? They won't eat our kind of food."

"My friends love ethnic fare. Look at Sallie. She's a gourmet and adores good Ukrainian, Polish, Russian cuisine. Most of Henryk's friends are Polish. They'll be happy, too. Mama, it's the only wedding I'll have. I'd like it to be the way I want it."

"Anyway, you can't have cold borscht. It's much too heavy. A little beef consommé?" Mother tried to salvage something.

"I don't want consommé. I want *šaltibarščiai*."

Aunt Dozė reentered the room at a run, shot me a fiery

glance, started calming my mother down, motioned me outside and followed.

In the yard she turned on me angrily, "Do you want to kill your mother? Her heart—"

I didn't, but would my wedding my way send her into the next world?

Mother succumbed, though she did get me to compromise on a different beet soup, lighter than the one I wanted. For the next week she stalked around the house, muttering disconsolately, "What will the Americans think?"

The second of June dawned fair. The bride was not late, though the ceremony was, for Bond Chapel was non-denominational and lacked the necessities for a Catholic wedding ceremony. Reverend Antanas, always resourceful, disappeared briefly to borrow a chasuble and a chalice from a local Jesuit church. Then all was ready, but we were still out in the Quadrangle of the university cooling our heels.

One of Henryk's witnesses, Tomek, was caught in a traffic snarl. He arrived, panting and spouting apologies, and we got underway.

Dr. Rubenstein stopped in at the ceremony to congratulate us.

Our friends—Judy from New York, others from Chicago, Boston, Washington, Mindaugas and Violeta Gedgaudas, my relatives from California, with Uosis and family from Providence—partook of quantities of Lithuanian dumplings and drank plenty of wine, until we retired to my parents' house for the comfort of conversation and watermelon on the lawn.

The next day the wedding party drove to Chicago's Greek Town for a brunch of *mezedes* and *retsina* at the "Greek Islands."

On Monday Henryk and I left for Jamaica and our second honeymoon. Besides the pleasure of soft, transparent water that rocks the body like a warm cradle, we savored Blue Mountain coffee, which almost converted me, an inveterate tea drinker, but was strong enough to give Henryk the jitters.

* * *

Momentous events were taking place in Lithuania. The grassroots movement *Sąjūdis* had taken hold and spread. People gathered in squares and parks, in the city center, in stadiums waving flags. Thunderous applause accompanied poet Sigitas Geda who spoke in veiled, meaningful phrases about giants toppled by dwarfs.

On March 11, 1990, Lithuania declared independence and resumed the statehood that had been interrupted by almost fifty years of occupation. Many western nations considered this not only foolhardy, but harmful to the future of the Soviet Union itself and to the stability of the world. Gorbachev counseled the Lithuanians to wait five years. The man heading the Lithuanian parliament at the time, Vytautas Landsbergis, did not wait.

Then the first free elections in Lithuania after a half-century of communist rule brought former communists, under the name of the Democratic Labor Party, back into power. Algirdas Brazauskas, the former First Secretary of the Communist Party, was elected president of Lithuania. Why the re-election of communists at the first sign of freedom?

January of 1991 arrived. The situation in Lithuania was heating up. One government collapsed, a new one was formed. Soviet soldiers made threatening noises and milled about, taking their tanks out for a spin around Vilnius. The pro-Moscow branch of the Communist Party issued vociferous statements. Lithuania was not toeing the Soviet line. There was menace in the air.

Our phone rang late evening Sunday, January 13, 1991. The boss was terse: "Trouble in Lithuania—come in to work."

Soviet tanks had attacked a crowd of singing civilians at the television tower in Vilnius. Thirteen were dead, a fourteenth would shortly succumb to wounds. Hundreds were injured. Lithuanian broadcast facilities had been seized by the Soviet Army, which intended to take over the parliament. Tens of thousands gathered to protect it. The legislature, led by Landsbergis, barricaded itself in the building.

The eyes of the world were on the crisis in the Persian Gulf. Only when the United States warned Gorbachev that the crackdown in Vilnius threatened mutual relations, and the European Community informed Moscow that aid and cooperation were at risk, that the Soviet Army backed off.

## 23. The "List of lists." Eglė discovers the internet and meets diabetics who have different takes on life with it.

"Got a great computer game. Everyone's playing it," yelled Alison, a Radio computer specialist, over her shoulder, as she raced to the aid of a Kazakh Service intent on taking out some of its frustration with the Mac on the Mac. "You want it?"

By the time I turned my head, Alison was long gone.

The next assault was offhanded and came from a member of the Lithuanian Service.

"I spend evenings here discussing philosophy," Mykolas Drunga said, threading an arm into his coat.

"Here? Where here? Who is there to philosophize with here? This is the Radio. You mean in Munich?"

"The Internet." I didn't realize how fatal that word was.

Soon I learned to access it through my computer at work and ran down the "List of lists," fingers itching like a gambler's at a Reno slot machine, until the word "diabetic" appeared. Bells rang, whistles blew, and a load of nickels whooshed into my lap. A support group—just what I needed.

I signed on. In recent years the number of diabetics has been multiplying at an appalling rate. Many countries have associations that provide information on some aspects of the disease, but numberless diabetics lack know-how about the illness or depend on physicians unaware of changes in treatment. A support group, whether meeting on computer screen or in person, deals with the daily problems of diabetes care for which health professionals do not always have the time.

This particular group, which has since metamorphosed and split into different lists, specialized in the nuts and bolts of daily life with diabetes mellitus. An endocrinologist on the list made sure that information given wasn't false or inappropriate, though everyone who joined to exchange information was careful not to recommend questionable therapies. The most common sentence appended to a message was, "Remember, your mileage may vary." People did disagree, though they were mindful of others' feelings. If the mood of messages strayed into annoyance, someone nudged the author back to tolerance.

List members lived not only in the United States and Canada, but also Brazil, Germany, Australia, France, Sweden, Holland, Japan.

"It seems to me," wrote one diabetic from cyberspace, "that it's a combination of the information, knowing that you're not the only one with diabetes mellitus, seeing how others manage to control their BG's, not being 'yelled at' to have better control but choosing that for yourself by yourself, all these things combine to 'help' folks deal with DM in their lives."

Here are excerpts from my file **"Diabetic List Miscellaneous."**

**On good control:** "And, yes, I do jump off the wagon occasionally. I have experimented with different foods to see how much insulin I need to cover occasional treats. It helps me avoid major binges. I accept that about myself. I have had periods where my intensity with keeping my blood sugars controlled has helped drive them out of control and others when related illnesses took everything out of my control."

**On depression:** "I am beginning to get over the WHYMES and hope soon to be very rational about my lifestyle."

"It's somebody else's turn to have it. I'm tired of it. I'm tired of dragging around feeling exhausted all the time. I'm tired of having to check my blood glucoses and having to eat something simply because of having a low score, not because I'm hungry. "

**On uninformed people:** "There is a stigma on diabetes and sugar that comes from the oversimplified and mythological connection and the outdated regimens to treat it. Sugar is not bad, per se, nearly all carbohydrates end up as glucose, many forms of it faster than sucrose, it turns out. I had to get a progressive doctor who was treating me to explain to my mother the subtleties of intensive therapy and that strict avoidance of sugar was a canard because she absolutely would not believe me."

**General support:** "If you want to keep what you have left of your sight, you've got to follow the doctor's dietary recommendations. It's tough, I know, but you've GOT to do it...."

**On the usefulness of the list:** "The most powerful things this list has given me is when someone else's post touches me emotionally or I get feedback that something I said "touched" you."

"My own efforts to gain and keep very good control are happening almost entirely because of this list."

**On hypoglycemic reactions:** "I was taught to use gel, honey, or icing orally and allow the patient to swallow, a reflex action, but I think more recently the advice is never give anything by mouth to someone who is unconscious. If you don't have glucagon, call 911."

**On what diabetes demands of a person:** "…diabetes requires constant attention from the patient, no matter what the circumstances are: social pressures, emotional strain, any other medical problems, etc. The illness interacts with all that. As such, people with Diabetes Mellitus tend to become headstrong. I, for one, don't like to take suggestions about the treatment of my DM without a thorough review of the reasoning, even from my trusted and well-liked endo."

**Reaction to diagnosis:** "I felt that the disease was some cruel hoax played at my most personal weakness."

**On what it's like living with diabetes:** "I would compare diabetes to having a cold that never ends. I can function with it, but it drags me down a little bit even on the good days. I seem always to be recovering from the last blood sugar event."

"My husband says I make it look too easy, and to some extent he's right, but it's really hard to be forthcoming about how hard it REALLY is. I don't think it hurts to let people know occasionally that some people have life tougher than others. "

**On public injections:** "Of course people don't like to see people giving injections. We don't love taking them. So what? They faint? Let them look away. No one is saying that diabetics should stand on tables and tap and sing while they stick large needles in their abdomens. We are saying that we shouldn't be compelled to hide ourselves in dirty, unsanitary toilet stalls so that the squeamish can sip their tea placidly. We are discussing the difference between discretion and repression."

**On admitting to being diabetic:** "I would just want to caution against the assumption that letting the information out would be detrimental to your career. In general, friend or foe will try to read how you feel about being diabetic and base their feelings and actions on that. If they think you are trying to hide something, they will dig until they find and exploit it. If you act as if it is unimportant in relation to work, and make no big deal about hiding it, chances are others will act the same way."

"I'm in excellent physical condition and very active. This doesn't seem to jive with the diabetic stereotype that many people have. This stereotype of the sickly, I'm-going-to-die-any-minute diabetic can get in the way of both career and friendships."

"If there is anything I'm careful to do is to make sure my colleagues at work know I am diabetic and sometimes prone to hypoglycemia. When this occurs and I am unaware of it, and if the dear people who work around me don't know I'm diabetic, the trauma I put them through is simply not fair."

"A friend deserted you when you mentioned your diabetes!!! But why? Why is it that people will do that? Is it a medieval fear of diabetes being contagious?"

**Positive aspects of diabetes:** "This is a general sweeping comment, BUT... I think I am a stronger person having lived with this condition. I think diabetics in general are stronger than those who have never had any problem like this. If there was a positive side to all of this, I guess that would be it."

**On similarities between diabetes and alcoholism:** "Here is an example of how alcoholics and diabetics are alike. There comes a point when we have to take responsibility for attempting to control our disease. When I reach for a donut, I am making the same type of choice an alcoholic has to make when he reaches for a glass. And the results can be the same. Death! Or a better life."

**On relationships and dating:** "It's impossible to spend any time with someone without having to test my blood sugar or give myself a shot—and if there is any possibility that this person is going to remain in my life, I make it clear what's going on. Sometimes there is immediate acceptance or immediate rejection, but far more often, the reaction is curiosity and interest."

**On hospital Emergency Room problems:** "While you have great faith in Emergency Room personnel and it's well-deserved, some of them are not very competent, and this is what we worry about. There are lots of judgment calls. We have sometimes quite unreliable and dangerously ignorant people treating us and possibly not being aware of important things we try to tell them."

**Greatest fear:** "I think losing my sight is my greatest fear about having diabetes. Running a real close second is nephropathy. The "scariest" thing about complications of diabetes for me lately is realizing how little warning some of the complications give before they burst upon the scene."

**On doctor-patient relationships:** "You made me realize that as a doctor I'm always balancing empathy with objectivity. I keep an attitude of letting you know how I feel about an issue, but it's up to you to do it or not. I don't scream at you or penalize you. The reason I don't give solemn orders to my patients is not that I'm nice or humble, but that at times the patient is right and I am wrong."

**On the subject of careers:** "Well-controlled diabetes should make no impact on career planning. This renders good control an important goal. The character-building effect of good control may actually make you better at whatever you do. 'Old fashioned' advice to avoid certain careers because of diabetes has not been very helpful."

## 24. A gray two-tonner enters our life in many variations. Eglė sews (!) a token for Henryk's trips. Safari in Africa. George cooks an Afrikaaner breakfast in the wild.

Then there was the elephant fetish, although it is a little unfair to call it that. To Henryk and me it was something quite different, but I admit that it might appear that way to others. It began one Christmas when Judy came for a visit from New York and Katama joined us for the holiday. We had all passed out gifts to one another to our mutual pleasure, when Henryk pulled a last package from under the tree.

I ripped through the wrapping paper and there it was—a stuffed tan toy with teddy bear ears and an elephant trunk. Although like no elephant I had ever seen, it was unmistakably *loxodonta africana*. I loved it. After everyone had admired it, the beast got the place of honor on our bureau, next to Henryk's wedding present to me, and became the second of what was soon to be a large troop.

My love for elephants was intensified that Christmas. The African animal excited more interest than Indian, because of its impressive ears, bigger than the sorry, lopped-off auricles sported by their Asian cousin. I felt a strong affinity for elephant ears because my own are sizable. When

I was a toddler, on special occasions my five hairs were gathered up at the top of my head and tied with a satin bow that stood out above my very visible ears. In high school I attempted to hide my hearing appendages, but for my senior photo the hair was too short. The photographer felt sorry for me because not only did he retouch my complexion, pinken my cheeks, and pale out my nose, but he also dabbed in some strands of hair to cover the ears.

During my studies at the university I stopped agonizing over ear size, but until Henryk appeared in my life no one admitted to liking them.

Not being frivolous people all of the time, we began to worry about the condition of the elephant in the world. In some African countries they were being massacred for their ivory tusks and had become an endangered species. We contacted the African Wildlife Association, made a small donation, plastered an ONLY ELEPHANTS SHOULD WEAR IVORY sticker on our door, and started to acquire elephant things: white porcelain plant stands, black and white plant holders, drinking mugs, stuffed toys, birthday, no occasion greeting, and Christmas cards.

Henryk's sister, Joanna, sent us, as a wedding present from Australia, a small wooden elephant to hold toothpicks. Friends have been imaginative. Judy has brought an Indian elephant hat, a racy Japanese elephant mug, a gray stone that someone with fantasy, paint, and talent had cleverly turned into an elephant.

"Henryk, help! I'll never remember to take this with me to wherever we were going," I would shriek waving an ad from a magazine, or my down jacket's stuff-me bag, or a shoehorn, a bus schedule, a Sleep-eze neck supporter.

"Put it in the elephant," would come the measured

response.

The one thing it never held was insulin pump equipment—catheters, batteries, Tegaderm. These, together with syringes and medicines, were impossible to forget.

Once, on his return from Paris, Henryk wistfully told me of a talisman Beata had stitched together for her husband whose work took him away for months at a time to oil rigs. Jurek had shown Henryk the little cloth animal.

"I don't suppose you could sew me something like it?" he asked.

Sewing was in the genes I could have inherited from the maternal side of my family. Grandmother Konstancija could visualize a dress and make it without using a pattern. My mother needed patterns to make clothes from rompers with rows of furbelows on the seat to elegant dresses in which I swished to concerts. Our entire family benefited from her sewing, though the men were usually recipients of pajamas.

"Sewing men's clothes," she shook her head, "is just too difficult. They have no patience for fittings."

What new immigrants could afford to outfit two small children every several months? She bought swatches of material on sale, a Singer, the expense of which my mother quickly amortized, and taught herself to sew.

The genes were there to pass on but they didn't reach me. Whether the pattern was simple or complicated, sewing just didn't interest me. In high-school home economics class I learned the basics with marked reluctance. I was bad at it and had neither the patience, nor the desire to "waste" my time plying needle and thread. If I couldn't cut a skirt, baste it, sew it, and wear it within three hours, I wanted no part of the process.

Standing straight and immobile, turning one centimeter at a time on command was bad enough. To be the one eyeing, measuring, pinning and tucking? Not me.

Mother had patience. Or maybe it was just her stubbornness that would not let her give up. In any case, she stitched the dresses, the skirts, the pajamas, the pillow covers, the sheets, tore out the seams when they weren't right, and painstakingly repeated the process until they became what the patterns promised: perfection in linings, inside seams, inside cuffs, buttonholes.

I was recalcitrant. Much as she tried to prod me in this direction, I just wouldn't go. In response to Henryk's request for a talisman, I told him that I had never learned to do anything with needle and thread other than sew a button or darn a sock.

When he went off on one of his trips I proceeded to the store and bought a square meter of gray velvet. Not being my grandmother, I didn't even consider sewing without a pattern. But where would I find such a thing for a minuscule stuffed velvet elephant? I would have to create it. For someone not gifted with artistic abilities, this would be a feat. I drew. The first ones were odd. The ears seemed to be butterfly wings.

I improved with practice. Once I had gotten an acceptable elephant image on paper, I pinned it—some of the steps I had apparently learned by osmosis—on the velvet and began to cut. After several botches I was looking at a gray velvet elephant, flat as a board, but on its way to becoming. Only then did I discover that velvet unravels, sort of like jeans or corduroy, unless you stitch the edges. When Henryk came back I presented him with his new companion. An enduring attachment formed. He refused to acknowledge the defects even when I pointed them out to him. It accompanied him on every journey. I asked him what it does when Henryk is not on the road or a flight. He answered, "Drinks."

My bedside table is laden with miniature elephants: a gray porcelain midget that holds earrings, a black dancing one with gilt-edged ears, a gray leaden accordion player from Paris. What Henryk and I discussed over morning tea and evening wine was a live baby elephant, unrealistic as that was. Henryk was planning a trip to Kenya.

"You'll have to bring me pictures," I would whisper to Henryk before falling asleep. He promised, though he had different plans. Edward de Virion, a friend in South Africa who had visited us in Munich, camping out in the wide hall of our one room apartment on *Kaulbachstrasse* 68, had repeatedly extended an invitation to visit.

He had told us of the female giraffe that had fallen in love with him and the black mamba that he had had to kill—all part of the life he led after settling in Johannesburg.

Henryk loved the idea of South Africa. My going was out of the question. One day, he casually snuck in a few sentences about the high level of medical care in South Africa. I confirmed this, for Dr. Rubenstein had grown up and studied there. "If the doctors are good and you could get necessary care should you need it, why can't you go?" Henryk questioned.

When I saw Rubenstein on my next visit to Chicago, I asked for the names of diabetes specialists in Johannesburg and Capetown. Nothing was certain, but the idea was fulminating in my brain.

In January 1993 two stamps were placed in my passport: Lisbon and Johannesburg.

Henryk's plan was not to see cities. The highlight of the trip would be letting me experience animals in their natural habitat. The high point of our trip would be a safari in Kruger National Park. In the beginning we planned to book it, but when Edward offered to lend us his car and his son George, a native South African, as driver and guide, Henryk used his powers of persuasion on me.

I was not sure, as I had been imagining the two of us holding hands, lost in a world of our own among six other safari members who would function as a backdrop, but luckily I caved. George was a gem, a good driver, an amusing conversationalist, and a wealth of information about South Africa.

During the three days we saw elephants nineteen times, singly and in groups. Old, young, and every age in between, from a distance of several and several hundred yards. We saw them in the morning and in the evening going about their business, leaving piles of dung in the summer sun, clearing paths for themselves by destroying trees, shrubs, anything in their way, not with malice aforethought, but they were big beasts. The rest of the animals were raisins in the *muesli* rolls, but the elephants were like an Afrikaaner breakfast to three hungry trekkers. I kept trying to sneak in a touch of a gray hide, but Henryk was on the lookout for signs of impending tourist idiocy.

The expressed desire to caress an elephant brought a lecture on the meaning of the word "wild" and the misconceptions of people who have seen animals only in zoos separated from onlookers by bars. Chastened I dropped the idea of leaving the car and walking up to the elephant that was eyeing our vehicle and us with curiosity. We learned of a Japanese sightseer who had filmed the mauling and death of his brother. He had come too close to a pride of lions. There was the Volkswagen that was overturned by an annoyed elephant. At dinner in Olifants Camp we drank to our not becoming another anecdote.

The live wire between man and beast hums and sparks in the wild. In Kruger we knew we were trespassing on the elephant's, the lion's, the Cape buffalo's, the giraffe's, the antelope's territory. They were at home, we were interlopers. The dignity of the giraffes as they strode in pairs, or sampling the leaves on the highest branches of a tree, whose lower limbs elephants had decimated; the lions stretching in the shade of a tree, not taking their eyes from us for a moment while our car paused to let us watch; the yawning hippos, protective of their young and their water sources; the crocodiles almost invisible at the water's edge, one startled antelope sprinting across a meadow with all the rest veering to follow in instant response—these were not pictures, not images on a screen but living creatures to whom the land with its vegetation and the sky with its three-dimensional clouds belonged.

* * *

South Africa wasn't only the safari. Back in Joburg we got on a train to Cape Town. Henryk had booked us a coupé for the trip, which was almost twenty-four hours long, and we were able to enjoy in solitude passing through occasional towns, seeing the changing nature, even a thunderstorm with ball lightning.

Table Mountain, towering above the city in swirling mist, further on the meeting of the two oceans, Indian and Atlantic, the Cape of Good Hope, a tale from grade school history books—it was the other side of the world.

The diabetes behaved. The kidney as well. There was only one anxious moment when we were in Kruger. I saw that the pump needle had caused an infection as it had in Australia. Should I say something or should I wait? I wanted to wait.

It was so tedious to have to stop everything and call out the troops. Two days to go before we would hit civilization. I thought better of silence.

"Henryk, I think I have an infection."

"Where?"

"Belly. Where the needle is. Same thing as in Australia."

"We have to get out of here. We have to find a doctor."

I had seen a sign that the camp had a doctor I noted these essential facts subconsciously. Just in case. It was, of course, six in the morning; the camp was barely stirring when we located the doctor's hut. Monkeys were clambering on the fence. The front and back doors were festooned with immense spiders. That was it for me. I backed off.

Henryk took over knocking until the door opened and we were asked inside. The doctor, a woman, listened to my story, examined the infected spot, confirmed that an abscess was forming, and equipped me with antibiotics. She stopped me once, as I was talking, to make sure that she had heard me right—I was sitting in Olifants Camp with a transplanted kidney.

Henryk was not pleased to hear that the malaria-carrying mosquito had bitten a number of people, as because of the transplant, I had not been allowed to take pills that would have protected me from it. For the rest of the trip through Kruger Henryk made sure that no mosquito would enter the car.

In Cape Town fresh fish, fresh fruit—papaya, mango, melon. Delicious, easy to calculate for insulin with my trusty exotic fruit carbohydrate guide. We were renting space with a jacuzzi bath from a Polish woman, whose career was in catering and who cooked her homeland's food like a chef of a three-star Michelin-guide restaurant. Ah, the incalculable... meat dumplings with fried bacon bits bubbling over them—and this in Africa!—as well as plum dumplings with sugar and sour cream.

I closed my eyes and let my diabetes suffer.

In South Africa, Poles surrounded me. Through their kind offices, I had a chance to meet my own countrymen in Cape Town. Knowing that I'm Lithuanian and having read that the yacht "Lietuva," on a trip around the world, was anchored at the Royal Yacht Club, they offered to take us there.

I had plunked my straw hat with ribbons in the yellow, green, and red of the Lithuanian flag jauntily over one ear and begun my perusal of the dozens of yachts anchored in Club waters, when Henryk gave a shout. He had spotted the yacht flying the flag of Lithuania and seeing a member of the crew had the presence of mind to hail him, "*Labas!*"

Hearing his native tongue at the ends of the earth, the man turned.

A reporter from one of the Vilnius—or was it another city?—dailies, he had been allowed to put his job on hold for the duration of the journey and had, in turn, agreed to write articles from all of the yacht's ports of call.

In my experience Lithuanians had been a rare sight in most places, but it was more than novel to meet some at the other end of the world and as citizens of a free country.

## 25. Congress trims the budget. The Radio edges closer to oblivion. Eglé takes a step forward.

On the return trip from South Africa our TAP jet developed a problem and searched for an airport to land. We would have come down in Zaire, but rebels had killed the French ambassador in Kinshasa and the city was in turmoil. The pilot landed in Brazzaville.

During eight hours of negotiations with the airline's home country, Portugal, we stayed on the airplane without air-conditioning. Then we stumbled off, gave up our passports—temporarily, we hoped—and boarded buses to a 5-star hotel that had all of the amenities and more.

The stewardesses disappeared the instant we were off the plane, despite passengers' cries for assistance.

In the hotel we helped ourselves to a buffet breakfast of scrambled eggs, pancakes, croissants, omelets, toast, sausage, bacon, sweet rolls, and various tropical fruit. The hotel responded to the money from Air Portugal for our care with a lunch, consisting of a slab of unidentified tough meat.

Each of us paid twenty dollars for passports we kissed for joy. Then locals herded us onto a new plane, flown in from Lisbon.

At one point during lunch Henryk turned awkwardly and felt his back muscles contract. Having arrived in Lisbon in the early morning, we spent hour after hour looking for an Emergency Room to get him the cortisone injection he needed.

* * *

The morning after we returned to Munich I walked into a Radio buzzing with rumors. Groups of employees clustered in smoke-filled hallways. Smoking in rooms had been banned a short time earlier. "Did you hear?" someone called to me, as I passed.

"Sorry, not now. I'm late," I scurried on, glancing at my watch.

"Late for what? The Radio's closing, so what's the rush?" The sentence followed me down the corridor, ricocheted off the wall, and wound itself around my neck.

"Closing? The usual rumors? They never pan out."

"This is different. The president is a Democrat."

Jimmy Carter of the same party had canceled the tax exemption that US citizens working at the Radio abroad could take on part of their salary. It had been a painful bite, since we were paying German taxes as well.

"You know that. I know that. The new administration wants to use that analogy in a different way, to make a gesture, a clean sweep."

Before long mops, rakes, shovels, and vacuum cleaners began to appear in my dreams. Allusions to cleaning and burials started to crop up in conversations at and outside the workplace. One senator publicly exposed the top fifteen executive salaries at the Radio. They outstripped the official wage of the president of the United States.

During the past several years RFE/RL had doubled

the number of management-rank positions, though the organization began to skimp on broadcasting equipment. The computer department with its Macintoshes had spread tentacles into every broadcasting service, the carpets were constantly changing, but news transmission booths continued to be suffocating and dysfunctional at times, though ten minute newscasts every hour were considered the most important part of the broadcasts.

As months passed, Congress cut the Radio's budget, and rumors of the end began to have the hard ring of truth. Our employees clamored at the door of the Works Council and various unions, demanding a clear answer from the administration about their ultimate fate. Would the Radio close? What would happen and when? Was there a ticking clock?

A new possibility arose—consolidation with Voice of America. Some duplicate services would be canceled, all international broadcasting services would come under the aegis of a new supervising agency, and the Board for International Broadcasting would cease to exist.

Then someone tossed out the suggestion that to save money—costs were extremely high in Germany—RFE/RL should go to Washington or Prague. The President of the Czech Republic, Vaclav Havel, offered to house it in the former Federal Building for the nominal sum of three cents a day.

Those Radio employees who were employable elsewhere, colleagues from English or German speaking countries, began to look for other work, though this option was open to a limited number. Many had their national language as a salable commodity, but no one was buying. Germany was extending them the privilege of living on German soil only as long as they were employees of RFE/RL. The Radio seemed about to fade out of existence, "not with a bang, but with a whimper."

Some of those hired by the Radio after they fled their respective communist-controlled countries thought America was not living up to what they considered its promises. They had planned on jobs that would last forever. Numerous nationalities, which had lived under Soviet totalitarianism, had the expectation that someone would take care of them.

Though a number of them had suffered persecution under communism, it had always been there to furnish work, shelter, food, education, medical care, as well as chastisement. The extensive social security system of Germany had provided a soft landing for their leap West, and the Radio smoothed all the rough edges. They reacted with outrage to losing the soft padding.

There were many intelligent minds working here, people who had come selflessly, for the cause. Just as undeniably, there were sundry who had come and stayed for the money. Those employees who had lived and worked in America were quick to look for other employment, or just leave. Their expectations were realistic.

The administration kept calling for patience. Tempers were short, conversations—bitter. For two years time dragged. The Radio finally shut its doors in Munich on June 30, 1995, having fired a large number of its employees, closed the Hungarian, Azerbaijani, Polish and Czech Services, cut the staff of others, and transferred some 300 willing employees to Prague, where Radio Free Europe/ Radio Liberty, Inc. would continue broadcasting on one-third of its Munich budget.

I left on a disability pension several months before the end. I found my years at the Radio a rewarding experience and was grateful to work at a job I loved, in a language I had not dared hope to use to earn a living, and to live well in the process. The job had its problems, I'd be the last to deny, but in a real sense, I had contributed in part to Lithuania, to its freedom and independence. I was lucky enough to be at my post when its people achieved that goal. I heard my cue. In one of Tennessee Williams' plays an old actress says, "I knew that it was time to stop."

The Radio did not close its operations in Germany with flair and dignity. President Clinton had not considered this event momentous enough to warrant his or a representative's trip to Munich to send Radio Free Europe/Radio Liberty, Inc. out with pomp and circumstance. Some of those who had prepared and voiced the scripts of the Radio had spent thirty or more years working for the United States of America. They had to the best of their ability, certainly for an excellent salary, but just as certainly far from home and, in most cases, believing in the goal of Radio Free Europe/ Radio Liberty, contributed a great deal.

The end should have called for Veuve Clicquot, tears, handshakes, and congratulations for a job well done. It did not happen.

## 26. About things Eglė heard and didn't hear. Henryk publishes in *Paris Transcontinental*. After five years of waiting, the phone rings.

On the first Wednesday of January 1994, long before the Radio was to transfer out of Munich, I woke up and after a moment muttered, "That's odd. I can't hear anything with my left ear."

"What about work?" Henryk reminded me.

"I can't go in like this. Besides, tomorrow's a holiday, so I won't be able to go to a doctor then." I pounded my bent head to dislodge whatever it was that was blocking my hearing, but to no avail.

I called an ear doctor down the street for an appointment to have the wax removed from my ears and informed my boss that I would be in later.

"Frau Juodvalkis, it is necessary to have your ears cleaned by a licensed specialist twice a year to avoid wax buildup. You have probably been poking your ears with Q-tips. This only results in more difficulties. Wax gets pushed up into the canal and cannot then be dislodged. That causes all sorts of hearing problems," the doctor droned on and on, flushing my left ear with a stream of warm water.

"Well, that should do it. Can you hear now?"

"No, no... I can't."

"Are you sure?" He turned from the instruments he was cleaning and came back to me.

"Can you hear this?"

"No."

"You need a specialist. Take this note to the hospital."

There I waited hour after hour, frustrated and terrified. I could not help thinking the worst—my hearing would disappear totally. I would be deaf. Ten paces to the receptionist's window to ask when, when would I be seen, then ten paces back to my seat. A spot closer to the door of the examining room, which opened again and again, but not for me. Thoughts pounded in my head: How would I live? Weren't the complications I had enough? Would there be more and more? Tears rolled down my cheeks.

Henryk held me, but he too was pale—the future looked grim. For the first hours in the hospital I could find nothing positive about what was happening to me. Admitted to the examining room, I was told to pack a bag and report to a private clinic for a week of infusions as an inpatient and another week as an outpatient.

By morning my optimism had returned. I was ready to take things as they came. Drip, drip, drip, day in, day out. No change. As a last resort the physicians recommended sessions of a pressure chamber. No guarantees. No certainty that the insurance would pick up the tab for the relatively experimental treatment during which air pressure is changed to that of a certain water depth.

The insurance did agree. Every morning for three weeks I trudged bleary-eyed to the building where twelve of us sat in silence for two hours in a small chamber twiddling our thumbs and trying desperately to hear.

Nothing.

After two weeks of sessions I reported hearing birds twitter twice in a square, and my therapy was prolonged for a week, but the chirpers retreated to silence.

My right ear was doing the work of two. I could still hear, though I couldn't identify whether a car was honking on the right or the left. The hearing in my right ear was acute. Toward the end of February I woke one night, moved my head and promptly threw up. The slightest movement resulted in more vomiting. I had to go to the bathroom, but no chance. Henryk called an ambulance.

At the hospital, after the first misdiagnosis of my illness as flu was quickly revoked, the doctors were stymied. They agreed that my difficulties were apparently a balance problem caused by the loss of hearing on one side.

Walk? Sit? Impossible.

Two weeks went by before I could leave the hospital on my own. For seven days Henryk led me around as I, gradually more balanced, negotiated the hallways. My body had to learn to accommodate sounds coming from only one direction. It was one more straw, and the camel was already on the ground.

There was no question of my returning to work. I was waiting for an answer to my application for a disability pension. Step by step life eased, daily actions became easier. That summer saw several more hospitalizations, brief ones for severe hypoglycemia and an ear operation, a last-ditch effort to see if fluid in the ear canal was causing the hearing loss. Negative.

I was permanently deaf in my left ear.

* * *

In Paris and Munich Henryk had begun writing in English and submitting stories to various periodicals. April 1994 was a signal month. When a letter came from France announcing that the English-language literary periodical *Paris Transcontinental* had accepted his story "A Poet, Gamblers and Blackjack," we popped a champagne cork and toasted each other. The story would see print in the fall of 1995, formally marking the beginning of his life as a writer in English.

Henryk said he was following tradition because in the sixteenth and seventeenth centuries some writers of the Polish-Lithuanian Commonwealth were writing not only in Polish, but also in Latin. In his case, English replaced Latin.

\* \* \*

Late on the evening of November 6, 1994, a Sunday, as Henryk and I were indulging in spaghetti and lasagna with Chianti, the phone rang.

"Frau Juodvalkis?"

"Ja, bitte?"

"This is the Grosshadern Clinic's Transplant Center."

"Yes," I said, thinking that they wanted to remove me from the transplant list because I had been on it for so long.

"Are you still interested in a pancreas?"

"Yes."

"Are you suffering from any illness, cold or flu?"

"No." My heart was beginning to thump.

"Are you available at this telephone tonight?"

"Yes."

"We cannot be sure at this point, but we may have a pancreas for you."

"Yes."

"We will call you later tonight to confirm, if it proves to be so."

Henryk and I sat staring at one another.

"We might as well finish our meal," I said after a time, raising my wineglass. Then I paused and put it down, pushing back the plate.

"Do you think I can drink?"

"Better not."

"Right. Probably not eat either."

A bit distractedly I packed for the hospital just in case. At midnight I went to bed though we both were unable to sleep.

The phone rang several hours later.

"The pancreas is confirmed. Please be at the hospital at six in the morning."

We took a taxi, holding hands the whole way. The transplant ward of Munich's university hospital has the latest in technology and comfort, but I didn't notice it. Blood was drawn. and we both waited. After several hours of not much happening Henryk was told to go home. The operation had not even been confirmed yet.

When confirmation came, I took a shower, changed into a hospital gown, my groin was shaved—all standard procedure. I measured my blood sugar—48—and realized I was having an insulin reaction. "No problem, you don't need to treat it." the nurse responded to my frenzied call. I was terrified I would have to pass on the transplant if I had a reaction. "You don't need to take anything for it, because you're removing the insulin pump. We prefer a low blood sugar."

I called Henryk moments before I was wheeled into the

operating room. The transplant lasted five to six hours and resulted in a vertical scar down my middle detouring only around the belly button.

*   *   *

When I woke up, Henryk, smiling ear to ear and scarcely able to keep his feet on the ground, was pressing my fingers in both hands.

"It's over," he said. "You're not diabetic any more."

## 27. The end of the book. About a fairy tale and not a fairy tale.

Now, if this were a fairy tale, the end would be "and everyone lived happily ever after."

This is not a fairy tale, and the pancreas was not the end of my diabetes or my health problems. But then neither was it my end. Life carries with it changes and problems and joys, expected and unexpected.

What happened after the pancreas is, as Rudyard Kipling puts it, "...another story."

**28.** And life is a never-ending story. Lithuania catalogs changes, basketball Lithu-Mania sweeps the Olympics, and a new pancreas arrives. Mama is awarded the title of Parent of a Lifetime. Dialysis taps Eglė on the shoulder. She laments the fate of the Forest Brothers. The silver 25 materializes. Dr. Jeevanandam mends a heart.

In 1997 Lithuania held its second presidential election and chose a man with no ties to the Soviets. Valdas Adamkus had lived in America for over forty years and attained the position of Director for the Midwest at the Environmental Protection Agency.

Some changes had already occurred, denationalization of large factories was underway and the cornerstone of capitalism—private property—had been laid. Cosmetic improvements such as better lighting, newly asphalted roads, a number of new stores, renovated buildings, and a generally spruced-up look were evident.

Lithuania has its own army. The Communist Party no longer exists. The use of the word "party," has gained a wider meaning.

Any person can leave the country and return at will. All can play tourist, visit relatives, earn money abroad. The Lithuanian language can be heard in the ruins of the Parthenon as readily as on Machu Picchu. Before a trip the traveler will not be asked to secret police headquarters and blackmailed.

The Cathedral of Vilnius is no longer an art gallery but has resumed its function as a place of worship.

Christmas is celebrated by most Lithuanians.

Censorship belongs to the past.

Restaurants and cafes, serving Thai, Japanese, French, Indian, Georgian, Italian, and Lithuanian food, dot streets in the center of Vilnius. Every Lithuanian knows the mythology of how it was built.

Lithuania is an independent, self-governing country.

\* \* \*

At the 2000 Summer Olympic Games in Sydney the jerseys of Lithuania's basketball team sported "as usual" the name "Lietuva" instead of the cyrillic "CCCP," as athletes bent their heads for Lithuania's third Olympic bronze medal in basketball.

Washington writer Alan Siegel remembers in his internet blog the 1992 Olympics in Barcelona, "The squad had a sponsorship from the Grateful Dead, and some excellent accompanying dunking skeleton iconography."

In the internet paper "*SFGate*" in 1996 CW Nevius wrote another blog on that event. Golden State Warriors basketball player Šarūnas Marčiulionis tried to organize a basketball team for his freshly independent country which was low on cash. The Grateful Dead responded with a check and tie-dyed T-shirts and shorts which they had designed, skeletons, basketballs and all. CW Nevius quotes off-season coach for the Lithuanians, Donnie Nelson's recollection of the team's reaction after the years of the "Soviet colors, nothing but blues and grays, the guys went nuts for those shirts. They ended up wearing them to bed, to practice, everywhere."

There was more in the Nelson article. Not only did the team qualify for the Olympics and become a cult favorite in Barcelona, but also they played a big game against the Russians, for whom they previously had been forced to play.

"When they won that game, there was delirium in Lithuania, not to mention the team's locker room. The guys went crazy," Nelson said, "and then all of a sudden everybody quieted down. And at that moment the President of the country walked in and everybody started singing the National Anthem. There wasn't a dry eye in the place."

That wasn't all. A new sponsor of the Lithuanians had surfaced, which, as Nelson points out, "outfitted them with spiffy warmups to wear on the victory stand. But the guys figured they should honor the group that had backed them from the first. They took the stand in full Grateful Dead regalia. Overnight, 'Lithu-Mania' struck, and they had the hottest T-shirts at the Games."

\* \* \*

The new pancreas worked perfectly for the first month and a half. Having spent Christmas at home, Henryk and I decided to take the three of us—the pancreas seemed to be an entity with almost human properties—somewhere to celebrate the New Year.

We packed a basket of goodies, a bottle of Bollinger and took a train to Augsburg—all of forty minutes away. Passing along the narrow streets, gawking at the decorations and couples in their holiday finery, we meandered down to our hotel.

At midnight when the church bells started pealing we toasted each other.

I barely tasted the champagne—the new pancreas was still young, and there would be time enough—and watched the carbohydrate count. An hour or so later, I measured.

The blood sugar was higher than it should have been.

In another couple of hours the sugar level had gone down to normal but I kept remembering Christmas when I had stuffed myself with roast duck skin which in retrospect was sticking in my throat, as Henryk repeated over and over that even a healthy person would have gotten sick from such an amount of fat.

Had this self-indulgence overloaded the pancreas?

Heaven forbid! But fear was now constant. After the holiday I presented myself to Professor Landgraf who ran the requisite tests and hospitalized me.

Rejection.

For nine days I lived on hope and Atgam, a strong immunosuppresant made from horse serum.

The pancreas fought valiantly, but was lamed in the battle.

I subsequently needed to help it along with a minimal dose of long-acting insulin and an occasional unit of fast-acting. I used a pen for both: a fire-engine red Novopen for the three or four units of Protophan—the German equivalent of Ultralente—and a Becton-Dickinson half unit mini for the other.

Before returning to the Unted States, I asked the doctors a question important for my peace of mind and the serenity of our home: had I precipitated the crisis by downing all that crisp, fat roast duck skin? The answer was: no, I had not.

Each time I came back to Chicago from a trip to Lithuania I experienced culture shock. Returning to America to live after twenty years in Europe was a blow to the system that required longer adjustment.

Attention to the small things that make life extremely, even lavishly, comfortable is a way of life in the United States, at least for the middle class. Americans are practical and competent. Service with a smile. The customer is always right. Product return or exchange often with no questions asked. Daily life in America is easier than elsewhere.

\* \* \*

My mother died at the age of ninety-one. Going through the annual agony of choosing a birthday gift ten years earlier, I had had an idea: I would nominate her for Diabetes Forecast's Mother of the Year.

She was selected one of four Parents of a Lifetime! At her birthday celebration I gave her the magazine issue in which this was announced and a copy of the letter in which I had written about her.

\* \* \*

Somewhere inside I did not give up believing in myself, the descendant of Lithuanian warriors, like the ones who had fought the Swedes at the Battle of Kircholm in 1605. This book affirmed the need not to loosen my grip on life, to fall and rise again, to love myself, but not to the exclusion or the detriment of others. To scale Sugar Mountain.

* * *

In 2002 Uosis and I decided to fête Dad for his ninetieth birthday. It would be a gathering of all the colleagues my father had worked with in the many Lithuanian organizations that exist in Chicago. Wherever he was needed, he was there. The celebration was not planned as a surprise party. I needed his help to gather the troops.

Nearly ninety people came. My brother spoke. Many speakers evaluated my father's contributions to Lithuanian life and presented him with a sizeable framed address, a gauge of his life that all of us had signed.

No one paid attention to the ban on gifts and envelopes passed freely from guests to my father, who acknowledged them in his thank-you address by saying, "All of you were told no gifts. Thank you for your generosity. I will not keep any of the money, but will publish a list in the daily Draugas of organizations that will receive it and how much each will get." He tried to be fair to all the recipients.

* * *

My father died at the age of 91 in 2003. The two-story house we lived in with him and my mother was too big for the two of us. Henryk and I began to think where to live.

Father had always told me that to maintain a house was impossible, unless someone stayed to look after it while we were traveling.

He had done that for us. In his absence because of our lengthy travels we thought that it would be easiest to take care of a condominium. We happened on one in La Grange, a western suburb of Chicago. End of housing story.

\* \* \*

About nine years after the pancreas transplant in Munich my nephrologist Michelle Josephson at the University of Chicago informed me that my first kidney transplant was failing after almost twenty years.

Though I had talked about the possible transience of the transplant, I had become accustomed to it as the years passed and had not considered its loss.

My doctor set a conundrum before me. I could opt for another kidney transplant. That would mean a wait of about five years, part of them on dialysis and I would be left with my maimed pancreas transplant that might not get along with the new kidney or I could go for a double transplant—kidney and pancreas—that would require only a two year wait also with dialysis.

I was not hard to match and had not developed numbers of antibodies to certain cells of foreign organs that could get in the way of accepting a transplant.

Almost to the day two years later the new organs arrived.

I avoided dialysis, as my first kidney transplant pulled me through until the operation. The new-to-me parts were a pair of organs from one donor, God bless him or her, duly flown to Chicago and transferred into me.

The pancreas kicked in on the third day but the kidney— at once. The hospital stay was nine days, while in 1983 it had been seventeen. I was grateful to heaven and a host of angels big-winged, and small, who were protecting me from the harm that I managed to inflict on myself.

Bliss with the new organs lasted eighteen months. The year was 2005. That spring and fall I went to Lithuania, did everything I wanted to do, went everywhere I wanted to go and hadn't an inkling that it would be some time before I saw Vilnius again.

Henryk and I had planned our schedule to meet back in La Grange—I from Lithuania and he from Poland. From there, after our garage gave the car a once-over, we would throw a couple of dozen bottles of water into it to keep my kidney well-irrigated on the trip and drive down to Arizona to visit Uosis and Jacquie.

After overlapping a couple of days, they would go up to Chicago and our apartment while we spent some time in their place before meeting again and going our own ways. Henryk and I would then retrieve his sister Joanna who was flying into Phoenix from Melbourne, go see the Grand Canyon, and return to La Grange. We should have paid more attention to Robert Burns, who wrote,

"The best laid schemes o' mice an' men,
Gang aft a-gley."

We reached Prescott in good time, hugged Uosis and Jacquie, had a scrumptious dinner, cooked by my sister-in-law, and caught up with each other's news. Then they left the house to us and hied themselves to Chicago.

In a couple of days we picked a Japanese restaurant for lunch, then came home and puttered.

I felt nauseous and vomited. Again. We agreed to let a doctor see what was wrong. Here was I, a double-transplant clearly not doing well, and the doctor, after asking where and what I'd eaten, suggested that I had indigestion and without ordering any blood tests sent me home.

I threw up all night, and we went to the health center again.

A different doctor was there. He ordered blood tests, got the results, and called for an immediate journey by chopper to the Arizona Mayo Clinic a hundred miles away in Scottsdale. All its physicians could do was to diagnose a dead kidney.

I would need dialysis at the clinic and at home. At the same time Henryk had to pick up Joanna and drive back to La Grange, Uosis would take me to Phoenix airport while neighbors from our condo, Chester and Pat, would pick me up at Chicago's O'Hare.

If someone asked me which of my then fifty-three hospital stays all over the world was the worst, I would say—that one, not because of incompetent physicians, unpleasant conditions, the wrong medication, or anything of that sort. Had the circumstances been different, had they resuscitated my kidney or had I been there for any other reason, I would have found surroundings, medical personnel, equipment, and physicians-all good.

I was stunned by what had happened.

Why had it happened? Doctors at Mayo and at home posited that I had been dehydrated and that I had not drunk enough during the trip. Had this been my first kidney transplant or had I not understood the necessity of continuously flushing the kidney, perhaps doctors could have briefly entertained the thought. I had taken care of the first transplant for twenty years, watered it, medicated it morning and night, patted it, spoke soothing words to it. I had done nothing less with my new buddy.

The reason could have been a blood clot brought in by the new kidney. No way to prove or disprove it. The fact was that it stopped filtering my blood. When I left the Mayo Clinic Uosis and Jacquie took me out, but my food possibilities had narrowed considerably. Before we left a mirror reflected a very swollen face. The doctors, working under the weight of their theory that I was dehydrated, pumped me so full of water that it temporarily distended my body.

Horrors of dialysis began.

Two out of every three days I would feel like a corpse. Say, today was Monday, and I would have dialysis at the Center in Westchester, Illinois, at 10:00 AM. I could barely drag myself to the car, no energy, no ability to concentrate, even to read. Paperbacks were too heavy to hold. For four hours I'd be in an armchair, attached to a machine that sucked out my blood, filtered it clean, and returned it to my body.

I would be done for Monday. Disdaining Henryk's help, I would walk to the car on my own, though I wouldn't be feeling all that strong. I'd get home, eat the curtailed diet that allowed me to survive at least one more day and suddenly couldn't keep my eyes open.

The next day, Tuesday, in this case, would be my day to do things—check bills, go for a walk, shop for food that I could eat, plan meals for myself, answer letters, talk to Henryk about all sorts of nonsensical things, go off into peals of laughter from the sheer fun of laughing.

Wednesday morning getting up would be difficult. I'd manage, but the effort it required to get ready for dialysis was in short supply. Henryk would say he'd go start the car, but instead would walk me to the elevator. On the first floor

I would lean on the front door until he'd bring the car and it would start again.

The worst mornings would be Mondays. If you had dialysis M-W-F, by that time your blood would have collected an extra day's worth of impurities and everything'd be just a smidgen harder.

Dialysis is known for causing bones to be brittle and break. I complied and broke five in the almost two years that I waited for my kidney—both feet, leg, spine, pelvis. Doctors managed to alleviate the problems caused by the last two, though it took months.

The specialist I saw after I broke my leg went on and on how this was a direct result of my diabetes though not only had I not been diabetic for a while and had always been lucky with my lower appendages, but they healed well. I was a "toppler" from way back, but this had resulted in lots of skinned knees over the years but falls with bone breakage had been nonexistent. Another foot doctor told me that once the word "diabetes" is mooted about, total ear block on the part of some physicians occurs.

The hospital doctor who diagnosed gout, when I broke my foot on dialysis, told me I could immediately resume walking and even jumping on that foot. For three days the hospital, which did the x-ray, could not locate me or the physician who had ordered it, though he was on its staff. To that trauma I date the beginning of a condition that plagues me to this day—Charcot's joint.

As if that were not enough, my blood pressure rose out of control. Doctors prescribed me four different medications, not one at a time, but together. Still, the blood pressure read high.

I lost consciousness at home and was taken to the

hospital's Intensive Care unit, where I lay in a coma for seven days.

Machines registered—no brain activity.

I grew up with Vidas Nemickas, a physician and friend, who warned my husband that I might wake up a vegetable. He and his wife Marytė were close friends with whom we shared dinners, tapas, Spanish wine, stories of bullfights and travels.

While I was in the coma Henryk brought tapes of people reading my poetry in public and played me CD's of Lithuanian songs. After a series of hallucinatory dreams connected to nurses on the floor, my poetry displayed on the hospital room's television, Henryk with long green hair, for which he expressed eternal gratitude, dialysis in garages and rolling trucks, I opened my eyes the morning of the eighth day with one thought uppermost in my mind.

I would say to Henryk, "You thought you would never hear this voice again."

I was awake, but when I tried to speak, I could make only unintelligible sounds, so I practiced until my mouth could make sounds for letters, put letters together to make words, and make the words into that sentence.

When he arrived in the afternoon, I articulated it and smiled. His reaction could not have been better. It took me some months to recover my memory, but gradually it did come back.

Twice yearly in the spring and the fall I flew to Lithuania to read my poetry. In 2007 having heard a friend discussing dialysis in Vilnius, I jumped on the idea, got in touch with the proper institute there by e-mail and announced that I would go for the Poetry Spring Festival.

Henryk washed his hands of me.

The Vilnius dialysis center was across the street, through a courtyard entrance, and in the back, not more than seven minutes from my apartment.

I knocked on the door with trepidation and stepped inside.

"You are A-me-ri-kan?"

"*Laba diena, esu Eglė Juodvalkė. Atskridau iš Jungtinių Valstijų ir man reikės dializės.*" Good day, I'm Eglė Juodvalkė. I flew in from the United States and I will need dialysis.

"*Kalbate lietuviškai?*" "You speak Lithuanian?"

That was all it took.

I was equipped with a bed, blankets, and pillow, attached to a machine, brought a hot drink, then dialyzed. This was all similar to what I experienced in Westchester except for the tea, the smiles. I don't denigrate the care I received in the USA. It was excellent. This was with heart. The three weeks left an indelible impression. Whenever I could, I read verses to groups of poetry fans, slept a little less than at home, and survived.

After nearly two years of dialysis in the States, I got a staph infection of the blood. The worst part for me was that UofC doctors had to change the location through which the unfiltered blood would flow out and clean return. I would no longer be able to avoid a fistula which I saw as disfiguring.

All this was happening after my trip to Lithuania in May. As the vein was being prepared for the graft and the first part of the procedure had just been completed, came the news that a kidney for me had arrived.

\* \* \*

Let's go back to the pair of organs from a single donor that I received in 2004. Once I had received the new organs from one donor and they started working properly, I began to feel better and more alive. The twenty years I had spent with my first transplanted kidney and the rejection of my initial pancreas that only the doctors in Munich revived until the slowdown with my failing kidney—all gave me experience for the double transplant.

In a week the physicians at the University of Chicago Mitchell Hospital were ready to let me go home. After some trouble with my insurance, that had to be coaxed into paying for the anti-rejection medication without which the hospital would not release me, it was time to pick up the reins and let the high-steppers now harnessed into my chariot go forward.

The kidney collapsed in the shafts in 2005, a year and a half later. That began the period of dialysis, though the pancreas did not leave me.

The next forewarning of a pending miracle was two phone calls in July 2007.

"We think we may have a kidney for you."

Several hours later the phone rang again. I wanted it badly, but I was not alone in the waiting line. Lucky? Incredibly lucky. I fit all the medical criteria for this particular kidney.

I was whole again. Not the way I was born perhaps, but fully functional, which I had not been for a while. Here I had a working pancreas, and the kidney which set to work at once, filtering blood, whistling as it worked.

I could imagine the kidney in overalls because sometimes filtering the blood was not the neatest job. I was getting ready to get back to my life with my latest miracle.

*  *  *

In the fall I again went to Lithuania, this time with my third transplanted kidney.

Half the book I had published in 2002 in Vilnius, *Veidrodis ir tuštuma/The Mirror and the Void*, were poetry originals written in Lithuanian and the other half were originals written in English, as well as a compact disc of me reading them. They were not translations, because I do not "translate" my poems. If they are not originally written in Lithuanian, I adapt and change them, as the spirit of the language demands.

With that book I was one of the writers that were sent to the International Frankfurt Book Fair 2002 in Germany, where Lithuania was the guest of honor.

A year later an exhibit came to the Balzekas Museum of Lithuanian Culture in Chicago from the homeland. The subject was one of which I had some, but not enough knowledge, and in which I had a great interest.

In 1944 when the Soviets advanced into Lithuania for the second time, a section of the population did not submit. Tens of thousands took to the forests to fight against far more numerous Soviet troops. Known as Forest Brothers, though there were women among them, they had little or no fighting experience and certainly no experience of guerilla warfare.

High school classes, teachers, farmers, clerks, railroad workers, bank tellers, all those who were not willing to give in without a struggle, went into the underground.

The battle lasted from 1944 to Stalin's death on March 5, 1953. It portended the end of active resistance with some notable exceptions.

In those nine years the Soviets eradicated the Forest Brothers. Mutilated corpses were dragged to marketplaces and villagers were paraded past them, examined and punished with deportation to Siberia or death for signs of recognition. This was a vivid picture of communism in full swing.

One medical student's diary from that time has already seen it's seventh printing in contemporary Lithuania. Lionginas Baliukevičius-Dzūkas was killed at the age of twenty-five. He had kept a diary of his thoughts about the future of the country, his run in with a traitor, who later morphed into a Soviet poet, the daily routine of the fighters, the subsistence on what farming families brought to them or left for them, the "coffee" they drank by boiling dried and roasted tree bark, the priests who held Mass in the forest. After the country declared independence in 1991, a part of the diary was found in a Soviet archive.

Juozas Lukša—who fought under the name Daumantas, reached the West twice to seek contacts and aid. While there, he wrote what he had experienced fighting in the part of Lithuania known as Suvalkija. He left a manuscript to be published in Chicago, parachuted back into Lithuania to continue the struggle, was betrayed and killed in 1951. In the book he told the stories of battles from which I gleaned the length, breadth and depth of the combat.

All of this I ingested, reading books, speaking to Forest Brothers, broken in body but strong in spirit, the same spirit that had led armed Lithuanians and Poles to fight together against the Teutonic Knights and conquer them at the Battle of *Grünwald*, "*Žalgirio mūšis*," in 1410. That same determination which imbued Lithuanians then, also led them to resist Russia in 1831, 1863, and to fight against the

Red Army in 1944 to 1953.

Lithuania regained its freedom in 1990, and honored those who laid down their lives for it.

What had I done for Lithuania? What could I look back on and say, this was needed and I did it? I prepared *Sugar Mountain* in Lithuanian. There was no literature about living with diabetes by a diabetic. I did that. It was not a how-to manual, but the story of one diabetic's life.

In 2005 I went to the administration of the Victims of Genocide Museum in Vilnius and asked if they would be interested in my poetry about the Forest Brothers. They read the poems, suggested that I have a public reading of eight of them, and promised to look in their archives for the photographs of the partisans, their families and colleagues, that had been exhibited in Chicago and had inspired my poetry. One by one slides of them projected on the wall behind me illustrated the poems I read. Four years later, manuscript in hand, I went to see Birutė Burauskaitė, Director of the Lithuanian Genocide and Resistance Research Center in Vilnius. Soon after, my book, *Sakalai naktį nemiega* (Falcons Don't Sleep at Night), was published. A picture of the partisan about whom I wrote accompanied each poem.

\* \* \*

Our two weddings, the civil vows in Paris and the religious in Chicago, gave us the opportunity to extend the festivities at the twenty-five year mark from September 2014 to June 2015.

It was balmy on September 2nd as we assembled in

our favorite restaurants near the lake. We took a hotel just off Michigan Avenue, were joined by Judy Vale and Oded Regev from New York, Sallie Wise Chaballier from Paris, Basia and Andrzej Skwarczyński from Warsaw. Marytė and Vidas Nemickas, domiciled downtown, were stretching their wings after a difficult leave-taking from his patients. Stanley Balzekas Jr., founder of the Balzekas Museum of Lithuanian Culture in 1966 and Honorary Consul of Lithuania in Saint Petersburg, Florida, added his presence to the gathering.

Judy, who had swiveled, shimmied, and swayed her appropriate body parts in a mean tsifteteli in Munich, had now asked me to bring a compact disc player to the hotel.

In the midst of the festivities Judy and Oded came to our room, bringing a long, flat package made up of parts, one of them small and square. As the wrapper fell away, a CD appeared. On the jacket were flags of Poland and Lithuania around a picture of Henryk and me exchanging rings in church. On the inside were two more photos of the wedding, one with Judy who was a witness. The title of the disc read—*Parables of Love* by John Califra and it celebrated the 25th anniversary of Henryk Skwarczyński and Eglė Juodvalkė. It was made up of eight pieces: "Parables of Love", "Sacrament," "Growing Used to Happiness," "Ship of Fools" (*Overture to an Imaginary Opera*), "Deep Waters, Quiet Contentment," "To the Dance before Us" and ending with "Henryk Dances on the Head of a Pin" (*very, very Huckleberry*).

But the key to it all was the large, flat part of the packet, the musical score, whose cover stated that members of the Czech Philharmonic at CNSO Studios recorded John Califra's "Parables of Love" August 28, 2014, Prague, under the direction of Maestro Christo Pavlov. We knew where both parts of the unique parcel would be from then on—in our living room. The sounds of the music would bring Judy, the originator of this unique idea, her husband Oded, the composer John Califra, his wife and all the others to life in our home.

Our Japanese dinner for ten at Kamehachi on Wells street allowed us to indulge in *gyoza*, shrimp *tempura*, *sashimi*, a variety of *sushi*, washed down with sake, tea, or wine. At sunset we moved to Stanley's apartment at the Hancock Building and a Chicago tradition—deep-dish pizza with a mellow Marquis de Riscal 2004. From the 33rd floor of the Hancock we mooned over the hawk's-eye-view of Lake Michigan, watched the city light up, oh-ed and ah-ed over Stanley's collection of armour and weaponry, like the matchlock, halberd and arquebus from a Lithuania of earlier centuries. Then we trooped off to sleep, taking time the next morning to explore downtown Chicago.

In the afternoon we met at the restaurant Greek Islands. Brunch after our June wedding in 1990 had been there and I had the pictures of laughing faces to prove it. The old owners had seen us off after our repast that fateful afternoon with a round of Metaxa, the brandy named for Ioannis Metaxas, who on October 28, 1940, said "Ohi" to Mussolini's ultimatum to Greece: allow our troops to enter, or face war. As we fondly remembered the previous owners, plates of *tsadziki*, *melitzanosalata*, *tarama*, *skordalia*, *kolokithakia*, *oktapodi* crowded the table and then made way for more food.

\* \* \*

On October 20, 2014, I went under the knife. Dr. Valluvan

Jeevanandam, Chief of Cardiac Surgery, wielded it at the University of Chicago Medical Center and mended my "broken" heart. I had a triple bypass. The two transplanted organs had to be kept alive while the arteries were cleaned and patched. I was hospitalized for nine days and emerged, heart, balance and looks in much better shape. This was elective surgery, so I had delayed my sojourn in the ward till after the wedding anniversary celebration. When I saw my cardiologist Dr. Sorrentino after some weeks and Dr. Jeevanandam stopped by, Henryk, who was with me, introduced himself by giving his novel *Feast of Fools* and saying, "Skwarczyński, that's Jeevanandam in Polish."

\* \* \*

Spring saw the continued celebration of our silver anniversary, this time June 2, 2015, at an outdoor restaurant, Boston Fish Market, with a second set of friends plus Vidas and Marytė. A filmmaker raised and schooled in Brasil and responsible for the first political campaign clip about Obama, Michał Siewierski, came with Ela, his wife, and their months old daughter, Vivian, who beamed and slept in turn throughout the feast. Joining us was my cousin, Rimvydas Tveras, toy inventor turned writer of the riveting novel *Hole*; artist Vilija Eiva, whose painting of a nude for Henryk's birthday hangs in our apartment where we see it every day; epicure Dr. Mark Stasiulis, his wife Donna, a bookworm, who shares my love for mysteries, like those of Elizabeth Perry, their daughter Cydney, a fresh baked Cambridge alumna, all three enamored of traveling the world, tasting new places; Marytė and Vidas Nemickas—she, world master of an apple cake, that leaves one drooling, he, a regular at Plaza de Toros de Las Ventas and La Maestranza.

Michał, Ela and Vivian arrived with a bouquet of exotic flowers, that we watched bloom for days. Vidas and Marytė had given us two wine glasses in a box that formed a heart. Vilija brought a tiny cardboard container with a hole at the top into which we each had to stuff our part of a symbolic chain of what the twenty-five years had put us through—joys, horrors, sorrow, and satisfaction. Best of all, another set of our friends gathered with us under trees to feast on lobster, shrimp, fresh bass, and smelt, with plates of vegetables, potatoes and other accoutrements of a banquet, laced with New Zealand chardonnay.

Among the missing, though invited, were my brother Uosis, whose marriage to Jacquie Rice we had celebrated with them in Rhode Island, and my California relatives, Mindaugas and Violeta Gedgaudas. They couldn't come to Chicago, but invited us to Laguna Beach to recuperate after my heart bypass.

A Canadian couple also couldn't make the anniversary. Włodzimierz Krysiński, a poet and a professor of comparative literature at the University of Montreal, has published books and articles in French, English, Italian and Spanish from Peru to Italy. He had studied under Henryk's father, Zdzisław, in Poland. The other half of this literary pair, Bretagne-born professor Annie Brisset is a connoisseur of the poetry of W. H. Auden and consultant to UNESCO on projects for the development of multilingual communication in parts of Europe.

They came to visit us in La Grange and we paid them a return visit to Ottawa, getting lost briefly in Montreal on the way. We had driven to Rouses Point, New York, for an outdoor wedding. Uosis's son, Isaac, had married Maria on the shore of Lake Champlain. His brother Ben and sister Rebecca with her son Gabriel had come from California to join in the festivities. Then we were off to Canada. Włodzimierz introduced us to a poet and scholar in Brazil, Henryk Siewierski, and was responsible for my Henryk's meeting another writer and colorful character, Keith Botsford. He, with Saul Bellow, founded and continues to publish a literary journal, *News from the Republic of Letters*. Excerpts from two of Henryk's novels, *The Straw Sea* and *Feast of Fools*, the latter published in Poland with a superb afterword by Włodzimierz, appeared in *TRoL*. We saw Keith in Warsaw a couple of summers ago, a cigarette constantly in his mouth, words rolling out in a velvety, mesmerizing voice.

Like spinning a spider web, one writer connects to a second, a third to a scholar or two, crossing countries, continents, rivers, seas and oceans. The Krysiński's, world travelers like us, have served as our lighthouse in the domain of literature without borders.

We're thinking of having another celebration for those who couldn't make the first two.

\* \* \*

"My Lord, the gods want you to build an impregnable castle on a high hill. The Iron Wolf, howling in the voice of a hundred, is the city, the capital of your country, which you will build around the castle and whose inhabitants will spread tales of your prowess and glory far and wide."
—Dream of Gediminas, the Grand Duke of Lithuania, and founder of Vilnius. Fourteenth century.

# Acknowledgments

My wholehearted thanks to the physicians who helped me not just survive, but LIVE. My magicians: endocrinologist Dr. Arthur Rubenstein of the UofC, and Prof. Dr. Rüdiger Landgraf of Munich. They gave me back my belief in those who took the Hippocratic oath. Two shining stars of my private sky are nephrologist and defense against diseases Michele Josephson and cardiologist Matthew Sorrentino, both from the University of Chicago. In that firmament gleams Robert Harland, Valluvan Jeevanandam, and all of the other surgeons whose hands did the operations. Dr. Garrity keeps the lungs in working order, Dr. Naclerio concentrates on the functionality of nose and ears, Dr. Seenu Hariprasad focuses on repeatedly saving my sight, Dr. Sherwin Ho makes sure the body stays erect and they all help me be pain-free, which is no small feat. Dr.Daniel Mass keeps my hands working. My osteoporotic bones still carry me, thanks to Dr. Tamara Vokes, a specialist of bone problems; and my feet have not succumbed to wounds, breaks and other diabetic trials and tribulations due to timely interventions by Dr. Ann Zmuda, podiatrist, both doctors specialists at the UofC clinics. Dr. Anthony Peterson at Loyola Medicine keeps me free of skin problems, like cancer, from my scalp to my toes.

My UofC post-transplant team, nurses Roseann Sweda, Mary Beth McNamara, and particularly Jo Sutor, have seen me through three kidney, one pancreas transplant and countless ailments. They are better sources of information and advice than even cyber space. I can't thank them enough.